TOWARDS COHERENCE BETWEEN
CLASSROOM ASSESSMENT AND ACCOUNTABILITY

TOWARDS COHERENCE BETWEEN
CLASSROOM ASSESSMENT AND ACCOUNTABILITY

103rd Yearbook of the
National Society for the Study of Education

PART II

Edited by
MARK WILSON

20 04

Distributed by THE UNIVERSITY OF CHICAGO PRESS • CHICAGO, ILLINOIS

National Society for the Study of Education

The National Society for the Study of Education was founded in 1901 as successor to the National Herbart Society. It publishes a two-volume Yearbook, each volume dealing with a separate topic of concern to educators. The Society's Yearbook series, now in its one hundred-third year, presents articles by scholars and practitioners noted for their significant work in critical areas of education.

The Society welcomes as members all individuals who wish to receive its publications. Current membership includes educators in the United States, Canada, and elsewhere throughout the world—professors, researchers, administrators, and graduate students in colleges and universities and teachers, administrators, supervisors, and curriculum specialists in elementary and secondary schools, as well as policymakers at all levels.

Members of the Society elect a Board of Directors. The Board's responsibilities include reviewing proposals for Yearbooks, authorizing the preparation of Yearbooks based on accepted proposals, and appointing an editor or editors to oversee the preparation of manuscripts.

Current dues (for 2004) are a modest $40 ($35 for retired members and for students in their first year of membership). Members whose dues are paid for the current calendar year receive the Society's Yearbook, are eligible for election to the Board of Directors, and are entitled to a 33 percent discount when purchasing past Yearbooks from the Society's distributor, the University of Chicago Press.

Each year the Society arranges for meetings to be held in conjunction with the annual conferences of one or more of the national educational organizations. All members are urged to attend these meetings, at which the current Yearbook is presented and critiqued. Members are encouraged to submit proposals for future Yearbooks.

Towards Coherence Between Classroom Assessment and Accountability is Part II of the 103rd Yearbook. Part I, published simultaneously, is titled *Developing the Teacher Workforce*.

For further information, write to the Secretary, NSSE, College of Education m/c 147, University of Illinois at Chicago, 1040 W. Harrison St., Chicago, Illinois 60607-7133 or see www.uic.edu/educ/nsse

ISSN: 0077-5762

Published 2004 by the
NATIONAL SOCIETY FOR THE STUDY OF EDUCATION
1040 W. Harrison St., Chicago, Illinois 60607-7133

First Printing
Printed in the United States of America

Board of Directors of the
National Society for the Study of Education
(Term of office expires in the year indicated.)

Contributors to the Yearbook

Dedication

To Allistair Merrick Wilson, may your future paths bring you joy.

Preface

The generating idea behind this volume is that in discussions and debates among educational policymakers, professionals, and researchers about the role of assessment in educational accountability there has been insufficient attention paid to the central place of the classroom. The aim of the volume is to correct this oversight by encouraging reflection and scholarly exchange on the topic. Hopefully, it will prove a useful addition to the ranks of annual volumes that the National Society for the Study of Education has contributed to the progress of education over the last 100 years.

The volume has been designed with a structure that I hope will actively promote discussion and debate. It begins with an introductory chapter that outlines a vision of an accountability system that is very different from the one most commonly conceived of in the United States today. By positing a decidedly contrarian point of view in this opening chapter, I hope to stimulate a broader range of thinking about accountability and its relationship to the classroom than what commonly occurs.

Following the introductory piece is the first of the two main parts of the volume. This first part consists of five "source" chapters that constitute what one might call "exhibits"—examples of research and development studies in the broad area of assessment that cut across the issues of classroom assessment and make possible new approaches to accountability. Each source chapter describes a specific study, or series of studies, that informs discussion and debate in this general area. Each also comments on how the project described highlights certain links between classroom assessment and accountability. I selected these chapters mainly because I felt that each had something unique and interesting to say about assessment and would open up possibilities about how assessment might be related to accountability. The source chapters do not constitute a comprehensive set of relevant studies. Instead they are a representative selection designed to prompt a range of reflection and discussion among the readership.

The source chapters are followed by responding commentary chapters. In these commentaries, strategically chosen individuals offer their reflections on the issues arising from the source chapters with respect to classroom assessment and accountability. Some are educational professionals and some are researchers working in related areas; they were chosen largely because of their different and interesting viewpoints and the clarity with which they deliver those viewpoints.

There are far too many issues raised in the volume to attempt to usefully summarize them all, and such an effort would, in part, be contrary to the purpose of the volume, which is to encourage others to join in the discussion and debate. Instead, in my concluding chapter, I focus on comments and points that relate to the current context of assessment and accountability, which is so strongly influenced by the federal No Child Left Behind legislation. I then summarize the points made in the commentary chapters and link these to current topics and issues.

The expected audience for the volume comprises a broad range of educational policymakers, professionals, and researchers with interests in assessment (both classroom and large scale) and accountability. I also anticipate that the volume will make for a stimulating source of material on which to base a graduate student seminar on accountability and assessment. In order to provide an opportunity for ongoing debate and discussion, the NSSE is sponsoring a Web site (http://bear.soe.berkeley.edu/NSSE/) with threaded discussions focused on the issues raised within these pages. I invite you to log on.

I would like to thank Robert Calfee for making the initial suggestion that inspired this volume. The concept of having a set of "source chapters" and "commentary chapters" is closely related to the structure used in the new journal from Lawrence Erlbaum and Associates, *Measurement: Interdisciplinary Research and Perspectives*, which focuses on the areas of measurement and assessment, though in a setting that is broader than the focus of the current volume. Debra Miretzky has, with good grace and timely e-mail messages, ably shepherded the volume through its many stages of construction. June Hartley set up the Web site that we used for the chapter editing, assisted the chapter authors in utilizing it, and contributed to the copyediting of many of the chapters—many thanks to June. Thank you to the chapter authors for putting up with the complexities of the process by which the volume was put together and also to the commentary authors who helped in the reviewing process for both the source chapters and the commentary chapters. In addition, I would like to thank the NSSE members who helped by reviewing chapters: Beverly Falk, Gary Ivory, and Richard Siegesmund.

MARK WILSON
Editor

Table of Contents

Part One

CHAPTER
Introduction

Part Two
Source Chapters

Part Three
Commentary Chapters

Part Four
One Step Further

xii

Part One
INTRODUCTION

CHAPTER 1

Assessment, Accountability and the Classroom: A Community of Judgment

MARK WILSON

The generating idea behind this volume is that there has been insufficient attention paid to the central place of the classroom in our thinking about the role of assessment in educational accountability. This introductory chapter is intended to be somewhat provocative. In it I attempt to help the reader see beyond the current state of affairs in terms of the relationship between classroom assessment and accountability and to consider some wider perspectives and possibilities. Hopefully, this will also help the reader step into the spirit of the discussion that is inherent in the chapters that follow. For those who are unfamiliar with the topics of classroom assessment and accountability, I direct them to Shepard's (in press) up-to-date and extensive review in the latest edition of *Educational Measurement* (Brennan, in press); for somewhat more traditional views, see its predecessors, Nitko (1989) and Frechtling (1989), in previous editions of that series or refer to a classic textbook such as Anderson (2003).

In considering the relationship between assessment and educational accountability, it is important to keep in mind the two-way flow of information that it involves—from the classroom out into the system and from the system back into the classroom. In the "standards-based" framework that is currently the most common accountability approach in the United States, the direction of this "flow" is mainly from the system into the classroom. States sample student performances using some form of standardized test and then distribute the results 1) into

Mark Wilson is a Professor of Education at the University of California, Berkeley. He specializes in measurement and assessment, particularly in education, and also in educational statistics.

an accountability system (usually at the school level, but other levels are also possible), 2) back into the classroom, and 3) to other stakeholders such as parents and school administrators. However, it is important to realize that assessment information drawn from standardized tests represents no more than a drop in the bucket of all the assessment information that is gathered in a typical classroom. The assessment enterprise, as it exists in schools today, consists overwhelmingly of the assessments that teachers themselves design, score, and act upon in their classrooms every day and every week of the school year. Thus, improving the usefulness of assessment in schools will primarily consist of assisting and harnessing this flood of assessment information to the advantage of learning *within* the classroom and as the source of crucial information flowing *out* of the classroom.

In order to consider this complex issue in a coherent way, we must start with a consistent view of assessment. One such view, the "assessment triangle," appeared in the recent NRC report *Knowing What Students Know* (Pellegrino, Chudowsky, & Glaser, 2000), shown here in Figure 1. According to KWSK, assessment consists of 1) a cognition aspect (the model one has of a student's cognition), 2) an observation aspect (the methods one uses to assess the student's cognition), and 3) an interpretation aspect (the methods one uses the relate the observations to the cognition model). In the classroom, one could interpret these three parts of the triangle as 1) the curriculum and the instructional plan, 2) the assessment tasks (tests, homework, etc.), and 3) the interpretation and use of the student's scores on these tasks. With this in mind, there are three challenges we must face in designing assessments that place the classroom context at the center of our accountability systems.

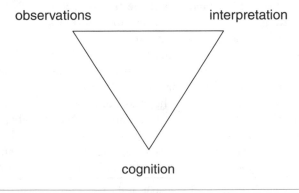

FIGURE 1
The KWSK assessment triangle.

First, the challenge for *system-level standardized assessments* is to find ways to design tests and information delivery systems that produce results that are directly useable in the classroom setting. For if the test results are directly useable in the classroom, then they must indeed have sound content and construct validity. But, such tests can also provide a framework that will help teachers do a better job of interpreting the results from the system-level standardized tests and that will be a model for teachers when they are designing and interpreting their own assessments.

Second, the challenge for those who design *assessments for use in classrooms*, both stand-alone systems and those that accompany specific curricula, is to find ways to make their assessments consistent with and supportive of the curriculum, efficient to administer and interpret in the classroom, and useful to the planning and instructional tasks of the classroom (at both individual and class levels).

Third, the challenge for our *assessment and accountability systems*, beyond those outlined above, is to find ways to recognize the strength and usefulness of both classroom-based assessments and system-level assessments and to channel useful information from one level to the other (i.e., from the top down and from the bottom up). The aim is 1) to make the accountability system more valid by finding ways to use teacher judgments of student performance that are the classroom reflection of student learning, 2) to give an appropriate place in the accountability system to the professional knowledge and standing of teachers, and 3) to encourage teachers to use in their classrooms assessment frameworks and styles that are consistent with good practice and are coherent with system-level assessments.

To address all three of these challenges will require what the NRC committee termed *coherence*—the integration of assessment frameworks and methods across all levels of the assessment system, from the classroom to the system levels.

A Community of Judgment

An educational system must be held accountable for its expenditures on students' education. It must be able to show that students are making suitable progress on important educational variables, and it should be able to determine when particular programs accelerate (or impede) that progress. In the United States, these two purposes have traditionally been fulfilled by gathering the results of standardized tests in a small range of subject areas (to determine whether suitable progress has been made) and analyzing those results using group comparisons (to evaluate specific educational programs). As a result, standardized tests have penetrated very deeply into the everyday educational environment.

An assessment monoculture has thus been created for our educational system, and, as for biological monocultures, otherwise innocuous characteristics of minor "species" (in this case, the multiple-choice item) have come to dominate the entire educational environment. A monoculture has the advantages of uniformity, which promotes efficiency and comparability. But it also has the disadvantages of uniformity—it limits our monitoring of what is important to that which it is suited to, thus defining "educational importance" in ways that many educators would likely not endorse. Asking students to recognize, rather than produce, is one obvious limitation, but others, such as limitations on student expressiveness and on the possibilities for them to react to contingencies in an extended way, are also important. The challenge, then, is to come up with a different sort of assessment culture, one that does not limit us to just one assessment mode, and, in particular, one that does not reject the standardized multiple-choice test. It should be a system that encourages assessments of a type that reflect the best instructional practice, yet also preserves the essential features of efficiency and comparability that have been the strengths of the traditional monoculture.

This chapter is an explication of one possible response to this challenge. There is no claim that the approach described here is uniquely advantageous. Moreover, it is as yet only realized in its parts—no full-scale implementation comprising all of its components exists, although examples of the components are certainly extant.

This approach is based on the idea that the professionals who are currently entrusted with the education of our students—teachers—are also the ones with the most direct access to the information needed for an accountability system. Direct use of their knowledge is the best way to achieve validity, reliability, and efficiency. Moreover, teachers are also the ones who are best placed to interpret such information in an educationally sound way. Thus, the approach described below puts teachers and their judgments at the heart of the accountability system. It does so by situating them in a *community of judgment*—an interpretive system that connects their judgments of student work to

1. a substantive *framework* for describing the level of students' performances in terms of their achievement in particular subjects— this will define certain *achievement progress variables* that we value;

2. a broad range of tasks, projects, and performances that are real-
izations of the achievement variables and that embody our best
instructional practice—this will be composed of a set of *assessment modes* for each achievement variable with accompanying
scoring guidelines for rating student responses;

3. a *moderation* of the actual judgments that are made using these
guidelines—this will include both rater improvement and rater
adjustment components;

4. methods of *quality control* regarding the interpretation of evidence from the assessment modes—these will include methods
of ensuring that ratings of the evidence are both valid and reliable and methods of verifying that the evidence is sound.

These four parts of the community of judgment correspond to the
three vertices of the KWSK assessment triangle: the framework is a
model of student cognition, the assessment modes are observations,
and moderation and quality control are aspects of interpretation—the
first at the teacher level, the second at the system level.

The moderated assessments gathered from such a community
would then be available for standard reporting purposes, but they would
also be uniquely suitable for the purposes of evaluating specific educational programs. An evaluation component for such a system would
take as raw materials the location of individual students—or schools, or
other groups of students—on the achievement variables and analyze the
progress that they make along those variables. This information would
then be evaluated by taking account of the conditions under which the
instruction takes place and the scope of the educational interventions.

How would such a system be better than the present one? One
clear advantage has already been referred to above: The system is explicitly designed to incorporate a wide range of modes of assessment. This
means that "standardized tests" would no longer determine what is valued in education because the community of judgment system can
incorporate assessment types that arise out of valued instructional practices and thus can more authentically assess student progress. Instead
of spending significant portions of the school year practicing for standardized tests, students would be "practicing" for tests while working
on their regular instructional activities (Resnick & Resnick, 1992).

A second major advantage is that by placing teachers in the system's central position, we are engaging them fully as professionals in
the instruction of their students. This means that the effort to get such
a system implemented will involve crucial professional development

for teachers in the following areas: 1) knowledge of the frameworks mentioned above, 2) new instructional practices that relate to the frameworks and new assessment modes related to those instructional practices, 3) new ways for teachers to work together, and 4) resources to help teachers contribute to the evaluation of their own success. One way to look at this list is to see it as a set of problems to be overcome before such a community could be said to be in operation. Another is to see it as a means of motivating teachers to enhance these significant aspects of their professional roles.

The cost of such a system is another important issue. The staff development mentioned above and the specific materials and skills development that the system would require would necessitate large-scale investments. However, one should see the professional development as being funded for its potential to improve the education of our students, as well as for accountability purposes. Once in operation, the practice of collecting information for the community of judgment would become part of the regular school day and thereby productively use the time presently devoted to testing and test preparation. The money spent on purchasing standardized tests could instead be applied to giving teachers time to develop the professionally enriching roles mentioned in the previous paragraph.

Perhaps the most vexing issue regarding this approach is the question of whether one can trust teachers' judgments of their students' progress. In a certain light, this might seem an absurd question—if we can trust teachers to teach the students, why can't we trust them to assess the students? Nevertheless, the community of judgment described in brief above and in greater detail below has interlocking structures in each of its parts that are designed to ensure that teacher judgments are educationally sound, and verifiably and visibly so:

1. The frameworks ensure that the variables to be measured are understood by all involved in the accountability system, from teachers to parents to administrators to policymakers;
2. the use of specific types of assessment means that there is commonality in the contexts under which student responses are observed and thus comparability can be achieved;
3. the moderation processes ensure that teachers are acting coherently with their peers in making specific judgments, and these judgments can be subject to outside scrutiny; and
4. the system of quality control will ensure comparability, verifiability, and fairness across the system.

In summary, *every* part of the community of judgment is designed to contribute to the usefulness and validity of the judgments made within the community.

I describe below each of the four components of the community of judgment, noting recent relevant developments. Following this I discuss how information from those judgments could be used for program evaluation. I conclude the chapter with a discussion of the implications of adopting such an approach and suggest some directions for further development.

Frameworks

To attain consistency in the operation of a community of judgment, the various parts of the system must speak the same basic "language" regarding their educational goals. This language must be based on agreed upon ideas regarding the curricula to be taught. This agreement begins with the idea that our ultimate goal is student *progression* along the achievement variables of the curricula. Such progression must be part of a shared understanding on the part of the agents and audiences of the system. This understanding must include fundamental ideas about student development (i.e., what the progression is *in*), an agreed upon set of important achievement variables, and an agreed upon set of discernible levels of performance along the achievement variables.

A *framework* is a set of achievement variables within a defined curriculum area, along which are located defined levels of performance, and along which students are expected to make progress. The achievement variables extend from lower, more elementary knowledge, understanding, and skills to more advanced levels. The levels describe understanding in terms of qualitatively distinguishable performances along the achievement variables.

The idea of a framework is not new. Examples include the Western Australian *First Steps* project (West Australian Ministry of Education, 1992), the Australian National Curriculum Profiles (Australian Education Council, 1992), and the U.K. National Curriculum strands (Department of Education and Science, 1987a, 1987b). Note that the contemporary notion of "standards" is really a simplification of the idea of a framework. Educational standards, as they are commonly expressed in state educational documents, consist of lists of individual objectives of education. In contrast, the framework idea takes such lists and organizes them into meaningful and interpretable progressions of children's educational development (which will often result in alterations in the original list). Where progress is expressed in terms of a framework as part of a community of judgment, the interpretation of that progress is fundamentally qualitative. A quantitative approach can be based on the fundamental underlying qualitative levels and may be used to help maintain comparability within the system, but the numbers are meaningless without the qualitative grounding of the achievement variable.

A concrete example of such a framework appears in chapter 6 of this volume (Wilson & Draney). In that chapter, Figure 1 shows a framework spanning a middle school science curriculum, and Figure 4 shows the levels from one particular progress variable. More detail can be found in Wilson and Sloane (2000) and Wilson and Scalise (2003).

A Range of Assessment Modes

A decade ago, the authentic assessment movement (Wiggins, 1989) and the closely associated efforts to develop performance assessment (Baron, Forgione, Rindone, Kruglanski, & Davey, 1989) and portfolio assessment (Wolf, 1989) promoted new views of student learning and assessment that demanded that the use of information-gathering procedures extend beyond the tradition of standardized multiple-choice tests. Aschbacher (1991, p. 276) described the key features of such assessments as follows:

1. Students perform, create, produce, or do something that requires higher level thinking or problem solving skills (not just one right answer).
2. Assessment tasks are also meaningful, challenging, engaging instructional activities.
3. Tasks are set in a real-world context or a close simulation.
4. Process and conative behavior are often assessed along with product.
5. The criteria and standards for performance are public and known in advance.

Many of these features were not new even then. For example, fifty years ago, Lindquist (1951) wrote that

it should always be the fundamental goal of the achievement test constructor to make elements of his test series as nearly equivalent, or as much like, the elements of the criterion series [in this context, the elements of instruction] as consequences of efficiency, comparability, economy, and expediency will permit. (p. 152)

However, it is probably fair to say that, in the last 50 years, concerns with "efficiency, comparability, economy, and expediency" (Lindquist, p. 152) have predominated. Historically, multiple-choice tests have been widely advocated because of their positive features with regard to such criteria. There will always be countervailing forces in assessment that, on one hand, pressure designers to seek more efficiency and, on the other, pressure designers to use assessments that are as education-ally useful as possible. A primary goal of the community of judgment is to find ways that those forces can be brought into alignment rather than opposition.

Advocates for alternative assessment have reminded us that there are many information-gathering formats that can provide useful infor-mation. I will use the ideas illustrated in Figure 2 to discuss different approaches to gathering information. I put this figure forward not because it provides a complete formula for describing all assessment modes but rather because it helps in conceiving and describing several aspects of assessment that are relevant to the arguments in this chapter. In the figure, the vertical dimension is used to indicate variation in control over the assessment task. At the "high" end of this dimension is assessment undertaken using externally set tasks that will allow stu-dents to respond only in a prescribed set of ways. Standardized multi-ple-choice tests are an example of this extreme, whereas short-answer items are not quite at this extreme because students may respond in ways that are not predefined. The "low" end of this dimension is char-acterized by a complete lack of task or response specification. Teachers' holistic impressions of their students belong at this end of the task-control dimension. Between these two extremes are information gath-ering approaches such as teacher-developed tests and performance tasks developed from central guidelines and adapted to local condi-tions. The horizontal dimension is used to indicate variation in control over how the student work is to be judged. The "high" extreme is typi-fied by tasks that are machine scorable; the "low" end is typified by unguided holistic judgments. Between these are variations in terms of the expert status of the judges and the degree of prescription of judg-ment protocols. For example, the judgments of teachers who are certi-fied as expert judges after successfully completing a training procedure are controlled to a higher degree than those of teachers who make their own interpretations of how to use centrally developed assessment materials.

Assessments that fall in different locations on Figure 2 are often valued for different reasons. For example, assessments that occur in

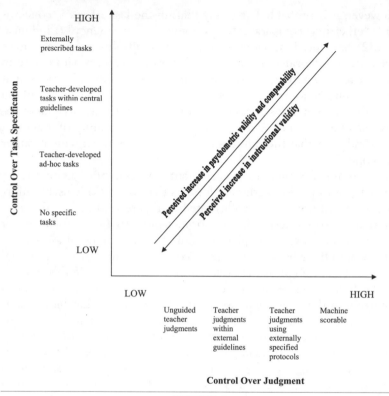

FIGURE 2

Control chart for assessment formats: Perceived advantages at extremes

the upper right-hand corner are typically valued because they are perceived to have greater reliability. They are composed of tasks that are the same for all students, that can be scored using objective criteria, and that are congruent with the historically prominent types of psychometric models. Alternatively, assessments in the bottom left-hand corner are typically perceived to have greater instructional validity. That is, they are closer to the actual format and content of instruction, are based on the accumulated experience of teachers concerning their own students, and allow maximum adaptation to local conditions. Although it is desirable to have the positive features of both of these forms of assessment, the figure illustrates that no single assessment format can encompass them.

Interestingly, according to this classification, the two forms of assessment with which we have probably the greatest familiarity fall at the two extremes—external, fixed-choice tests and teacher grades. Teacher grades have an advantage in that when we use them for assessment, we are acknowledging that those who provide the instruction are best qualified to know what is an appropriate assessment task for an individual and are also best qualified to judge the work of the individual. In contrast, external examinations have an advantage in that the context of the assessment, and the rating system applied to the resulting performances, are both very uniform and thus, at least at a superficial level, are highly comparable across classrooms and relatively impervious to criticism on the grounds of fairness. These two extremes form the end-points of the diagonal in Figure 2. I will call this diagonal the "control–validity dimension," with greater control and lesser instructional validity in the top right-hand corner and lesser control and greater instructional validity in the bottom left-hand corner.

The most important motivation behind the use of a range of assessment modes is that no single assessment format can satisfy simultaneously the need for both instructional validity ("authenticity" in the jargon of alternative assessment) and control. The use of diverse assessment modes, then, is an attempt to use information from a variety of different forms of assessment (i.e., forms that fall at a variety of locations on Figure 2) so that we can capitalize on the opportunities that some assessments might provide for enhancing validity as well as the opportunities that others might provide for increasing reliability. Newer standardized tests that include both open-ended and multiple-choice items (e.g., the complete version of *Terra Nova* from CTB-McGraw Hill) represent a step toward this multiform approach, but because one of these choices falls on the control–validity diagonal and the other falls just slightly off the diagonal, it is a small step indeed.

A System of Moderation

Having a range of assessment modes, while sending a much-needed message to educators (i.e., that matching assessments to instruction is important), is insufficient to ensure the successful operation of an accountability system. What is needed, in addition, is a way to integrate teachers' judgments of students' responses to the various assessment modes with those of other teachers and those of teachers expert in the content and format of the assessments. The *moderation* system described below should be viewed not only as essential for the integration of student responses into the accountability system but also as a way to transmit into the classroom the genuine spirit of new assessments. To do this, we must go beyond mere exemplification and establish a network of information and support for teachers.

Assessment Moderation

The first part of a moderation system concentrates on the *process* of judging student work. Moderation begins where the frameworks and assessment tasks leave off. A core of teachers must first have professional development in the instructional implications of the frameworks, in the use of the specific assessment modes in the system, and in the rating of student responses using scoring guidelines. This core group would then act as leaders for local groups of teachers, called *moderation groups* (Bell, Burkhardt, & Swan, 1991). These groups would meet on a regular basis to help one another with the staff development described above, the application of consistent and fair grading practices in the assessments, and the development of assessment tasks and instructional practices for use in local schools. A sample agenda for a moderation group meeting is shown in the appendix to this chapter. The moderation groups operate principally as a way for teachers to compare the work of their own students with that of other teachers' students. This engages them directly in professional conversations regarding some of the core issues of teaching—how well their students are doing and how teachers can help their students improve. Thus the scoring acts as a prompt for the professional development aspects of the meetings.

Verification

The second part of a moderation system is the verification of teachers' ratings. There are typically two ways that this can be carried out, and the two can be combined. One technique is based on sampling of student work. In this process, rated student work is sampled from teachers and then rerated by expert raters. The aim is to allow the teacher input to make the assessment more "authentic" while maintaining certain standards of comparability and scrutiny. This has been termed *moderation by inspection* in the U.K. (Smith, 1978) and *external verification* in Australia (Stephens, 1992). In both the U.K. and Australia, it has been used on a sampling basis to achieve comparability among teachers' ratings.

A second verification technique, called *statistical moderation*, is also available. If students are measured with assessments at two (or more) different levels of control (say, a test and a rated work or ratings by teachers and ratings by external experts), then statistical moderation can be used to analytically combine the two different types of information. Historically, this technique has been applied using the two most extreme categories in Figure 2 (Clarke, 1987). It starts from the assumption, on the one hand, that teachers know best the relativities among their own students but know much less about the relativities between classes. On the other hand, external raters or tests are assumed to be good at comparisons between classes but not so good at measuring within classes (or perhaps are too expensive for this task). Consequently, one builds a formula for applying these assumptions to the ratings produced by teachers and external experts. Typically, statistical moderation gives complete control over relativities within classes to teacher ratings and complete control over relativities between classes to external ratings or test scores (McGaw, 1977). This approach has been used for many years to adjust students' teacher-supplied university entrance scores in a number of Australian states. There are several variants of this approach (a number of which are described in McGaw, 1977, and Viviani, 1990). For the purposes of this discussion, the statistical moderation approach should not be viewed as being restricted to the two most extreme categories of control. It could be used, for example, to adjust portfolio ratings using an external test or to adjust teacher grades using external experts' ratings.

In Summary

A system using moderation both for helping teachers achieve more coherent judgment and for verifying those judgments has several advantages over a more traditional system based only on high-control modes of assessment. It allows teachers to decide the most appropriate forms of assessment for their students, and this decision will predominate over any other sort of information that is used to measure the relativities of students *in that class*. It places the measurement of relativities into a framework where the teacher is a participant with other teachers and with curriculum leaders. In a way, this is the ideal for the teacher, as he or she will still have input into how the students are assessed but will also be able to show how the fairness of the assessments has been confirmed. This direct involvement of the teacher in the moderation process, and the various forms of feedback described above, not only can result in an alignment of teacher assessment practices with those of his or her peers but also can become an instrument of professional development for teachers in ways that reach far beyond assessment, out into the whole range of instructional practices. It removes teachers from the forms of oversight that predominate in a production-line environment (where workers are most often judged by information over which they have no control) and places them in a position similar to that of other professionals, where they have control over significant parts of their own assessment, tempered by peer participation and procedural oversight by external experts.

Quality Control

Quality control procedures are needed 1) to examine the coherence of information gathered using different formats, 2) to map student performances onto the achievement variables, 3) to describe the structural elements of the accountability system—tasks and raters—in terms of the achievement variables, and 4) to establish standard characteristics of system functioning such as validity and reliability studies and bias and equity studies. The most complete set of techniques available to meet this need is one centered on generalized item response models. Generalized item response models such as those described in the recent NRC report (Pellegrino, Chudowsky, & Glaser, 2001) have now reached levels of development that make their application to the complexities of large-scale assessment systems feasible. The output from these models can be used as quality control information and to obtain student and school locations on the achievement variables, which may be interpreted both quantitatively and substantively. Examples of such outputs are shown in chapter 6 (Wilson & Draney, Figures 6 and 7).

A judicious choice across a range of modes of assessment, along with a suitably meshing system of moderation, could provide a state with an assessment system that could not only fulfill accountability and staff development requirements but also provide the basis for the evaluation of educational programs and the educational system as a whole. This system need not be the same from state to state. One state could use portfolios as its low-control assessment, another could use teacher grades, and each could use a different mode of high-control assessment. Nor would the assessment system need to remain the same over time within a particular state. A gradual transition would make public acceptance of the newer forms of assessment more likely and would also provide a "running-in" period, during which practical difficulties with different assessment modes could be ironed out without their having to bear the full burden of being the primary mode of data gathering for an accountability system. Longitudinal comparability across such a change in modes of assessment would require evidence that essentially similar things were being measured by the different modes of assessment and that data was gathered from a representative sample of students who had performed under the two modes of assessment. In the case where modes were not changing, longitudinal comparability could be maintained by the standard item response modeling techniques.

The community of judgment provides measures of the changes that students within schools have made along the achievement variables. Background characteristics for those students, and the contextual characteristics of the schools they are in, will influence the magnitude of this growth. Some school characteristics might be, for example, average socioeconomic status of the students in the school, geographical location of the school, or both. Because these characteristics are beyond the control of the school, and because they are likely to influence the performance of students within the school, it would appear unreasonable to compare only the net growth. The evaluation system should incorporate the possibility of taking into account such influences in comparing schools. One such approach would use a multilevel model (Bryk & Raudenbush, 1992) based on the student measures from the measurement model to estimate how the progress of students in each school compares with students' progress made in similar schools.

Conclusion

The implementation of a community of judgment as described in this chapter would have a profound effect on educational accountability and on the educational system in general. Quite a lot of the discussion in this chapter has concentrated on the technical system of moderation and program evaluation. This is necessary for the sound and fair operation of the system for accountability purposes. But by placing teacher judgment at its center, the community of judgment becomes a catalyst for educational improvement. By capitalizing on the professional interest that teachers have in their students' performance, we can gain exceptional leverage to bring about 1) the concrete implementation of curriculum innovations in the nation's classrooms, 2) the fostering of professional development among teachers in instructional and assessment practices, 3) the creation of an accountability system in which the chief participants—teachers and their students—have a vested interest in its success, and 4) the development of a more professional role among our corps of teachers, involving a commitment to self-maintenance of professional standards. The implementation of such a system would not be inexpensive. But its running costs would consist mainly of the expenditures necessary to give teachers time to be more evidence-based and reflective about their teaching, and to allow teachers to come together for professional development purposes. Long-term implementation would need to recognize this effort by teachers with changes in their working conditions and career structures. This should be compared to the present situation, in which the equivalent expenditure of class time and school funds is devoted to practicing for standardized tests. Today, the value added by the accountability system is almost exclusively value added to the profit margins of publishing companies. In contrast, the community of judgment aims to return added value directly back to our students in the schools by ensuring more relevant and fair assessment, by assisting in the dissemination of educational innovations, and by encouraging a more independent and better-trained corps of teachers.

First steps toward the implementation of such a community of judgment have already been made, as I have noted on in several places in this chapter. National frameworks in many school subjects are available (two of the earliest are given in National Committee on Science Education Standards and Assessments, 1993, and National Council of Teachers of Mathematics, 1989). A range of assessment modes has already been developed (e.g., consult the many example projects described in Pellegrino, Chudowsky, & Glaser, 2001). Consensus moderation systems are operating in several parts of the world, and statistical moderation is also currently being used in a number of places. The development of more flexible item response modeling approaches is currently a topic of intense work, and the development of the type of quality control system described here has been proceeding within the item response modeling literature for some time (Pellegrino, Chudowsky, & Glaser, 2001).

Further work on the idea and practice of a community of judgment will need to take several forms:

1. Further work on each of the components: This would require the continuation of present efforts on frameworks and diverse modes of assessment but would need some augmentation on the developmental side for consensus moderation and on the technical side for moderation and the quality control system.
2. Work on integrating all of the components. Piecemeal implementation of the components will not necessarily bring about the value added results described above. Moreover, many aspects of the mutual interaction of the components will not be examinable until the whole system is up and working. Therefore, my recommendation is that a small-scale but complete community

of judgment be implemented to fully develop the practical dimensions of the ideas presented here.

3. Work on disseminating the ideas presented here, recruiting participants, and adapting the ideas and procedures to different contexts.

Such work would need people of vision, ability, and commitment to carry it out. The current demands for change in accountability reflect the failure of our present vision, if *vision* is indeed the right word for what we have now. Many people have displayed their ability and commitment with their excellent work on alternative assessment over the last decade, but efforts have been isolated and thus have not prospered. What the community of judgment adds is a view of how these new ideas might be integrated into a working system of accountability.

AUTHOR'S NOTE

Parts of this chapter are adapted from an earlier work (Wilson, 1994). I would like to thank Karen Draney and June Hartley for comments on an earlier version of this chapter.

APPENDIX

SEPUP Moderation Process

Moderation Roles
- *Group Leader: Permanent Responsibility*
- *Discussion Leader: Rotating Responsibility*
- *SEPUP Teachers*

Before the Moderation Meeting

Group Leader lets SEPUP teachers know which question is to be moderated at the next meeting (this might have been decided at the previous meeting) and makes arrangements for the next meeting. Teachers score student work from a selected class prior to teacher moderation meeting. Prior to the meeting, teachers choose a range of example papers to represent as many score levels as possible and also choose a few difficult to score papers. A total of 5 to 6 papers are selected.

The Teacher Moderation Process

Part 1: Initial Reactions to Scoring Student Work (5 minutes)
Led by Discussion Leader

Part 2: Scoring Guide Discussion (15 minutes)
Led by Discussion Leader
- A group discussion to review the scoring guide(s).

Part 3: Pair Discussion and Selected Re-scoring of Student Work (45 minutes)
Led by Discussion Leader
- Teachers score student responses and reach consensus.
- Teachers tell group of interesting issues that arose in making their comparisons.

Part 4: Group Identification of Student Work Examples for Each Scoring Guide Level (15 minutes)
Led by Discussion Leader
- Group discussion to identify student work examples.

- Group may need to add to scoring guide at this point.

Part 5: Instructional Implications (20 minutes)
  Led by Discussion Leader
  - Group discussion to focus teachers on instructional strategies for each scoring guide level and how to connect scoring information to grading.

(Repeat steps 1 through 5 for each example paper.)

Part 6: General Discussion (15 minutes)
  Led by Discussion Leader
  - Discussion of general issues.

REFERENCES

Anderson, L.W. (2003). *Classroom assessment: Enhancing the quality of teacher decision making* (3rd ed.). Mahwah, NJ: Erlbaum.

Aschbacher, P.R. (1991). Performance assessment: State activity, interest, and concerns. *Applied Measurement in Education, 4*, 275-288.

Australian Education Council. (1992). *Mathematics profiles, levels 1-6.* Melbourne, Australia: Curriculum Corporation.

Baron, J., Forgione, P., Rindone, D., Kruglanski, H., & Davey, B. (1989). *Toward a new generation of student outcome measures: Connecticut's Common Core of Learning Assessment.* Paper presented at the annual meeting of the American Educational Research Association, San Francisco.

Bell, A., Burkhardt, H., & Swan, M. (1991). *Balanced assessment and the mathematics curriculum.* Nottingham, UK: Shell Centre for Mathematical Education.

Brennan, R. (Ed.). (in press). *Educational measurement* (4th ed.). Washington, DC: National Council on Measurement in Education and Greenwood Publishing Group.

Bryk, A.S., & Raudenbush, S.W. (1992). *Hierarchical linear models.* Newbury Park, CA: Sage.

Clarke, E. (1987). *Assessment in Queensland schools: Two decades of change, 1964-1983.* Brisbane, Australia: Department of Education.

Department of Education and Science. (1987a). *Education reform: The government's proposals for schools.* London: HMSO.

Department of Education and Science. (1987b). *National curriculum task group on assessment and testing: A report.* London: HMSO.

Frechtling, J.A. (1989). Administrative uses of school testing programs. In R. Linn (Ed.), *Educational measurement* (3rd ed., 475-484). New York: Macmillan.

Lindquist, E.F. (1951). Preliminary considerations in objective test construction. In E.F. Lindquist (Ed.), *Educational measurement* (pp. 119-184). Washington, DC: American Council on Education.

McGaw, B. (1977). The use of rescaled teacher assessments in the admission of students to tertiary study. *Australian Journal of Education, 21*, 209-225.

National Committee on Science Education Standards and Assessments. (1993). *National Science Education Standards: An enhanced sampler.* Washington, DC: National Research Council.

National Council of Teachers of Mathematics. (1989). *Curriculum and evaluation standards for school mathematics.* Reston, VA: National Council of Teachers of Mathematics.

Nitko, A.J. (1989). Designing tests that are integrated with instruction. In R. Linn (Ed.), *Educational measurement* (3rd ed., pp. 447-474). New York: Macmillan.

Pellegrino, J., Chudowsky, N., & Glaser, R. (Eds.). (2001). *Knowing what students know: The science and design of educational assessment.* National Research Council Committee on the Foundations of Assessment. Washington, DC: National Academy Press.

Resnick, L.B., & Resnick, D.P. (1992). Assessing the thinking curriculum: New tools for educational reform. In B.R. Gifford & M.C. O'Connor (Eds.), *Changing assessments: Alternative views of aptitude, achievement, and instruction* (pp. 37–75). Boston: Kluwer.

Shepard, L.A. (in press). Classroom assessment. In R. Brennan (Ed.), *Educational measurement* (4th ed.). Washington, DC: National Council on Measurement in Education and Greenwood Publishing Group.

Smith, G.A. (1978). *JMB experience of the moderation of internal assessments*. Manchester, UK: Joint Matriculation Board, Universities of Manchester, Leeds, Sheffield and Birmingham.

Stephens, M. (1992). Comprehensive assessment at senior secondary level in Victoria. In M. Stephens and J. Izard (Eds.), *Reshaping assessment practices: Assessment in the mathematical sciences under challenge* (pp. 257-271). Hawthorn, Australia: ACER.

Viviani, N. (1990). *The review of tertiary entrance in Queensland*. Brisbane, Australia: Ministry of Education.

West Australian Ministry of Education. (1992). *First Steps*. Perth, Western Australia: Ministry of Education.

Wiggins, G. (1989). A true test: Toward more authentic and equitable assessment. *Phi Delta Kappan, 70*, 703-713.

Wilson, M. (1994). Community of judgment: A teacher-centered approach to educational accountability. In Office of Technology Assessment (Ed.), *Issues in Educational Accountability*. Washington, DC: Office of Technology Assessment, United States Congress.

Wilson, M., & Draney, K. (2004). Some links between large-scale and classroom assessments: The case of the BEAR Assessment System. In this volume—M. Wilson (Ed.), *Towards coherence between classroom assessment and accountability. The 103rd yearbook of the National Society for the Study of Education*, Part II. Chicago: National Society for the Study of Education.

Wilson, M., & Scalise, K. (2003). Reporting progress to parents and others: Beyond grades. In J.M. Atkin & J.E. Coffey (Eds.), *Everyday assessment in the science classroom* (pp. 89–108). Arlington, VA: NSTA Press.

Wilson, M., & Sloane, K. (2000). From principles to practice: An embedded assessment system. *Applied Measurement in Education, 13*(2), 181-208.

Wolf, D.P. (1989). Portfolio assessment: Sampling student work. *Educational Leadership, 46*, 35-39.

Part Two
SOURCE CHAPTERS

CHAPTER 2

The Formative Purpose: Assessment Must First Promote Learning

PAUL BLACK AND DYLAN WILIAM

The work described in this paper started with a review of the literature on formative assessment (Black & Wiliam, 1998a). That review presents evidence from more than 250 articles by researchers from several countries that helped us to establish three main points. First, there is strong and rigorous evidence that improving formative assessment can raise standards of students' performance. There have been few initiatives in education with such a strong body of evidence to support a claim to raise standards.

The second point concerns the quality of current classroom assessment practices in schools. Here again, the published evidence from classroom research gave a clear and positive answer: the assessment methods that teachers use are not effective in promoting good learning; marking and grading practices tend to emphasize competition

Paul Black is Professor Emeritus of Science Education in the Department of Education and Professional Studies, King's College, University of London. Dylan Wiliam is formerly Professor of Educational Assessment and Assistant Principal of King's College, University of London. He is now Senior Research Director of the Center for Learning and Teaching Research at Educational Testing Service, Princeton, NJ.

We acknowledge the initiative of the Assessment Policy Task Group of the British Educational Research Association (now known as the Assessment Reform Group), which gave the initial impetus and support for our research review. We are grateful to the Nuffield Foundation, which funded the original review and the first phase of our project. We are also grateful to Professor Myron Atkin and his colleagues at Stanford University, who secured funding from the U.S. National Science Foundation (NSF Grant REC-9909370) for the last phase. Finally, we are indebted to the Medway and Oxfordshire local education authorities, their six schools, and above all their 36 teachers who took on the central and risky task of turning our ideas into practical working knowledge.

rather than personal improvement; and assessment feedback often has a negative impact, particularly on students with low attainment levels who are led to believe that they lack "ability" and are not able to learn.

These conclusions naturally lead to our third concern, which was whether we could learn from the evidence how to improve formative assessment practices. Although the literature did provide many ideas for improvement, it lacked the detail that would enable teachers to implement these ideas in the classroom. We concluded that teachers need a variety of living examples of such implementation, by teachers with whom they can identify and from whom they can derive the conviction and the confidence that they can do better, in order to see what doing better means in practice.

We followed our research review with a 25-page booklet for teachers entitled *Inside the Black Box* (Black & Wiliam, 1998b). Since that booklet was published, we have planned and implemented a program in which groups of teachers are supported in developing innovative practices in their classrooms. This work has produced a wealth of new findings that are both practical and authentic, so we are now confident that we can set out soundly based advice for improving classroom assessment. A second booklet for teachers entitled *Working Inside the Black Box* (Black, Harrison, Lee, Marshall, & Wiliam, 2002) describes this program and its results and has proved very popular with teachers.

In this paper, we first give a brief account of our work with teachers to develop formative assessment practices, including a brief outline of the quantitative results and the impact of the project. Second, we give a full account of the changes in classroom practice that the project schools developed, together with some reflections on their significance in relation to theories of learning and of motivation. Finally, we focus more specifically on those parts of the project that addressed ways in which the teachers dealt with the tensions at the interface between formative and summative assessment.

Working With Teachers and Schools

At the outset of the project, we found that we had to be very clear about the precise meaning of the term *formative assessment*, which is central to our work. In general, a formative assessment has as its prime purpose the promotion of learning, that is, the first priority in its design and practice is to serve the purpose of promoting students' learning. This distinguishes it from any assessment designed primarily to serve the purposes of determining accountability, ranking, or competence. An assessment activity can promote learning if it provides information that can be used, either by teachers or their students when assessing themselves and each other, to modify the teaching and learning activities in which they are engaged. Such assessment becomes formative assessment when this information is actually used to adapt the teaching work to meet learning needs.

We found that providing a detailed, precise definition of formative assessment was essential because many teachers and researchers seem to have misunderstood the term. Some have thought, for example, that it refers to any assessment conducted by teachers and, in particular, that giving a test every week and telling the students their marks constitutes formative assessment. It does not. Unless some learning action follows from the outcomes, that practice is merely frequent summative assessment. Others have believed that it includes portfolio assessment when that assessment is developed with the aim of replacing or supplementing the results produced by externally imposed tests. Again, there is no formative aspect to such practice except insofar as there is active feedback that enables students to change and improve their work as they build up their portfolios. In general, any test or assessment given at the end of a piece of learning cannot be formative because there is no opportunity to use its results as feedback to improve performance.

The King's Medway-Oxfordshire Formative Assessment Project

To carry out the necessary exploratory work, we needed to collaborate with a group of teachers willing to take on the risks and extra work involved, and we needed to secure support from their schools and their school districts. After receiving funding for the project through the generosity of the Nuffield Foundation, we chose to work with two school districts—Medway and Oxfordshire—because we knew that their advisory staff understood the issues and would be willing to work with us. Each authority selected three secondary schools (for ages 11 to 18) spanning a range of catchment areas; they included one boys' school and one girls' school, and four coeducational schools. Each school selected two science teachers and two mathematics teachers to participate in the project. We discussed our plans with the principal of each school and then called the first meeting of the 24 teachers. Thus, in January 1999, the King's-Medway-Oxfordshire Formative Assessment Project (KMOFAP) was born.

We decided to start with mathematics and science because we had expertise in the subject-specific details that we thought essential to practical development. In the following year, we augmented the project with one additional mathematics teacher and one additional science teacher, and we also began working with two English teachers from each school.

Our "intervention" with these teachers had two main components. The first was a series of nine one-day inservice (INSET) sessions conducted over a period of 18 months, during which teachers were introduced to our view of the principles underlying formative assessment and were given the opportunity to develop their own plans. The second consisted of regular visits to the schools, during which the teachers were observed teaching by project staff and had an opportunity to discuss their ideas and their practices. Feedback from the visits helped us to attune the INSET sessions to the developing thinking and practices of the teachers.

Because we were aware from other studies that effective implementation of formative assessment requires teachers to renegotiate the "learning contract" that has evolved between them and their students (Brousseau, 1984; Perrenoud, 1991), we decided that implementing formative assessment would best be done at the beginning of a new school year. For the first six months of the project (January 1999 to July 1999), therefore, we encouraged the teachers to experiment with some of the strategies and techniques suggested by the research, such as rich questioning, comment-only marking, sharing criteria with learners, and student peer and self-assessment. We then asked each teacher to draw up an action plan of the practices he or she wished to develop and to identify a single, focal class with whom these strategies would be introduced at the start of the new school year in September 1999.

The following examples are typical of these plans. One teacher proposed to work with a higher ability group of students ages 15-16 by formulating his questions so that they would encourage students to reflect on their own work, by giving the students samples of course work to assess in groups, by generally giving more time to peer work in groups, and by reducing his own burden of marking students' books by concentrating on those ways of marking that are most useful to students' learning. Another teacher in a girls' school proposed to work with a group of students ages 13-14 as follows: giving only one formal homework assignment per week; asking each girl to write her own question at the end of the assignment; having the student's own question marked in class by another girl; thinking about questions she asked in class, giving thinking time, and not accepting just the first answer, even if it were correct; and starting each lesson with an aim and ending with a summing up. (Further details about these plans can be found in Black, Harrison, Lee, Marshall, & Wiliam, 2003.)

The Learning Gains

Our intervention did not impose a model of "good formative assessment" upon teachers, but rather supported them in developing their own professional practices. Because each teacher was free to decide which class to experiment with, we could not impose a standard experimental design—we could not standardize the outcome measures, nor could we rely on having the same input measures for each class. In order to secure quantitative evidence, we therefore used an approach to the analysis that we have termed *local design*, making use of whatever data were available within the school in the normal course of events. In most cases, these were the results of the national tests for 14-year-olds or the national school leaving examinations for 16-year-olds, but in some cases we also made use of scores from school assessments. Each teacher consulted with us to identify a focal variable (i.e., a dependent variable or output) and in most cases, we also had reference variables (i.e., independent variables, or inputs). We then set up, for each experimental class, the best possible control class in the school. In some cases, this was a parallel class taught by the same teacher (either in the same or a previous year); in others, it was a parallel class taught by a different teacher. Failing that, we used a nonparallel class taught by the same or a different teacher. We also made use of national norms where these were available. In most cases, we were able to condition the focal variable on measures of prior achievement or general ability. By dividing the differences between the mean scores of the control group and the experimental groups by the pooled standard deviation, we were able to derive a standardized effect size (Glass, McGaw, & Smith, 1981) for each class. The median effect size was 0.27 standard deviations, and a jackknife procedure (Mosteller & Tukey, 1977) yielded a point estimate of the mean effect size of 0.32, with a 95% confidence interval of (0.16, 0.48). Of course, we cannot be sure that increased emphasis on formative assessment was responsible for this improvement in students' scores, but this does seem the most reasonable interpretation. (For further details of the experimental results, see Wiliam, Lee, Harrison, & Black, in press.)

This quantitative evidence that formative assessment does raise standards of achievement on the external "high-stakes" tests current in the U.K. was important in showing that innovations that worked in research studies in other countries could also be effective in our classrooms. Part of the reason that formative assessment works appears to be an increase in students' "mindfulness" (Bangert-Drowns, Kulik, Kulik, & Morgan, 1991), but then its effect on test performance will depend on the kind of knowledge that is assessed in the tests. More will be gained from formative feedback where a test calls for the mindfulness that formative assessment helps to develop. Thus it is significant that almost all the high-stakes assessments in the U.K. require constructed (as opposed to multiple choice) responses and often assess higher order skills.

In all of this development work, we emphasized to the teachers that the project must not involve them in working harder, but only in working smarter. The classroom times, the material to cover, and the formal tests of their students were to be no different from normal practices. The teachers reported that some of the changes—for example, formulating better questions when reviewing lesson plans or making comments more relevant when correcting homework—took longer initially, but also that they were able to overcome this with practice. For example, some marked less homework in order to find time to mark the rest more thoroughly. Other teachers found that questioning at the beginning of a topic sometimes revealed that students already knew what was to be taught. For example, one of the science teachers began a lesson on optics by asking the students a series of probing questions. He found that the students already knew all the content he was planning to teach, but that the links between the elements of their knowledge were missing. He quickly replanned the lesson "on the fly" to focus on the links between the concepts involved, rather than on the concepts themselves.

How the Project Changed Practices

This section sets out our main findings about classroom work under three headings: questioning, feedback through marking, and peer and self-assessment. Most of the quotations are taken from pieces written by the teachers; the names of the teachers and the schools are pseudonyms, as our policy was to guarantee their anonymity.

Questioning

The research of Rowe (1974) showed that many teachers leave less than one second after asking a question before, if no answer is forthcoming, asking another question or answering their own question. The key to changing such a situation is to allow a longer "wait time." However, even with short wait times, the only questions that work are those that can be answered quickly, without thought; that is, questions that call for memorized facts. Consequently, the dialogue is at a superficial level. So changing wait times can only work when corresponding changes are made in the questions asked:

Not until you analyse your own questioning do you realise how poor it can be. I found myself using questions to fill time and asking questions which required little thought from the students. When talking to students, particularly those who are experiencing difficulties, it is important to ask questions which get them thinking about the topic and will allow them to make the next step in the learning process. Simply directing them to the "correct answer" is not useful.   Derek, Century Island School

Other changes followed. In order to ensure that all students were actively involved in classroom dialogue, some teachers vetoed the practice of students putting their hands up to volunteer answers—all were expected to be able to answer at any time even if only to say "I don't know." Consequently, the teachers had to create a climate in which students would be comfortable giving a wrong answer so that these students, by exploring their wrong answers, could be helped to restructure their thinking. One particular strategy that increased participation was asking students to brainstorm ideas, perhaps in pairs, for two to three minutes prior to the teacher asking for contributions. Overall, such changes allowed teachers to learn more about the students' prior knowledge, as well as about any gaps or misconceptions in that knowledge, so that their next moves could address the learners' real needs.

An example is the use of a "big question": an open question or a problem-solving task that can set the scene for a lesson by evoking a broad-ranging discussion or by prompting small group discussions, thus involving many students. One teacher illustrated this as follows:

Nowadays, when we start a new unit, we start by looking at what we already know. This might be by having an in-depth question and answer session—with open-ended, challenging questions—such as, "If plants need sunlight to make food how come the biggest plants don't grow in deserts, where it's sunny all the time?" A *far better* lead in to the recall of photosynthesis than "What is the equation for photosynthesis?" The former question allows all those students who don't even remember the word photosynthesis to begin formulating ideas, and to be part of a discussion which gradually separates those who do remember and understand photosynthesis, from those who don't.
                                     Philip, Century Island School (teacher's emphasis)

The combined effect of such changes was to alter students' understanding of their classroom as a place for learning. As one teacher put it,

There have been two very positive results from this approach. The most significant one is that because they have to explain their answers each time orally this has carried through to their written work and now they set out their answers fully without being prompted. The second one is with a girl with a statement [of special educational need] for being unable to talk or communicate with an adult. Having got used to the extra thinking time she now offers answers orally and will now tentatively explain her answers.

Gwen, Waterford School

Effective questioning also has to become an important aspect of the impromptu interventions teachers make once the students are engaged in an activity. These often include simple questions, such as "Why do you think that?" or "How might you express that?" or—in the "devil's advocate" style—"You could argue that..." This type of questioning can become part of the interactive dynamic of the classroom and can provide an invaluable opportunity to extend students' thinking through immediate feedback on their work.

Put simply, the only point of asking questions is to raise issues about which the teacher needs information or about which the students need to think. Where changes to questioning practices have been made, students have become more active as participants and have come to realize that learning may depend less on their capacity to spot the right answer and more on their readiness to express and discuss their own understanding. The teachers began to realize that in the past they had not planned and conducted classroom dialogue in ways that might help students to learn, and that they had to shift in their role, from presenters of content to leaders of an exploration that develops ideas in which all students are involved.

Feedback Through Marking

The second area in which the KMOFAP developed formative practices was feedback. Feedback to learners should both assess their current achievement and indicate the next steps for their learning. Here we created discussion and influenced the teachers' practices by describing research by Butler (1988) about the types of feedback that students receive on their written work. In a controlled experimental study, Butler set up three different ways of providing feedback to learners—percentage scores (40 to 99), comments, and a combination of scores and comments. The study showed learning gains for the group given only comments, with the other two treatments showing no gains. Some of the teachers participating in the KMOFAP were shocked by these findings and initially could not envisage how giving comments without scores would be possible in their schools. Many were goaded by these research findings to explore reasons for such findings in order to make sense of why and how comment-only marking might raise achievement. For these teachers, the study had created "cognitive conflict" which led them to debate with colleagues in an effort to resolve their conflict. However, the study created "cognitive inhibition" for some teachers, who felt that their school situation prevented their even considering the possibility of giving comments without scores.

Those who were able to discuss the possibilities of implementing comment-only marking pointed out, in justification, that students rarely read comments, preferring to compare scores with peers as their first reaction on getting work back; that teachers rarely give students time in class to read comments on written work; and that probably few, if any, students consider these comments further at home. They also realized that comments are often brief, not specific, or both—for example, the same written comments (such as "Details?") frequently recur in a student's exercise book, which reinforced the impression that students do not act on the comments.

Such reflections, together with the impetus the Butler study provided, encouraged the teachers to envisage how feedback might be employed differently. This involved more than simply not giving a percentage score or a letter grade. It involved finding the best way to communicate to the learners about what they had achieved and what they needed to work on next, then leading them to take action on the feedback and providing them with appropriate support.

We began guiding this change by first interviewing students in three of the schools and investigating their reactions to the way that their exercise books were marked and the value they gave the feedback comments that they received. The very clear messages from the students were that they wanted their teachers 1) not to use red pen (students felt that it ruined their work); 2) to write legibly so that the comments could be read; and 3) to write statements that could be understood. Given these messages, the KMOFAP teachers, through discussion with project colleagues, worked on producing quality comments that could direct and motivate their students to improve their work. Collaboration among the teachers in sharing examples of effective comments was helpful, and experience led to more efficient assessment.

Most of the comments that we saw at the start of the project either stated a general evaluation, such as "good" or "well done," or were geared to improving presentation, or merely requested completion of the work. Such comments had to be replaced by comments that informed students about what they had achieved and what they needed to do next. Examples of the new style are:

James, you have provided clear diagrams and recognised which chemicals are elements and which are compounds. Can you give a general explanation of the difference between elements and compounds?

Susan, you have got the right idea here about trying to explain your rule. Think: does it apply to all triangles?

Initial fears about how students might react to not receiving scores turned out to be unjustified. Students came to realize that the comments helped them in their future work:

At no time during the first fifteen months of comment-only marking did any of the students ask me why they no longer received grades. It was as if they were not bothered by this omission. I found this amazing, particularly considering just how much emphasis students place on the grades and how little heed is taken of the comments generally... When asked by our visitor how she knew how well she was doing in Science, the student clearly stated that the comments in her exercise book and those given verbally provide her with the information she needs. Derek, Century Island School

Also, neither parents nor senior management teams nor government inspectors have reacted adversely. Indeed, comments help parents focus on and support the student's learning rather than make uninformed attempts to interpret a score or grade or simply urge their child to work harder. In fact, we believe that the effort many teachers devote to scoring may be misdirected: a numerical score does not tell a student how to improve his or her work, so an opportunity to enhance learning has been lost.

The KMOFAP teachers used a variety of ways of accommodating the new emphasis on comments. Some teachers ceased to assign scores at all; some entered scores in record books but did not write them in the students' books; others gave scores only after students had responded to their comments. A particularly valuable method is to devote some lesson time to redrafting one or two pieces of work, so that emphasis can be placed on feedback for improvement within a supportive environment. This can change students' expectations about the purposes of classwork and homework.

As they tried to create useful feedback comments, many of the project teachers realized that they needed to reassess the work that they had asked students to undertake. They found that some tasks were useful in revealing students' understandings and misunderstandings, but that others focused mainly on conveying information. The teachers also took time to reflect on schemes of work for specific topics and to recognize those activities in which there was the opportunity to create a range of good comments, to be followed by appropriate activities in which students could respond to the feedback comments.

As both teachers and learners became more familiar with and more skillful in dealing with comment-only marking, the classroom culture began to change. All came to understand that it was worthwhile putting in the effort to work with feedback through comments because they could sense that learning was improving. The comments provided the vehicle for personal dialogue with each learner about his or her work to which the learner could respond. However, the development was more important than that because the teachers also came to realize that they needed to create learning environments that supported and fostered good learning behaviors in their students.

Overall, improvement of learning through students' written work calls for tasks designed to encourage students to develop and show understanding, backed up by comments that identify what has been done well and that give guidance on how to make the improvements that are needed. To complete the learning process, students need opportunities and support so that they can follow up the comments with further work.

However, there is another dimension involved here. The way in which teachers give feedback to students can have significant effects on the students' motivation and self-esteem. Butler's (1987) work showed that feedback given as rewards or grades enhances ego rather than task involvement; that is to say, it leads students to compare themselves with others and focus on their image and status rather than encouraging them to think about the work itself and how they can improve it. Rewards or grades can also focus students' attention on their "ability" rather than on the importance of effort, thus damaging the self-esteem of low attainers and leading to problems of "learned helplessness" (Dweck, 1986). Indeed, as Craven, Marsh, and Debus (1991) demonstrated, in a competitive system, low attainers attribute their performance to lack of "ability," high attainers, to their effort; in a task-oriented system, all attribute performance to effort and learning is improved, particularly among low attainers. Newman and Schwager (1995) found that students who were told that feedback "will help you to learn" learned more than those told that "how you do tells us how smart you are and what grades you'll get"; furthermore, the increase in learning was again greatest for low attainers. In their comprehensive review of research studies of feedback, Kluger and DeNisi (1996) showed that feedback improved performance in 60% of the studies, but that in the cases where it was not helpful, the feedback turned out to be merely a judgment or a grade with no indication of how to improve.

These various studies underline the importance of the changes that we explored with the KMOFAP teachers. Feedback that focuses on what needs to be done can enhance learning, both directly through the effort that can ensue and indirectly by supporting the motivation to invest in such effort. A culture of success should be promoted, where all students can achieve by building on their previous performance, rather than by being compared with others. Such a culture is promoted by informing students about the strengths and weaknesses demonstrated in their work and by giving feedback about what their next steps should be.

Peer and Self-assessment

The starting point here was the work of Sadler (1989), who points out that self-assessment is essential to learning, because to achieve a learning goal students must both understand that goal and be able to assess what they need to do to reach it. In developing self-assessment skills, teachers find that the first and most difficult task is to get students to think of their work in terms of a set of goals. One teacher identified the key features as follows:

I have thought carefully about students taking *ownership* of their own learning. I have now thought more about letting students know what the intention of the lesson is and what they need to do to *achieve it*. This way they have to think about what they know and take more *responsibility* for their own learning.   Angela, Cornbury Estate School (teacher's emphases)

At the start of the project, students' initial attempts at self-assessment and target setting were unsuccessful. The source of the problem was that students lacked the necessary skills both to judge specific problems in understanding and to set realistic targets to remedy them. However, those teachers who introduced feedback through comments were providing the training that students needed in order to judge their own learning and to begin to take action to improve.

In practice, peer assessment turns out to be an important complement to, and perhaps a prior requirement for, self-assessment, for several reasons. First, the prospect of such assessment has been found to improve students' motivation to work more carefully:

The students know that homework will be checked by themselves or another girl in the class at the start of the next lesson. This has lead to a well-established routine and only on extremely rare occasions have students failed to complete the work set. They take pride in clear and well presented work that one of their peers may be asked to mark.   Alice, Waterford School

Second, the interchange in peer discussions is in language that students themselves would naturally use. They communicate with one another in shared language forms and models of quality, so that the achievements of some can convey the meaning and value of the exercise to others who are still struggling. Furthermore, students accept from one another criticisms of their work that they would not take seriously if made by their teacher:

Students regularly read their own work or another pupil's as a matter of course. This has made them realise how important it is to write clearly. Previously I would have said that I could not read their work—their peers saying they cannot read the writing has more of an impact. Rose, Brownfields School

A third advantage is that feedback from a group to a teacher can command more attention than that from an individual, and so peer assessment helps strengthen the student voice, thus improving communication between students and teachers. This can also make the teacher's task more manageable, for it helps the learners to recognize their own learning needs and to inform the teacher about these needs.

One simple and effective idea is for students to use "stop light" icons, labeling their work green, yellow, or red according to whether they think they have good, partial, or little understanding. These labels serve as a simple means of communication of students' confidence in their work and so act as a form of self-assessment. Students may then be asked to justify their judgments in a peer group, thus linking peer and self-assessment.

So it seems that peer assessment is an important factor in helping students develop the essential skills that they require for self-assessment. KMOFAP teachers developed a variety of classroom strategies to explore these habits and skills. The following teacher used them as part of the work on "investigations" in mathematics:

I got them to mark their peers' investigational work . . . I was really surprised with the attention they paid to the work and to the levels. They also gave excellent reasons for giving that person's work the level they did. The work was swapped back and the pupil then had to produce targets for their own work . . . I found when marking the work that some had not quite got the gist of it, but that will come with repetition of the task in the future.

Lily, Brownfields School

Another approach is to ask students first to "stop light" a piece of work and then to indicate by a show of hands whether they chose green, yellow, or red; the teacher can then pair up the greens and yellows to deal with problems between them, while the red students can be helped as a group to deal with their deeper problems. This is instant differentiation. Because the response to their needs is immediate, students begin to realize that revealing their problems is worthwhile because the focus of the teaching is to improve learning rather than to compare one student with another:

They have commented on the fact that they think I am more interested in the general way to get to an answer than a specific solution and when Clare [a researcher] interviewed them they decided this was so that they could apply their understanding in a wider sense.   Belinda, Cornbury Estate School

Peer assessment can help develop the objectivity required for effective self-assessment, but it will only thrive if teachers help their students, particularly the low attainers, to develop the skill. Many students will need guidance about how to behave in groups, for example, listening to one another and taking turns, and once again this takes time and care if it is to succeed in the classroom. These skills of collaboration in peer assessment are of intrinsic value as well as serving to improve achievement.

Both the literature on learning and our experience in the project have convinced us that peer and self-assessment make unique contributions to the development of students' learning—they secure aims that cannot be achieved in any other way. This conviction leads us to recommend to teachers that the criteria for evaluating any learning achievements must as far as possible be made transparent to students. Such criteria may well be abstract—concrete examples should be used in modeling exercises to develop understanding. Suitable models may be drawn from the work of other students, modified where appropriate to highlight particular aspects. Only where students are encouraged to keep in mind the aims of their work and to assess their own progress will they be able to guide their own work and so become independent learners.

Formative Feedback and Learning

During one of our early meetings, the project teachers asked us to run a session on the psychology of learning. This was a surprise, but it was a welcome one that in retrospect should not have surprised us. The teachers were trying to feed back information to the learners to help them in improving performance, so they needed to know in advance what sort of information was going to be useful and how students might best make use of it; they needed to build models of how students learn.

The main lesson that emerges from constructivist approaches to learning theory is that the key to effective learning is to start from the students' own ideas and then help them to restructure their knowledge in order to build in different and more powerful ideas (Bransford, Brown, & Cocking, 1999; Wood, 1998). So it was clear that the first aim of classroom dialogue should be to evoke, and so put on the agenda, students' own ideas. The teachers came to take greater care in selecting tasks, questions, and other prompts to ensure that the students' responses actually helped the teaching process. When students make their thinking explicit through talking, it allows the teacher some access into the students' thinking, and they can intervene to address misconceptions or to promote further learning. This is nicely illustrated by the science lesson on optics described earlier.

As the KMOFAP teachers came to listen more attentively to the students' responses, they began to appreciate more fully that learning is not a process of passive reception of knowledge, but one in which the learners are active in creating their own understandings. As well as helping the teacher, getting students to make their thinking explicit is also important for the learner because it actually causes learning. It is tempting to view the process of questioning as "probing" to see whether the requisite knowledge is stored somewhere in a student's head. This may well be what is going on when the teacher asks low order questions, such as those that require mere recollection of facts. However, when the teacher asks higher order questions—questions that explore understanding and require thinking—the student is not just recalling knowledge but also building it. This is why allowing students enough time in questioning sessions is important (see chap. 4 in Black et al., 2003).

Such principles are also applicable to the setting of homework and other tasks requiring written responses. Here, thinking about the purposes of feedback and the ways to ensure that students made good use of it emphasized a related principle: no matter the pressure to achieve good test and examination scores, learning cannot be done *for* the student; it has to be done *by* the student.

Engaging in peer and self-assessment was also a significant step away from the culture of passive reception and toward active and responsible involvement. The developments in these practices involved much more than just checking for errors or weaknesses. They involved making explicit what is normally implicit, helping students to understand the criteria for quality in assessing their own work and the work of their peers. As one student wrote,

After a pupil marking my investigation, I can now acknowledge my mistakes easier. I hope that it is not just me who learnt from the investigation but the pupil who marked it did also. Next time I will have to make my explanations clearer, as they said "It is hard to understand" . . . I will now explain my equation again so it is clear.

Because the opportunities for students to articulate their thoughts in a whole-class session are limited, many of the KMOFAP teachers began to appreciate the usefulness of small-group work, which created more opportunities for students to talk about their work. Students articulated their own understanding; the contributions of others in the group were "scaffolded," but here the scaffolding was provided by peers.

The students also became much more aware of when they were learning and when they were not. One class, subsequently taught by a teacher not emphasizing assessment for learning, surprised that teacher by complaining, "Look, we've told you we don't understand this. Why are you going on to the next topic?"

These changes were also leading the students to develop an overview of their learning work. Teachers felt they had to ensure that feedback, in classroom dialogue and on written work, was selective in emphasizing those aspects of the work that were essential to its purposes. The work of peer and self-assessment took this one step further, for any such assessments could only be made by applying criteria of quality based on the underlying aims of the exercise. This stress on purposes and criteria was a way of taking seriously the notion that meta-cognition is a hallmark of effective learning. Further examples of the development of meta-cognition are discussed below.

A final aspect in which the work developed, reflected, and implemented basic principles of learning was in the ways it stimulated, even required, students to talk more, thus making the classroom a place where the community was regularly engaged in talk about their learning. The idea of social learning was being taken seriously and its practice developed, both in the whole-class dialogue and in work in peer groups.

That the various formative assessment practices did reflect and implement basic learning principles was not merely a happy accident.

Formative assessment is about developing interaction between teachers and learners, about evoking evidence from such interactions and using it as feedback, and about learners' capacity to make intelligent use of such feedback in order to improve. It is not possible to work to such an agenda without implementing these basic learning principles.

Differences Between Subjects

As stated earlier, we started this project with teachers of mathematics and science because we believed that the specifics of the subject matter might be significant in the development of new practices and these were the subjects in which we had expertise, and we later included teachers of English with the collaboration of a colleague expert in that subject. More recently, in training sessions with larger groups, we have had to engage with teachers of other subjects also. The issue that has concerned us is both practical and theoretical. The question is, to what extent are the practices we can describe and recommend generic, and to what extent should they be prioritized and detailed differently depending on the subject discipline involved? The practical importance is clear when one is engaged in advising school staff about developing a formative assessment policy for the whole school. We offer in this section some of the lessons that have emerged. (For more detail see chap. 6 of Black et al., 2003.)

To enrich classroom interaction and the learning value of students' written work, teachers must frame or choose tasks, activities, or questions in light of their own subject knowledge. This is not, however, the kind of abstract subject knowledge that is developed through advanced study. Advanced study often produces individuals who partially understand a great deal of advanced material, while effective teachers understand thoroughly the basic material in light of their students' learning needs (Askew & Wiliam, 1995). This idea has been summed up in Shulman's notion of pedagogical content knowledge (Shulman, 1986). For example, it is very easy to recommend to teachers a generic form of question such as "Why is X an example of Y?" but this is of little value until it is translated into concrete form, and then one has to make judgments according to the subject about such specific questions as "Why is photosynthesis an example of an endothermic reaction?" or "Why is a square an example of a rectangle?" or "Why is *A Perfect Spy* by John Le Carre an example of a love story?"

Comparisons between our experiences of work with teachers of English, science, and mathematics have strengthened our view that the subject disciplines create strong differences in both the mindsets of the teachers and the conduct of learning in their classes. Teachers of mathematics and science tend to regard their subjects as being defined by a body of knowledge that gives the subject unique and objectively defined aims. It is possible to "deliver" the subject matter without necessarily ensuring that students learn with understanding, and even where priority is given to providing help with understanding, it is help that is designed to ensure that every student achieves the "correct" conceptual goal.

In the teaching of writing, there is very little to deliver, unless teachers focus only on the mechanics in grammar, spelling, and punctuation. Rather than a single goal for the whole class, there is a range of goals that might be appropriate for a particular student at a particular time (and, of course, the range of goals will be different for different students at different times). If we view the process of intervening in students' learning as one of "regulating learning" (i.e., keeping learning on track), then the mathematics and science teachers generally appeared to try to bring all the students in a class to a common goal, while for the teachers of English, there was a "horizon" of different goals. Having said this, it is important to note that the English teachers did not operate with a policy of "anything goes." When a student was pursuing a track that the teacher believed would be unproductive, the teacher did intervene to bring the student back on track, but the range of acceptable trajectories of learning seemed to be much greater for English teachers than for the teachers of mathematics and science. It is also important to note that when their classes were undertaking open-ended activities such as investigations or studies of the social and ethical consequences of scientific discoveries, the mathematics and science teachers regulated students' learning in a way similar to that typical of English teachers.

This suggests that the differences in practice in different subjects are not inherent in the subject, but rather are consequences of the way that the subject is interpreted, in the school curriculum and by the teacher. When the goal is very specific, the teacher's regulation of the students' work will be tight, and when the goal is less well defined, the regulation will be looser. This regulation takes place on two levels (as pointed out by Perrenoud [1998]). The macro level is that of the task or activity. Where the goal is specific, the teacher will choose a task or activity that will lead students more or less directly to the required skill or competence, but where there is a horizon of possibilities, the task or activity will allow (and perhaps even encourage) students to head off in different directions. However, the teacher will also regulate learning at the micro level of the individual student, by observing the student's progress and intervening when the student appears not to be on track, and of course the more specific the goal, the tighter the regulation.

The question still remains, however, as to whether the differences that emerged in the practices of our teachers, and in the writing that we asked them to produce as reflections on their experiences in the project, are merely superficial and simply arise out of the examples they choose to discuss, or whether assessment for learning is substantially different in different subjects. Some of the perceived differences may be attributable to the fact that teachers of English, at least in secondary schools, are often themselves writers, and their students have more direct interaction with the subject, through their own reading and writing, than they might with science and mathematics, for example. These English teachers would have more personal experience of creativity, and of the problems of understanding the criteria of quality in creative work, than (say) science or mathematics teachers who, probably having only learned about the creative work of others without ever engaging in either original research or expert critiques of such work, would be more naturally prone to becoming trapped in a transmission model of teaching and learning.

One way of getting at the issue is to look at the broad generalizations we might make about different subject areas and the aims and debates that exist within them. At the risk of oversimplification, it is helpful to examine four groups of subjects: arts, sciences, humanities, and languages. Some subjects (e.g., English or technology) could, of course, easily be placed within more than one of these groups.

If we begin, then, by considering teachers of the arts, it could be said that, among other things, they desire to encourage creativity and expression in the students they teach. Success is usually judged by the outcome of the finished product. For some time, however, the process by which this final product is arrived at has been considered important for giving students an experience of what it means to be a practitioner in that subject and also a mechanism by which improvement may be achieved. This approach can stem from a philosophy that places experimentation and reflection at the heart of practice. For example, in drama the practice of peer feedback on role-playing activities and group performance has been long established. The summative assessments used have also reflected this trend, and students are often required to keep a log of the process by which they achieve their final product.

The debates in these subjects revolve around how the technical and craft aspects involved in the process of creation should be introduced and the extent to which analysis of these technical elements actually aids performance. In other words, do you have to have the basics first, and if so, what constitutes the basics, or should these so-called basics be introduced within the context of authentic tasks? The same debate appears in the teaching of technology and craft work. Yet whichever the approach taken, until recently the emphasis has tended to discourage the idea of a wrong answer. While it has always been perfectly possible to make factual errors, for example in the description of the plot of a novel, most teachers would still support the notion that as long as an opinion can be supported by evidence and argument it has some validity (Marshall, 2000). The same point could be made in the teaching of history. It may be generally acceptable to say that the Second World War started in 1939, but coherent and interesting arguments could be made that the war started in 1937 or 1942, or even 1919.

Now, on the one hand, this seems to be fertile territory for assessment for learning. Peer and self-assessment, drafting, and reflection are already well established in these subjects. On the other hand, some principles for teaching the arts can seem very vague, with no clear idea of progression. Part of the nature of the subject is to assess quality and learn how to apply those judgments to one's own work. Much of the role of the teacher is to apprentice students into this process.

To characterize the sciences as the opposite of the arts would be a mistake. Yet the ease by which arts teachers can set open-ended tasks, encourage debate and dissent, and see the relevance of this process to their overall aim appears, on the surface, less available in the sciences.

In science, for example, many students acquire ideas outside school that are contradicted by the scientific view. An example is the belief that animals are living, but trees and flowers are not because they do not move. Many of these alternative conceptions have been well documented. Also documented is that the mere presentation of the correct view does not change students' beliefs (Driver, 1983). The task in such cases is to open up discussion of these ideas and then provide feedback that challenges them by introducing new pieces of evidence and argument that support the scientific model. However, in both science and mathematics, open-ended investigations, let alone broader issues about the social or ethical implications of scientific achievements, call for different approaches. There is no single "right" answer, and so the work has to be open in a more fundamental way. The priority in giving feedback in science and mathematics, then, is to challenge students to tease out their assumptions and to help them to be critical about the quality of their own arguments.

Summative Tests

In planning the formative assessment project, we decided that we would avoid as much as possible any work concerned with summative testing. To achieve this, we asked the teachers not to choose classes in the two years of secondary school during which external national tests were held. This was not because we judged that the pressures of summative testing would be unimportant, but that we could do nothing about them. We expected that the U.K.'s high-stakes external tests would inhibit the formative work, but hoped to minimize such effects by advising the teachers to work with classes in years when such tests were not due. Most teachers ignored this advice with the result that some valuable work was developed on the formative use of summative tests. This work is described in the first part of this section. It led us, in the last phase of the study, to explore with teachers their perceptions of the formative-summative interface in their schools: the findings are discussed in the second part of this section.

The Formative Use of Summative Tests

Teachers came to ignore our attempted veto on summative testing because they felt the need to explore whether the new learning practices could be reflected in, and help with their inescapable concern with, summative testing. However, the findings in this section are mainly, but not exclusively, concerned with summative tests internal to the teachers' own schools, which the teachers themselves or their colleagues had created and over which they therefore had some control.

A first step proceeded from the following observation about his students that one teacher introduced:

> They did not mention any of the reviewing strategies we had discussed in class. When questioned more closely it was clear that many spent their time using very passive revision techniques. They would read over their work doing very little in the way of active revision or reviewing of their work. They were not transferring the active learning strategies we were using in class to work they did at home.   Tom, Riverside School

It was felt that practices of peer and self-assessment could help in tackling this problem. Some changed this situation by asking students to "stop light" a list of key words or a list of the topics on which the test would be based. The point of this was to stimulate the students to reflect on where they felt their learning was secure, which they marked green, and where they needed to concentrate their efforts, which they marked in yellow and red. These labels then formed a basis for review. Students were asked to identify questions on past examination papers that tested their red areas and then to work with books and in peer groups to ensure that they could successfully answer those questions.

A second idea was introduced by us: we told the teachers about research studies (Foos, Mora, & Tkacz, 1994; King, 1992) that have shown that students trained to prepare for examinations by generating and then answering their own questions out-performed comparable groups who prepared in conventional ways. Preparation of test questions calls for, and so develops, an overview of the topic:

Students have had to think about what makes a good question for a test and in doing so need to have a clear understanding of the subject material. As a development of this, the best questions have been used for class tests. In this way the students can see that their work is valued and I can make an assessment of the progress made in these areas. When going over the test good use can be made of groupwork and discussions between students concentrating on specific areas of concern.   Angela, Cornbury Estate School

The aftermath of tests was also seen to be an occasion for formative work. Peer marking of test papers was found helpful, as with written assignments, and was particularly useful if students were required first to formulate a scoring rubric scheme, an exercise that focused attention on criteria of quality relevant to their productions. After peer marking, teachers could reserve their time for discussion of the questions that give particular difficulty to many, while peer tutoring could tackle those problems encountered by only a minority. As one teacher reported,

After each end of term test, the class is grouped now to learn from each other. Clare has interviewed them on this experience and they are very positive about the effects. Some of their comments show that they are starting to value the learning process more highly and they appreciate the fact that misunderstandings are given time to be resolved, either in groups or by me. They feel that the pressure to succeed in tests is being replaced by the need to understand the work that has been covered and the test is just an assessment along the way of what needs more work and what seems to be fine.

Belinda, Cornbury Estate School

These developments challenged common expectations. Some have argued that formative and summative assessments are so different in their purposes that they have to be kept apart, and such arguments are strengthened by experience of the harmful influence that narrow high-stakes summative tests can have on teaching. However, it is unrealistic to expect teachers and students to practice such separation, so the challenge is to achieve a more positive relationship between the two.

It seemed that overall, classroom practice in relation to preparation for summative testing had to change, both in giving students help to engage in a reflective review of the work they had done so that they could plan their revision effectively, and in encouraging them to set questions in order to both understand the assessment process and gain an overview of their work. After a test, encouraging students to mark answers through peer and self-assessment helped them to grasp the criteria of quality and so to understand how their work might be improved.

The underlying message is that summative tests should be, and should be seen to be, a positive part of the learning process. By active involvement in the test process, students can see that they can be beneficiaries rather than victims of testing because tests can help them improve their learning.

Teachers on the Formative-Summative Interface

This section summarizes opinions of teachers who had worked through our project—so they were not typical teachers. The summary is based on individual and group interviews, teachers' diary entries, and teachers' responses to questionnaires. There are few generalizations; what is striking is the variety of practices across the six schools involved. The immediate purpose of this work was to explore the territory, the "no-man's land," between the ground occupied by classroom practices and the ground on which the alliance of external tests and the armies of accountability and public certification is firmly entrenched.

In school tests, there was very little use of questions set by the teachers themselves. They relied on questions taken from past external tests and from textbooks. A school test was typically assembled by one teacher, working alone on behalf of all, and was not usually reviewed with or by colleagues. Often, the same test was used year after year. The marking schemes were similarly prepared, without discussion, and teachers were aware that quality control was lacking. These external sources were used despite the teachers' low opinion of many of the questions. Some believed that their own tests were more useful for formative purposes but thought that, lacking as they were in any critical scrutiny, they would not have external credibility, whether with colleagues or with the students.

In marking, a few tried to use criterion referencing to help the test's results give a guide to progression against the targets of the national curriculum. Several involved their students in peer marking of their tests, with the teacher checking the outcomes. One teacher reported objections from a colleague not in our project that this gave such students an unfair advantage. It was common, both with homework and with some semiformal tests, for students to rework their answers after feedback. Most assigned only a single overall mark, but some used the components of the national curriculum (known as Attainment Targets) as the basis of a profile. Many said they would like to produce a profile, but that it involved too much work and they did not have the time. The teachers were well aware that aggregation of test marks loses all the information useful for feedback—but they nevertheless provided the data "for the school office."

The requirements for formal test occasions were prescribed either by the school, by the subject department, or by the individual teacher. The relative impact of these three sources, and the frequencies that ensued, were very variable. School requirements seem to range from none to four or five times a year, at fixed times or variable times. It was common to have a formal test at the end of a topic or module; some tested before the end of a module so that there would be time for formative use of the results. One teacher had a firm belief in testing topic by topic and avoiding any overall "big bang" test. Another teacher would only schedule a test when she thought the class ready—if the homework showed that they were not, she would defer the test and go over the common difficulties; this was the only evidence of adoption of a "mastery" approach. A few stated that they only scheduled tests because their schools required them. As one teacher put it,

I know a lot more about this class because of the formative assessment. I mean we discuss things, they do presentations, they talk to me, I talk to them, they talk to each other—and I could tell you for every one of this class their strengths and weaknesses. Derek, Century Island School

For practices of recording and reporting, it was again hard to find any regularities. For homework, some kept no record, some recorded only that the homework had been attempted, some scored but recorded the score only in their own record book, and some used peer assessment and perhaps checked this and recorded a score afterward. A complete record could involve a log of homework results, plus end-of-module test scores, plus scores on less formal class tests, plus effort grades judged by the teachers (or in one case, by the students). One school set up software so that students could enter their own records, update them, and review progress themselves and with their teacher. A few teachers said that it was too hard to review all the data, so they just used the scores on a terminal test to report to the school management, particularly when the need arose at the end of term when they did not have the time to collect and analyze the data. Among science teachers there was a common opinion that the variability across the various component topics made reviewing to produce an aggregate fairly pointless.

The quote from Derek, above, illustrates the fact that some teachers believed that they knew the students well enough without tests because of the interactions and feedback produced in the development of formative assessment. However, some holding this belief nevertheless realized also that their staff colleagues did not know the students in their classes well enough to assess each of them using personal knowledge. In addition, they were concerned that this variability in assessment expertise was exacerbated by the flux of teacher appointments and resignations and by the frequent use of substitute teachers. Thus the prospects of reliance on formative assessment as the sole basis for review on a department-wide or school-wide scale seemed to them to be remote.

For reporting to parents, two contrary views were expressed. One teacher explained how he felt he had to use only the test score:

Everyone is obsessed with numbers rather than what the kids really know. I think parents don't put a lot of weighting onto teacher assessment, they don't even put a lot of weighting onto coursework as a way of measuring their child's ability. Certainly they wouldn't put a lot of store by what I say as opposed to what a test says because at the end of the day society is driven by test results in schools . . . at the end of the day if you gave them the choice—they can have what I think or they can have an exam grade—they would take the exam grade every time because that is what they want. They want to be able to compare that with everyone else even though it is not about everyone else.

Philip, Century Island School

Given such a perception of parental expectations, the need to "avoid hassles" with parents, and the shortages of time, using only a score on a terminal test is the easy way out.

A contrary view was that parents appreciated the rich detail provided through good formative assessment, in that they and their children could be given specific and helpful advice on how to improve. This different appraisal of the situation may have arisen from a variety of causes that had to do with the success of the school as a whole in explaining learning needs to parents.

Teachers of English believed that training students to write in the timed conditions of external high-stakes tests absorbed valuable time.

This specific training was not necessarily connected to their view of valid English teaching. They acknowledged that writing to a deadline is an important skill but that teaching for this end detracted from time that could be spent engaging with and responding to texts. In addition, they believed that students often showed flair and originality that was not acknowledged in the assessment criteria and so was often missed. Teachers felt they just had to decode the requirements of the tests and were not able to approach all the set texts in ways they or the students might want. To this extent they believed there was "something desiccated about the process."

When asked how summative assessments affected what they taught and the way in which they taught it, science teachers mentioned several effects. They had to teach to the test, even though the test questions seemed to them to lack validity in relation to the national curriculum specifications. Summative test pressures inhibited teaching to cross-link concepts—everything had to be compartmentalized or isolated. The test pressures also limited practical work, affected the range of types of lessons, restricted teaching styles, and inhibited imaginative research-type lessons. Tying lessons to specific national curriculum statements restricted student involvement and enjoyment.

At the end of one discussion with a group of the project teachers about these issues, one of them summed it up as follows:

It is a bit depressing that isn't it?   Gwen, Waterford School

We could only agree with her. Because of the reality of their pressures, external tests had to be acknowledged and accommodated despite teachers' views of their low quality and their poor effects on learning. Things could get better if the validity of the tests could be improved, but even if it could be optimized, overall validity would still require some *independent* assessment by teachers as a complementary source of evidence. Overall, teachers seemed to be trapped between their new commitment to formative assessment and the different, often contradictory, demands of the external test system. Their formative use of summative tests had served to move the frontier significantly, but further territory seemed unassailable.

For the formative assessment work described in this paper, there emerges a dilemma: good formative practices may be used to prepare for tests in two ways. The *narrow* way is to continue to teach to the test, but to make such narrowly focused teaching more effective by helping students with better ways to prepare by revision, to "read" the intentions of test questions, and to anticipate the criteria by which their answers might be judged. The *broad* way is to teach for understanding of the concepts and processes that lie at the heart of the subject and trust that such deeper understanding will inevitably produce better test performances. While there is good evidence from this study and from others (Boaler, 1997; Newmann, Bryk, & Nagaoka, 2001; Nuthall & Alton-Lee, 1995), that the latter strategy will be rewarded, many might use both approaches, using the broad approach most of the time and switching to the narrow, test-focused approach in the immediate run-up to high-stakes tests.

Achievement and Impact

In this chapter we can only describe the evidence for the success of this project very briefly. In addition to the quantitative evidence of learning gains set out above, we have evidence of the changes in the classrooms from the direct observations of the researchers, the discussions among the teachers at our meetings, and the reflective writing about their experiences that 19 of the teachers produced for us. This evidence shows that almost all of the teachers achieved very significant, often radical changes in their instructional practices (Lee, 2000). It also shows that they were very pleased, in many cases enthusiastic, about the personal professional development that the work had helped them achieve. One teacher concluded that his main lesson was that he had been doing almost all of the work in class and that he had to start making sure that his students did most of the work. Two of the schools involved established, in response to the findings of four of their staff who participated in the project, a rule for the whole school: feedback on students' homework would be given through comments on how to improve, and scores or grades would not be given on any such work—an outcome that would have been unheard of two years earlier. Many of the teachers have since become ambassadors, in their own schools, in their school districts, and more broadly, for formative assessment.

There has also been a wider impact. The 24-page booklet describing, for a teacher audience, the outcome of the work (Black et al., 2002) has sold about 30,000 copies in the U.K. as of the time of this publication. Throughout the development of the project, the members of the research team have received, and are still receiving, more invitations to talk to meetings of teachers than we can possibly manage. We are also acting as consultants for regional development plans in three large districts. The invitations have ranged across all subjects and across both primary and secondary phases. In addition, there has been sustained work with some primary schools. All of this makes us confident that our general findings will be of value to all, although some important details may vary between different age groups and different subjects.

The KMOFAP was guided by a steering group that included, in addition to the King's researchers and the school district staff, nominees from the U.K. government ministry and several government agencies. The project benefited from this guidance, and contacts in the group helped us to ensure that its progress was well known to the organizations represented. These links have also ensured that assessment for learning is currently one of the central themes of a government initiative to improve teaching and learning in the 11 to 14 age range: 3,500 copies of our recent booklet have been bought for distribution to schools as part of that initiative.

A U.S. version of *Inside the Black Box* has been published (Black & Wiliam, 1998c), and a group at Stanford University obtained funding from the National Science Foundation to set up a similar development project, in collaboration with King's, in schools in California. The findings of that project are not included in this chapter. (For more information, see Sato, 2003.)

We have attempted elsewhere an analysis of the reasons for this success (Black & Wiliam, 2003). The key is not that we had new research results about learning to offer; it is that we have been reviewing, synthesizing, and learning how to deploy the numerous results of other researchers, results that for all their cogency had had little impact on classrooms. One key strategy was to interlink these findings into a unifying framework—the concept, central in formative assessment, that learning requires active and frequent interaction between teachers and learners.

A second key strategy was that, while providing the teachers with ideas about both the instructional processes and the subject contents that were backed by research findings, we nevertheless paid close attention to the processes by which teachers might achieve changes in their roles and practices. Through our work with teachers, we have come to understand more clearly how the task of applying research is much more than a simple process of translating the findings of researchers into the classroom. The teachers in our project were engaged in a process of knowledge creation, albeit of a distinct kind, and possibly relevant only in the settings in which they work (see Hargreaves, 1999). Furthermore, we attended to the process of professional development through an acknowledgment that teachers need time, freedom, and support from colleagues in order to reflect critically upon and to develop their practices. Too little is known about such strategies, perhaps because researching how teachers take on research, adapt it, and make it their own is much more difficult than researching the effects of, for example, different curricula or class sizes.

REFERENCES

Askew, M., & Wiliam, D. (1995). *Recent research in mathematics education*, 5-16. London: HMSO.

Bangert-Drowns, R.L., Kulik, C.L.C., Kulik, J.A., & Morgan, M.T. (1991). The instructional effect of feedback in test-like events. *Review of Educational Research, 61*(2), 213-238.

Black, P.J., & Wiliam, D. (1998a). Assessment and classroom learning. *Assessment in Education: Principles, Policy and Practice, 5*(1), 7-73.

Black, P.J., & Wiliam, D. (1998b). *Inside the black box: Raising standards through classroom assessment.* London: King's College London School of Education.

Black, P.J., & Wiliam, D. (1998c). Inside the black box: Raising standards through classroom assessment. *Phi Delta Kappan, 80*(2), 139-148.

Black, P.J., & Wiliam, D. (2003). "In praise of educational research": Formative assessment. *British Educational Research Journal, 29*(5), 751-765.

Black, P. J., Harrison, C., Lee, C., Marshall, B., & Wiliam, D. (2002). *Working inside the black box: Assessment for learning in the classroom.* London: King's College London School of Education.

Black, P.J., Harrison, C., Lee, C., Marshall, B , & Wiliam, D. (2003). *Assessment for learning. Putting it into practice.* Buckingham, UK: Open University Press.

Boaler, J. (1997). *Experiencing school mathematics: Teaching styles, sex and setting.* Buckingham, UK: Open University Press.

Bransford, J.A., Brown, A., & Cocking, R. (1999). *How people learn: Brain, mind, experience and school.* Washington, DC: National Academy Press.

Brousseau, G. (1984). The crucial role of the didactical contract in the analysis and construction of situations in teaching and learning mathematics. In H.G. Steiner (Ed.), *Theory of mathematics education: ICME 5 topic area and miniconference* (pp. 110-119). Bielefeld, Germany: Institut für Didaktik der Mathematik der Universität Bielefeld.

Butler, R. (1987). Task-involving and ego-involving properties of evaluation: Effects of different feedback conditions on motivational perceptions, interest and performance. *Journal of Educational Psychology, 79*(4), 474-482.

Butler, R. (1988). Enhancing and undermining intrinsic motivation: The effects of task-involving and ego-involving evaluation on interest and performance. *British Journal of Educational Psychology, 58*, 1-14.

Craven, R.G., Marsh, H.W., & Debus, R.L. (1991). Effects of internally focused feedback on enhancement of academic self-concept. *Journal of Educational Psychology, 83*(1), 17-27.

Driver, R. (1983). *The pupil as scientist?* Milton Keynes, UK: Open University Press.

Dweck, C.S. (1986). Motivational processes affecting learning. *American Psychologist, 41*(10), 1040-1048.

Foos, P.W., Mora, J.J., & Tkacz, S. (1994). Student study techniques and the generation effect. *Journal of Educational Psychology, 86*(4), 567-576.

Glass, G.V., McGaw, B., & Smith, M. (1981). *Meta-analysis in social research.* Beverly Hills, CA: Sage.

Hargreaves, D.H. (1999). The knowledge creating school. *British Journal of Educational Studies, 47*(2), 122-144.

King, A. (1992). Facilitating elaborative learning through guided student-generated questioning. *Educational Psychologist, 27*(1), 111-126.

Kluger, A.N., & DeNisi, A. (1996). The effects of feedback interventions on performance: A historical review, a meta-analysis, and a preliminary feedback intervention theory. *Psychological Bulletin, 119*(2), 254-284.

Lee, C. (2000, September). *The King's Medway Oxford Formative Assessment Project: Studying changes in the practice of two teachers.* Paper presented at the meeting of the British Educational Research Association, Cardiff University, London.

Marshall, B. (2000). *English teachers—the unofficial guide: Researching the philosophies of English teachers*. London: RoutledgeFalmer.

Mosteller, F.W., & Tukey, J.W. (1977). *Data analysis and regression: A second course in statistics*. Reading, MA: Addison-Wesley.

Newman, R.S., & Schwager, M.T. (1995). Students' help seeking during problem solving: Effects of grade, goal, and prior achievement. *American Educational Research Journal, 32*(2), 352-376.

Newmann, F.M., Bryk, A.S., & Nagaoka, J.K. (2001). *Authentic intellectual work and standardized tests: Conflict or coexistence?* Chicago: Consortium on Chicago School Research.

Nuthall, G., & Alton-Lee, A. (1995). Assessing classroom learning: How students use their knowledge and experience to answer classroom achievement test questions in science and social studies. *American Educational Research Journal, 32*(1), 185-223.

Perrenoud, P. (1991). Towards a pragmatic approach to formative evaluation. In P. Weston (Ed.), *Assessment of pupil achievement* (pp. 79-101). Amsterdam: Swets & Zeitlinger.

Perrenoud, P. (1998). From formative evaluation to a controlled regulation of learning processes: Towards a wider conceptual field. *Assessment in Education: Principles, Policy and Practice, 5*(1), 85-102.

Rowe, M.B. (1974). Wait time and rewards as instructional variables, their influence on language, logic and fate control. *Journal of Research in Science Teaching, 11*, 81-94.

Sadler, R. (1989). Formative assessment and the design of instructional systems. *Instructional Science, 18*, 119-144.

Sato, M. (2003). Working with teachers in assessment-related professional development. In J.M. Atkin & J.E. Coffey (Eds.), *Everyday assessment in the science classroom* (pp. 109-119). Arlington, VA: NSTA Press.

Shulman, L. (1986). Those who understand: Knowledge growth in teaching. *Educational Researcher, 15*(1), 4-14.

Wiliam, D., Lee, C., Harrison, C., & Black, P.J. (In press). Teachers developing assessment for learning: Impact on student achievement. *Assessment in Education, 29*.

Wood, D. (1998). *How children think and learn: The social contexts of cognitive development* (2nd Edition). Oxford, UK: Blackwell.

CHAPTER 3

Bridging the Conceptual Gap between Classroom Assessment and System Accountability

MARGARET FORSTER AND GEOFF MASTERS

This chapter is part narrative and part commentary. In the first part of the chapter we tell the story of our experiences over the past decade in supporting the work of classroom teachers *and* the system-wide monitoring of student achievement. In the second part of the chapter we reflect on the connections between the pieces of this narrative. It is these connections that provide us with a framework that bridges the apparent conceptual gap between teachers' classroom assessments and assessments undertaken for system accountability.

The story begins with the development of a set of resource materials designed to support teachers in their assessment of students' English literacy skills in reading, writing, speaking, listening, and viewing. Each resource was built around a theme, used multiple assessment methods, and was designed so that it could be integrated into regular classroom activities. The approach underpinning the materials was subsequently used as a model for a national sample survey of literacy achievement in Australian schools. In sampled classrooms, teachers were trained to make judgments of students' responses and performances, and their judgments provided the national survey data. Following the survey, Australian state and territory governments funded a national Web site to support teachers in their classroom use of an emerging assessment system, and they provided a complementary resource kit to assist teachers in understanding assessment principles and practice.

Ms. Margaret Forster, BA Hons, Dip Ed, MEd Studs, is a Principal Research Fellow and Research Director (Assessment and Reporting) at the Australian Council for Educational Research (ACER). Ms. Forster has extensive experience in the area of assessment and reporting and works as a consultant nationally and internationally. Professor Geoff Masters, BSc, MEd UWA, PhD Chicago, FACE, is Executive Director of the Australian Council for Educational Research (ACER). Professor Masters is an international authority in educational measurement and student assessment and has published extensively in these fields.

When we began our work we did not plan to develop a single conceptual framework for classroom assessment and system accountability. However, as we undertook each separate piece of work we began to make piece-by-piece connections, and now, in retrospect, we see overarching conceptual connections. Reflecting on our experience over the past decade, we think that it is possible for classroom and large-scale assessments to be brought together conceptually in support of student learning.

Narratives: The History and Context of Our Work

Developmental Assessment Resource for Teachers (DART)

In 1994, the Australian Council for Educational Research (ACER) began an ambitious project: to develop an assessment resource for teachers that would provide a model for addressing explicit learning outcomes, gathering evidence of student achievement using a range of assessment methods, judging student work in a way that would provide comparable results, and reporting achievement descriptively against levels of a standards framework. A central intention of the project was to integrate assessment and curricula: to model a thematic approach to curricula that would allow standardized assessment tasks to be embedded in day-to-day teaching practice, and to model ways in which the results of these assessments might be used directly to improve student learning.

We designed and developed a resource kit (DART) to assist teachers in assessing students' knowledge, skills, and understandings in English (language arts) at the elementary (Australian "primary") level. The kit focused on a single theme. Central to the materials was a videotape that students watched to set the theme, and which also provided the stimulus for the viewing assessment. Teachers were encouraged to teach within the broad theme suggested by the video over a four- to six-week period and to embed the standardized reading, viewing, speaking, listening, and writing tasks at appropriate times, thereby integrating curriculum and assessment.

DART provided assessment tasks, detailed scoring guides and rating scales, examples of students' work, diagnostic information about students' strengths and weaknesses, and report forms that illustrated students' levels of achievement numerically and descriptively.

DART used a range of assessment methods to provide evidence of students' achievements: open-ended and multiple-choice items for reading, viewing, and listening; essay responses for writing; and performance assessment for speaking. Thematically related short texts, audio taped materials, and discussion topics provided stimuli for the assessments.

Marking guides were constructed carefully to assist teachers in making comparable judgments of student work. For example, when marking students' essay responses, teachers used separate rating scales for the "quality of ideas" (content and context) expressed through the writing and for students' control over "language mechanics" (spelling, punctuation, and grammar). The rubrics were supported by annotated samples of student work that illustrated the levels on the rating scales (see Figure 1).

Most important for this discussion, the DART assessment tasks addressed explicit learning outcomes from a range of levels as described in the Australian national English curriculum framework (Curriculum Corporation, 1994).[1] The English profile (a "content standards" framework) was organized into three strands—Speaking and Listening, Reading and Viewing, and Writing—corresponding to the language modes of English. Each strand consisted of a series of learning *outcomes*. These were descriptions of knowledge, skills, and understandings that students develop in English in the order in which they typically develop them.

The outcomes were structured into *substrands*: Texts, Contextual Understandings, Linguistic Structures and Features, and Strategies. These substrands provided different ways of looking at students' performances. The Texts substrand focused on what students do with what kinds of texts; the Contextual Understanding substrand focused on students' understanding of sociocultural and situational contexts; the Linguistic Structures and Features substrand focused on students' use of linguistic structures and features of text; and the Strategies substrand focused on how students go about composing and comprehending text.

Within each profile strand (and substrand), outcomes were structured into eight levels. These levels were broadly defined ranges of achievement for the compulsory years of school—eight levels for 10 years of schooling.

In DART, each reading, viewing, and listening task addressed one outcome from one strand and provided the opportunity for students to demonstrate their knowledge, skills, and understandings in relation to that outcome. Outcomes were sampled from across four levels of the profile to enable students of different levels of ability to demonstrate what they know, understand, and can do. Each writing and speaking prompt allowed students of all levels of ability to demonstrate their writing and speaking skills as described in the profile outcomes.

'Legendary Creature'—Work Sample Level 2

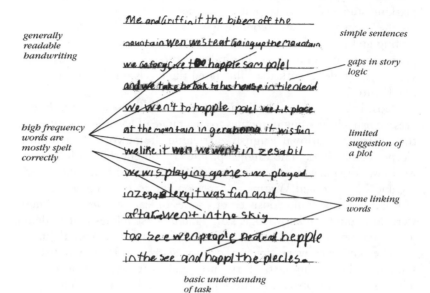

Content/Context 2
Language 2

generally readable handwriting

simple sentences

gaps in story logic

high frequency words are mostly spelt correctly

limited suggestion of a plot

some linking words

basic understandng of task

Me and Griffin it the bottom of the mountain when we started going up the mountain we go through caves to help some people and we take him back to his house in Thailand we went to help people we take place at the mountain in Jerrabomberra it was fund we like it when we went invisible we was playing games we played invisibility it was fun and after we went in the sky to see when people need help in the sea and help the people.

FIGURE 1

The DART writing marking guide consists of an annotated work sample and a transcript of the sample.

Most important for this discussion, teachers were assisted in interpreting and reporting student achievement in relation to the levels of the profile framework using a range of report forms. For example, Figure 2 shows a DART reading report. To the left of the report is the set of possible raw scores (1 to 28). (Equal distances on the vertical scale in this figure represent equivalent amounts of reading growth.) In the center of the report are descriptions of the knowledge, skills, and understandings addressed by the reading tasks. The descriptions are positioned in order of difficulty from the easiest task at the bottom of the report (retells the narrative without focusing on detail) to the most difficult task at the top of the report (makes specific connections between two types of texts; e.g., sees the relationship between two pictures and written text). Ordered in this way, the tasks provide a picture of what it means to develop in reading. To the right of the report are the levels of the profile framework aligned approximately with the raw score scale.

Using this report form, a teacher notes a student's raw score (the number of reading items a student completed correctly) and reads across the report to see the relationship between this score and the levels of the profile framework. A student is likely to be able to demonstrate the knowledge, skills, and understanding required by tasks below their score and less likely to be able to demonstrate the knowledge, skills, and understanding required by tasks above their score. For example, a student with a score of 15 on DART Reading Form A is estimated to have achieved at upper level 3 of the English profile and is likely to be able to demonstrate the knowledge, skills, and understanding required by tasks below a score of 15, and less likely to be able to demonstrate the knowledge, skills, and understanding required by tasks above a score of 15.

In the past decade several DART kits have been developed (Forster, Mendelovits, & Masters, 1994; Bodey, Darkin, Forster, & Masters, 1997; Recht, Forster, & Masters, 1998). Two literacy kits and one numeracy kit have been released for sale, and two additional literacy kits have been kept secure. All DART literacy materials (commercial and secure) have been equated and calibrated onto single scales, enabling DART assessments to be used to monitor students' growth over time. (For reading there are currently eight calibrated tests.)

DART has been successful in providing teachers with not only a model for designing assessments and for scoring tasks, but also a model for interpreting results in relation to the standards framework they are addressing in their teaching.

National School English Literacy Survey (NSELS)

In 1996 the DART model was adopted for the National School English Literacy Survey (NSELS), a sample survey of the literacy achievements (reading, viewing, speaking, listening, and writing) of year 3 (middle elementary) and year 5 (upper elementary) students across Australia.

In adopting the DART model, NSELS differed significantly from other data collection previously undertaken in Australia and overseas for surveys of this kind. As well as focusing attention on the collection of valid and reliable information, the model focused attention on the integration of the assessment process with normal classroom practice.

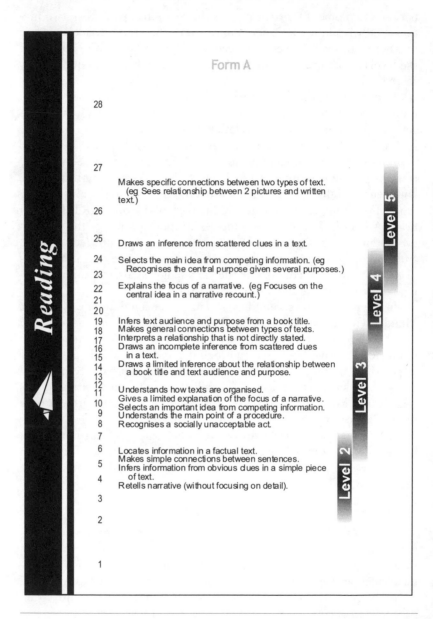

FIGURE 2
DART Reading Form A.

Because of the kinds of assessment methods used (e.g., performance assessment for speaking), it was necessary for classroom teachers to play a central role in the data collection process, and NSELS became a context for extensive professional development for participating teachers.

As with the original DART, in order to maximize the authenticity of the tasks and to model thematic approaches to learning, the tasks were presented in integrated settings. Literacy tasks for year 3 students were based on a myths and legends theme, with all tasks loosely integrated around a central videotape and picture book. Literacy tasks for year 5 students were built around a film entitled *Looking for Space Things*. The tasks were administered using standardized instructions within a four- to six-week period. (Although each participating teacher was required to administer the tasks to only 10 randomly selected students in his or her class, enough materials were provided to assess all the students in the classes.)

Evidence of students' achievements was collected using a range of assessment methods, including paper-and-pen assessments, performance assessments, and portfolio assessments. For example, evidence of students' speaking and writing achievements was collected from two sources: observations of speaking and writing performances on standardized speaking and writing tasks ("common tasks"), and records of observations of students' classroom speaking and writing ("best work"). Common tasks were administered, within specified time limits, by teachers using provided administration instructions.

In NSELS, the stimulus for the reading assessments was a set of thematically related short texts. For example, the myths and legends materials contained a poem, "Lovely Mosquito," which was directly related to the film that children watched, an African story titled *Why Mosquitoes Buzz in People's Ears*. The stimulus for the listening, writing, and speaking assessment was a set of thematically related audiotapes and prompts. For example, the listening materials included an interview with an Aboriginal elder telling some of the stories she was told as a child.

The initial responsibility for assessing student work rested with classroom teachers. They were provided with marking rubrics that were carefully constructed and supported by annotated samples of student work. Because of data reliability demands, additional procedures were put in place to ensure the comparability of teachers' judgments across sites. Ninety external assessors were trained over three days in the survey methodology and in the delivery and assessment of all survey tasks. These external assessors then trained 900 participating teachers, who were provided with handbooks for hands-on practice in assessing reading, writing, listening, and viewing work samples and in using assessment guides and record sheets. For speaking assessments, teachers viewed a series of videotaped speaking performances and completed guided and unassisted practice sessions. (In addition, teachers were provided with release time from normal classroom duties so that they could concentrate on the survey assessments.) To maximize further the comparability across teachers and schools, speaking assessments were made collaboratively by teachers and the external assessors, each of whom had the responsibility of working with ten teachers.[2]

Most important for this discussion, as with the original DART, the NSELS DART tasks were designed to address explicit outcomes in the National English Profile from a range of levels. The year 5 materials addressed levels 2, 3, 4, and 5 of the profile; the year 3 materials, levels 1, 2, 3, and 4.

Figure 3 shows an example of a NSELS year 5 viewing task (with a correct response) that focuses on the writer's craft. Figure 4 shows an example of a reading task (and a correct response) from the year 3 materials. This task assesses a student's ability to "read between the lines." Both items demand higher order literacy skills. More straightforward questions were also included in the survey materials.

Suppose that the filmmakers could have used any car they wanted in the film. Why do you think they chose this type of car for Mrs Flinders?

Because   the   Flinders   family   look   dorky
So   does   there   car.

FIGURE 3
A NSELS year 5 viewing stimulus and task and a correct student response.

Lovely Mosquito

Lovely mosquito, attacking my arm
As quiet and still as a statue,
Stay right where you are! I'll do you no harm—
I simply desire to pat you.
Just puncture my veins and swallow your fill
For nobody's going to swat you.
Now, lovely mosquito, stay perfectly still—
A SWIPE! and a SPLAT! and I GOT YOU!

—Doug MacLeod

Does the writer think the mosquito is lovely?
Explain your answer.

No because he is just ~~thing~~ trying to be nice to it so he can kill it.

FIGURE 4
A NSELS year 3 reading stimulus and task and a correct student response.

As with the original DART, the marking rubrics provided teachers who participated in the survey with a model for the assessment of students' understandings. For example, the levels of the rating scales for writing and speaking were constructed to correspond to the levels of the English profile. That is, rating descriptions at each level were constructed to address outcomes of the profile at each level. Separate rating levels were provided for quality of ideas and control of language features (spelling, punctuation, and grammar) in the case of writing and quality of ideas and engagement with the audience in the case of speaking. Teachers did not checklist the features of a student's performance but made a best-fit judgment of a level of achievement.

As with the original DART, in NSELS, year 3 and year 5 students' achievements were reported descriptively (as well as graphically) against a series of scales. The achievements of students from a number of subgroups also were reported: males and females, students from English- and non-English-speaking backgrounds, students from low, medium, and high socioeconomic backgrounds, and students from the special Indigenous sample. In the case of speaking and writing, achievements on common tasks and best work were reported separately and in combination.

The NSELS speaking scale is illustrated in Figure 5. The scale, which described increasing achievement in speaking, was empirically based. That is, it was based on an analysis of observed student performances.

The cluster of indicators at the bottom of the scale (corresponding to about level 1 of the profile) described the lowest level of achievement in speaking in the survey. The cluster of indicators at the top of the scale (corresponding to about level 5 of the profile) described the highest level of achievement in speaking in the survey. The italicized indicators described performance elements ("awareness of audience" and "ability to engage audience").[3]

Descriptions of the knowledge, skills, and understandings typically demonstrated by students at various levels along the scale were also provided. Shown in the appendix are transcripts of students' performances on the common tasks, one for each of the five levels of achievement described on the speaking scale. Each example is accompanied by a description of what students were typically able to do at that level of achievement and by the percentages of year 3 and year 5 students working at that level.

In using the DART model for system accountability purposes, NSELS broke new ground. As well as providing participating teachers with a model for designing assessments, for scoring tasks, and for interpreting results in relation to the standards framework they are addressing in their teaching, the survey methodology demanded a central role for teachers in the data collection process. Classroom teachers were the judges of students' performances on standardized tasks and on normal classroom work. Through the survey experience, teachers' professional knowledge and practice were recognized, supported, and developed.

Teachers and external assessors who participated in NSELS provided very positive feedback about this professional development experience. Teachers' exploration of the assessment materials had highlighted areas of strength and areas for improvement in teaching practice. Involvement in the survey, they reported, had led to better understandings about literacy assessment. Most important, teachers could continue to use the survey assessment models to assist with assessment at the school level.[4]

On the basis of this success in 1998, the federal government funded the development of a Web site by the South Australian Department of Education and Training to support teachers in their use of the NSELS materials: www.in2assessment.edu.au/index.html. The purpose of the Web site is to provide professional development strategies to support teacher judgment of student achievement. The site provides teachers with the opportunity to use and explore the survey assessment materials and to consider their usefulness as a model at the

Speaking Achievement

Level 5

600

Presents a well-reasoned account.
Displays a sense of key issues.
Presents challenging ideas.
Effectively uses appropriate language and/or organisational elements
appropriate to genre.
Consistently enhances presentation with relevant detail.
Gives considered reasons for opinions (generally justifies assertions).
Begins to engage audience through language, gesture, tone.

Level 4

500

Presents complete and well-organized account (eg well-rounded story
including details).
Attempts to justify assertions (eg 'It's a funny show because
of the way…').
Attempts to generalise about aspect of topic (eg includes synopsis of
show, as opposed to retelling one episode).
Presents a strong point of view (eg about a favourite character).
*Speaks clearly and articulately (allowing for some hesitation), with
good natural expression.*
Has a good, consistent sense of audience.

Level 3

400

Shows some evidence of organisation (presentation may be muddled or
incomplete).
Gives a full account of a character, experience or event including all key
information.
Justifies opinions with mostly descriptive information (eg 'Python was
a baddie because he scared rabbit out of her hole').
Offers a few arguments, mostly assertions.
Tells a complete story with a logical plot but lacking in detail.
*Speaks clearly and articulately (allowing for some hesitation), with
good natural expression **but** shows little awareness of the audience.*
*Shows a good, consistent sense of audience (looks around, smiles) **but**
speaks less confidently.*

300

Level 2

Tells a story with a recognisable plot.
Offers one or two comments or opinions with little or no justification.
Includes some key information.
Gives a largely incomplete or long and unstructured presentation
(some content may be irrelevant).
Shows a basic understanding of speaking task.
*Speaks audibly but with little sense of addressing audience
(eg may be little eye contact where culturally appropriate).*
Speaks with little attempt to modulate voice.

200

100

Level 1

Expresses ideas simply and conveys limited meaning (eg uses *and*
and *then* and repeats words).
Presents a disjointed or incomplete story (may need prompting).
Presents some unrelated ideas (may need prompting).
Shows limited understanding of speaking task
(may stray from original intent).
*Shows limited understanding of the need to communicate with
an audience.*
Speaks inaudibly at times.

FIGURE 5
Indicators on the NSELS speaking scale.

school level and as a springboard for teachers to examine their own students' work.

The site is divided into three main sections: Interactive Moderation, Frequently Asked Questions, and Resources. In the Interactive Moderation section, teachers can view student work samples and score them using the marking guides provided. They can then compare their assigned scores with those assigned by the survey. Examples from reading, viewing, speaking, listening, and writing are provided.

The Frequently Asked Questions section addresses eight literacy assessment issues: How do teachers assess the literacy needs of students with learning difficulties? How can learners be supported to use emotional responses to literacy in powerful ways? What is "guided reading"? What is "guided writing"? Where can I find information to help me, and my students, to use the Internet effectively? I'd like to widen my knowledge of research, trends, and ideas about literacy. Where can I find a range of articles on the Internet? I've planned a viewing unit focusing on the features of film but need a way to assess students' understanding of basic camera work. Any suggestions? How can I teach grammar in a more purposeful way?

The Resources section provides video interviews, and transcripts of these interviews, of various professionals in the education sector discussing literacy, as well as links to 100 literacy-related sites.

Assessment Resource Kit (ARK)

Recognizing the need to support teachers in their understanding of assessment principles and practice, from 1995 to 1998 the Australian federal government funded the Australian Council for Educational Research (ACER) to develop a set of more general materials: the Assessment Resource Kit (ARK).

ARK introduces basic measurement concepts in easily accessible formats and non-technical, everyday language and illustrates the concepts by drawing on examples from countries around the world, including the United States, Canada, England, Scotland, Hong Kong, Australia, and New Zealand. Four different communication media are used: full-color magazines, a videotape, a workshop manual, and wall charts.

The magazine format was chosen in preference to more traditional booklet formats in an attempt to make the content more interesting, attractive, and accessible. Features of the magazines include highlighted text, margin notes, photographs, diagrams, and drawings. The intention in using these design features was that, even by thumbing through a magazine, readers would be able to identify some key ideas.

The division of each magazine into a number of "articles" similarly was designed to make the content more accessible. The intention was that the articles, although building on each other, could be read in isolation.

Eight magazines have been published so far, three about measurement issues: *Developmental Assessment, Progress Maps*, and *Educational Measurement*; and five about assessment techniques/methods: *Portfolios, Performances, Projects, Products, and Paper and Pen*. All are printed in full color.

The second component of the ARK materials is a videotape, which complements the magazines. This videotape, *Understanding Developmental Assessment*, contains footage shot in the United States, Canada, England, Australia, and New Zealand and includes conversations with measurement specialists as well as classroom teachers. The videotape follows the same structure as the magazines and addresses the following topics: measurement variables (*progress maps*), assessment methods, judging and recording, estimating attainment, and reporting. The footage in the videotape shows student performances and assessment procedures not easily illustrated in paper format, as well as interviews with measurement specialists, assessors, and teachers.

The third component of the ARK materials is a set of three wall charts that were originally published with the literacy survey report. Each wall chart is a picture of a measurement variable constructed using item response theory and described and illustrated in terms of the items calibrated along that variable. Separate wall charts have been developed for reading, spelling, and writing. These charts also are designed for use in parent-teacher interviews.

The fourth component is a workshop manual. This manual, which is based on the authors' introductory workshop to assessment and reporting, provides overhead masters and accompanying text that can be used by curriculum and assessment leaders in conjunction with the ARK videotape to introduce groups of teachers to assessment principles and practice.

Topics covered in ARK include the concepts of validity and reliability in testing; the possibility of using a variety of assessment methods, including performances, projects, portfolios, products, and paper-and-pen exercises as sources of evidence in the measurement of student achievement; errors commonly associated with judgments and ratings; and options for, and issues associated with, the use of various response formats.

Most important for this discussion, the central concept in all ARK materials is the concept of a variable, or latent trait. This concept is introduced and described in the ARK materials as a *progress map*. Examples of measurement variables and of contexts that lend themselves to the construction of measurement variables are provided in the magazine *Progress Maps*. Each of the ARK assessment method magazines examines the concept of a progress map in educational measurement, the importance of selecting an appropriate assessment method to gather evidence of students' achievement along a particular kind of progress map; measurement as the process of estimating a student's location on an underlying progress map; and the use of graphical, numerical, and descriptive interpretations of achievement measures against a progress map.

This third piece of work brings us to the end of the narrative: our experience over the past decade in supporting the work of classroom teachers *and* system-wide monitoring of student achievement. What connections, in retrospect, have we made between the pieces of this narrative, and what do we take from this particular story that can assist us conceptually to bridge the gap between classroom assessment and system accountability?

Reflections

An Assessment System

Our experience suggests that a coherent assessment system will be one that places the assessment work of classroom teachers and system administrators within the same conceptual framework. For us, an ideal assessment system is made up of interconnected and mutually supporting components: a progress map that provides the conceptual backbone for the system; a range of assessment methods through which evidence of student achievement can be collected; opportunities for professional development activities to support teachers in their use of these methods; tools to assist teachers in assessing student work; procedures for collecting reliable system-wide information; and processes for reporting levels of achievement at both school and system levels and for monitoring levels of achievement over time. *In our experience, the conceptual bridge between classroom assessment and system accountability is a common conceptual framework for assessment.*

A Progress Map

Fundamental to a coherent assessment system is a progress map that provides the conceptual backbone for the system. A progress map (*continuum*, *strand*, or *variable*) describes growth in an area of learning—the knowledge, skills, understandings, attitudes, or values that students develop in an area of learning, in the order in which they typically develop them. The indicators of growth along a progress map sometimes are called learning *outcomes* or *indicators*.

The idea of growth or progress, development or improvement, is fundamental to all teaching and learning. This idea is invoked whenever teachers describe students as becoming better readers, using more sophisticated language, becoming more tolerant of others, developing deeper understandings, acquiring higher order skills, solving more difficult problems, or mastering more advanced knowledge. Teachers use words such as "better," "deeper," "higher," and "more" to describe the *direction* of student progress in particular areas of learning.

A progress map may not describe an individual's exact path of development in an area of learning. Rather, it describes students' typical development and thus provides a frame of reference for monitoring progress and for identifying, studying, and understanding idiosyncratic learning. The use of the same set of progress maps by classroom teachers and system administrators ensures that the conceptual frame of reference for teaching, assessing, and interpreting student learning is consistent across levels of the education system. It also provides a context and a language for conversations between theory and practice. Does practice support theory? Does theory need to be revised on the basis of practice?

One of the challenges for accountability programs is to design assessments that provide a model for teachers' own practice—a model that provides information that is directly useable in the classroom and that assists teachers to interpret results. When system accountability programs use the same conceptual framework (progress map) as teachers are using in the classroom, then teachers are able to make connections between accountability program tasks and information and their classroom practice. *In our experience, the conceptual bridge between classroom assessment and system accountability is the common use of one or more progress maps.*

Developmental Assessment

In the early 1990s we introduced the term *developmental assessment* to describe the process of assessing students' levels of achievement on a progress map (Masters, Adams, & Wilson, 1990). When we were first developing DART, we were focusing on supporting the work of teachers in the classroom, improving their assessment practice, and providing them with an assessment tool they could use directly or as a model for their own teacher-constructed assessments. Our interest was in demonstrating how teachers might use progress maps to gather evidence of students' achievement in order to feed this information directly into the teaching and learning cycle. In this context, our interest in developmental assessment was in assessing students' levels of achievement on a progress map in order to decide the best ways to facilitate learning.

Later, when we began applying the principles of developmental assessment to system monitoring and accountability programs, our interest was in assessing students' levels of achievement on a progress map in order to summarize and describe group achievements and as a basis for monitoring group trends over time. While the purpose of the assessments was different in these two different contexts, the shared process of assessing students' levels of achievement against a progress map provided the conceptual bridge between classroom assessment and system accountability.

When the work of classroom teachers and education systems is framed by developmental assessment, practice is guided by the same set of five principles:

1. Monitor students' growth against the learning outcomes of a progress map.
2. Consider a range of assessment methods to select an appropriate method for the outcomes addressed.
3. Judge and record students' performances on assessment tasks.
4. Estimate students' levels of achievement against a progress map.
5. Report student achievement in terms of a progress map.

Monitor students' growth against the learning outcomes of a progress map. In addition to providing a conceptual framework for understanding students' growth across the years of school, a progress map is especially useful because it is independent of the particular instrument used to assess learning—in much the same way as a scale for height provides a reference point regardless of the instrument used to measure height. A shared progress map also ensures that the same aspects of learning are valued explicitly at all levels of the education system.

The DART model addresses explicit outcomes on a progress map and provides students of different levels of ability a range of opportunities to demonstrate what they know and can do. To monitor student achievement effectively, classroom teachers and education systems need information along the full range of the achievement spectrum. A program that assesses high-level skills only will not provide information about the lowest achieving students. Conversely, a program that is pitched at the low end of the achievement spectrum will not provide information about the strengths of the highest achieving students. Teachers will find assessments most useful if they provide information about the strengths and weaknesses of all the students they teach: that is, along the full range of the achievement spectrum. Many DART and NSELS tasks were open–ended. Tasks of this kind are especially useful as they allow students of different levels of achievement to demonstrate what they know and can do in response to a single question.

Consider a range of assessment methods to select an appropriate method for the outcomes to be assessed. The assessment method must provide evidence about the learning outcomes identified on the progress map; different assessment methods will provide information about different kinds of outcomes. For example, if the outcomes require evidence of "students' abilities to write for a range of purposes and audiences," then a portfolio may be the most appropriate assessment method. If the outcomes require evidence of students' abilities to collect, analyze, and report information, then a project may be the most appropriate assessment method.

When we developed DART we intended to addresses a wide range of literacy outcomes. In the context of classroom use, DART provides teachers with a tool for assessing evidence of different kinds of student learning using a range of assessment methods, and with a model for developing their own assessments. In the context of system accountability, DART provides a model for the use of a range of assessment methods in the collection of valid system-wide achievement data.

Judge and record students' performances on assessment tasks. A variety of methods can be used to judge and record students' work. Some methods record whether tasks have been completed correctly, others record partial understandings. Sometimes ratings of student work are recorded, either based on separate judgments of aspects of a piece of work (analytic ratings) or based on a single, overall judgment (holistic ratings). The methods most useful to classroom teachers are those that expose students' conceptual understandings.

DART models a range of marking guides appropriate for different assessment methods. With procedures in place to ensure comparability of marker judgments, these methods can be used to collect reliable system-wide achievement data.

Estimate students' levels of achievement against a progress map. Because a progress map is a description of the path that students typically follow as they progress through an area of learning, the records made for any particular student will only more or less resemble this path. An on-balance assessment of the student's level of achievement will need to be made. The quality of this estimate will depend on the validity of the observations on which the estimate is based, the reliability of the estimate (the amount of evidence), and the objectivity of the estimate: Is the estimate unaffected by the choice of task and the choice of assessor?

DART provides a model for estimating students' levels of attainment against a progress map. The alignment of levels of a rating scale with levels on a progress map is a particularly useful strategy for classroom teachers.

Report student achievement in terms of a progress map. Because students' growth is assessed and monitored against a described continuum, students' estimated locations on a progress map can be reported descriptively in terms of the knowledge, skills, understandings, attitudes, or values typically demonstrated by students at these locations. *In our experience, the conceptual bridge between classroom assessment and system accountability is a developmental approach to the monitoring of student achievement.*

Supporting Research

The use of a progress map as a central support for teachers and students is consistent with recent research evidence. Research from the U.S. into how people learn (Bransford, Brown, & Cocking, 2000) suggests that three principles, when incorporated into teaching, result in the improvement of student achievement: (1) Learning is enhanced when teachers identify and work from learners' current knowledge and beliefs; (2) Learning is most effective when it results in well-organized knowledge and deep understanding of concepts and their applicability; and (3) Learning is enhanced by the ability to monitor one's own learning. A well-constructed progress map organizes knowledge in a way that brings conceptual understandings to the fore, assists teachers in identifying students' current beliefs, and provides a map of where students have come from and are going in their learning for both teachers and students.

The use of progress maps is also consistent with formative assessment research from the U.K. Research undertaken by the Assessment Reform Group (2002) suggests that in order to improve learning, teachers should discuss with pupils the purpose of their learning and provide feedback that will help the learning process; encourage pupils to judge their work by how much they have learned and by the progress they have made; help pupils to understand the criteria by which their learning is assessed and to assess their own work; help pupils to understand where they are in relation to learning goals and how to make further progress; and give feedback that enables pupils to know the next steps and how to succeed in taking them. Each of these strategies will be facilitated by the use of a progress map.

Finally, the reporting schema underpinning DART (alignment with a progress map) is cited in the National Research Council's summary of research on cognitive psychology and assessment as a "notable attempt to measure growth in competence and to convey the nature of student achievement in ways that can benefit teaching and learning" (Pellegrino, Chudowsky, & Glaser, 2001, p. 190).

In Summary

We began by describing the development of a set of materials (DART) to support teachers in their classroom assessment. These materials were based on the principles of developmental assessment. We then detailed the use of these materials for the collection of system-wide data (NSELS). Our experience in this second context has demonstrated that classroom teachers can assemble valid student achievement data on a wide range of learning outcomes, if they are provided with adequate tools. Furthermore, with adequate support, classroom teachers can be trained to assess student work with the level of reliability necessary for system-level data collection.

Feedback from teachers who were involved in NSELS suggests that the survey experience provided a useful professional learning experience. Involvement in the survey, they reported, led to a better understanding of literacy assessment. Most important, teachers were able to continue to use the survey assessment models to assist with assessment at the school level.

In our experience, the conceptual bridge between classroom assessment and system accountability is a common assessment system. We call the conceptual backbone of the system, which provides the connection between the components of the system, a *progress map*. We use the term *developmental assessment* to describe the process of assessing students' levels of achievement on a progress map. Through our work, we have found that a developmental approach to monitoring student achievement can provide a valuable conceptual bridge between classroom assessment and system accountability.

APPENDIX

Speaking Level 1

> My picture's . . . like . . . um . . . he puts sticks in his ears.

Students working at this level typically were able to

- express ideas simply and to convey limited meaning (e.g., using "and" and "then" and repeating words);
- present a talk that
  contained some unrelated ideas (may have needed prompting);
  was disjointed or incomplete (may have needed prompting);
  demonstrated a limited understanding of the speaking task (may have strayed from original intent);
  demonstrated a limited understanding of the need to communicate with the audience;
  was inaudible at times.

Two percent of year 3 students were working at or below this level.

Speaking Level 2

> Um . . . my favourite character is rabbit because he is a fast runner and he is a goodie (giggles).

Students working at this level typically were able to

- tell a story with a recognizable plot;
- offer one or two comments or opinions, but with little or no justification;
- include some key information;
- demonstrate a basic understanding of a speaking task;
- give a presentation that
  was audible but showed little sense of addressing audience (e.g., there may have been little eye contact, where eye contact was culturally appropriate);
  was largely incomplete or long and unstructured (some content may have been irrelevant);
  displayed little attempt to modulate voice.

Twenty-six percent of year 3 students and 7% of year 5 students were working at or below this level.

Speaking Level 3

> My favourite character is the owl because the owl woke up the sun every day. And my picture shows when the rabbit and the monkey and everything and the stick landed on the bird, and him dying,

and the snake and the rabbit getting out of his hole. And I thought the baddie . . . um...the baddie was the mosquito because he bothered everyone and no-one like him and the iguana put sticks in his ears to ignore him.

Students working at this level typically were able to

- tell a complete story with a logical plot but lacking in detail;
- give a full account of a character, experience, or event, including all key information;
- show some evidence of organization (presentation may have been muddled or incomplete);
- justify an opinion with mostly descriptive information;
- offer a few arguments, mostly assertions;
- speak clearly and articulately (allowing for some hesitation), with good natural expression but with little awareness of audience.

Fifty-five percent of year 3 students and 50% of year 5 students were working at this level.

Speaking Level 4

> Good afternoon. Um . . . my picture . . . um . . . is showing where the lizard's drinking water and the mosquito's coming to bother it and to tell it lies, and the iguana puts sticks in its ears. And I think that the . . . um . . . mosquito shouldn't have told lies but it wasn't necessarily at fault for doing all the rest and everything. And . . . um . . . I think the lion was a wonderful, a good character because he helped solve the problem and helped everyone to figure out and he didn't blame anyone until he found out the person who actually did it. And I liked, I liked the monkey as well as the iguana because I liked the way it broke the branch and it fell on the owl and that's all.

Students working at this level typically were able to

- present a complete and well-organized account (e.g., a well-rounded story including details);
- attempt to justify assertions (e.g., "It's a funny show because of the way . . .");
- attempt to generalize about aspects of a topic (e.g., include a synopsis of a show, as opposed to telling one episode);
- present a strong point of view (e.g., about a favorite character);
- speak clearly and articulately (allowing for some hesitation), with good natural expression;
- display a good, consistent sense of audience.

Seventeen percent of year 3 students were working at or above this level and 38% of year 5 students were working at this level.

Speaking Level 5

The bit that I picked was the last one and I picked it because I thought it talked about the poorer people and I'm concerned about them 'cos they're less fortunate than us. Um, a bit that John Paul said he thought was funny was that he only took the loaf of bread. Because the man was really hungry so he didn't take anything valuable. He knew he couldn't sell it and so he just took the loaf of bread. The last bit says, "Sitting by the fire I made toast, two buttered pieces each, but I couldn't eat for thoughts of the hungry man keeping warm with sheep." As I said before, I chose it because it talks about the poorer people in our community that haven't got enough to eat. They keep warm—well this was the olden days—so he would keep warm—and this was the country—by being near the sheep.

Students working at this level typically were able to

- present a well-reasoned account;
- display a sense of key issues;
- effectively use appropriate language and/or organizational elements appropriate to genre;
- consistently enhance presentation with relevant details;
- give considered reasons for opinions (generally justify assertions);
- begin to engage audience through language, gesture, tone.

Five percent of year 5 students were working at or above this level.

NOTES

1. During the period 1990-1993, as part of a collaborative effort of all Australian states and territories and the federal government, "statements" and "profiles" for eight areas of the school curriculum were developed. Each statement defines a learning area, and describes a sequence for developing knowledge, skills, and understandings. Each accompanying profile provides a framework for reporting student achievement. Some states and territories revised these documents to produce their own versions, others distributed and used them in their original form. In the United States, frameworks of this kind sometimes are called "curriculum standards." Most states of Australia have now refined these frameworks to better reflect their own curriculum expectations.

2. Finally, all answer booklets and teacher assessments were sent back to ACER for check marking. It is significant that the survey was able to demonstrate that teacher judgment of student achievement is reliable when supported by good assessment materials, professional development, and advice from trained external assessors. More than 96% of teachers' marks were left unchanged (Masters & Forster, 1997b).

3. Although performance elements and quality of ideas are described together on this scale, students' performances were assessed separately for each of these aspects of their presentation.

4. The middle elementary kit was made commercially available as the next kit in the DART series.

REFERENCES

Assessment Reform Group. (2002). *Testing, motivation and learning*. Cambridge, UK: University of Cambridge Faculty of Education.

Bodey, W., Darkin, L., Forster, M., & Masters, G. (1997). *DART English (middle primary): Developmental assessment resource for teachers*. Camberwell: Australian Council for Educational Research.

Bransford, J., Brown, A.C., & Cocking, R.R. (2000). *How people learn: Brain, mind, experience and school*. Washington, DC: National Academy Press.

Curriculum Corporation. (1994). *National English profile for Australian schools*. Carlton: Author.

Forster, M., Mendelovits, J., & Masters, G. (1994). *DART English (upper primary): Developmental assessment resource for teachers*. Camberwell: Australian Council for Educational Research.

Forster, M., & Masters, G. (1999). *ARK paper and pen*. Camberwell: Australian Council for Educational Research.

Forster, M., & Masters, G. (1998). *ARK products*. Camberwell: Australian Council for Educational Research.

Forster, M., & Masters, G. (1996). *ARK portfolios*. Camberwell: Australian Council for Educational Research.

Forster, M., & Masters, G. (1996). *ARK performances*. Camberwell: Australian Council for Educational Research.

Forster, M., & Masters, G. (1996). *ARK projects*. Camberwell: Australian Council for Educational Research.

Masters, G.N., Adams, R.J., & Wilson, M.R. (1990). Charting student progress. In T. Husen and T.N. Postelthwaite (Eds.), *International encyclopaedia of education: Research and studies* (suppl. vol. 2, pp. 628-634). London: Pergamon Press.

Masters, G., & Forster, M. (1996). *ARK developmental assessment*. Camberwell: Australian Council for Educational Research.

Masters, G.N., & Forster, M. (1997a). *ARK reading, writing and spelling growth posters*. Camberwell: Australian Council for Educational Research.

Masters, G.N., & Forster, M. (1997b). *Mapping literacy achievement: Results of the 1996 national school English literacy survey*. Commonwealth of Australia: Department of Employment, Education, Training and Youth Affairs.

Masters, G.N., & Forster, M. (1997c). *ARK progress maps*. Camberwell: Australian Council for Educational Research.

Pellegrino, J., Chudowsky, N., & Glaser, R. (Eds.). (2001). *Knowing what students know: The science and design of educational assessment*. Washington, DC: National Academy Press.

Recht, E., Forster, M., & Masters, G. (1998). *DART mathematics (upper primary): Developmental assessment resource for teachers*. Camberwell: Australian Council for Educational Research.

CHAPTER 4

Designing Assessments for Instruction and Accountability: An Application of Validity Theory to Assessing Scientific Inquiry

JOHN R. FREDERIKSEN AND BARBARA Y. WHITE

This chapter is concerned with how assessments of students' work in classrooms, although primarily intended to promote learning, can also become an important source of information for evaluating a school's effectiveness within an accountability system (Shepard, 2000). On the face of it, formative assessment practices used in the classroom to support learning and summative assessments used for accountability purposes seem to be incompatible. In their classroom activities, students know ahead of time the tasks on which they will be assessed, and they can prepare for them and get help in doing them. In addition, teachers' judgments of their students' work could be influenced if their classroom assessments were to be used for accountability purposes. For reasons such as these, assessments used for accountability typically are external assessments based on tasks that are not known to the students or the teacher; they often use items that are objectively scored; and they are scored externally (Baker, Linn, Herman, & Koretz, 2002; Linn, 2000).

To get a full picture of schools' and teachers' impact on students' learning, however, accountability assessments need to include measures of significant work that students are undertaking in the classroom. They need to include measures of the quality of students' work on important, consequential tasks that students have thought about and worked on for extended periods (Wiggins, 1993). These are tasks that, by their nature, are not just demonstrations of students' previously

John Frederiksen is Professor of Science Education and Cognitive Studies at the University of Washington, Seattle. Barbara White is Professor of Science, Math, and Technology Education at the University of California at Berkeley.

This research was supported by a grant from the National Science Foundation, Directorate for Education and Human Resources, Program on Research on Learning and Education (ROLE) to the University of California at Berkeley, Award No. 0087583. We would like to thank Larry Suter for his valuable comments on a draft of this chapter.

learned skills. Rather, they involve students in searching for new information and new ways of working, and in incorporating such newly developed knowledge into their work. Such tasks might include, for example, science fair projects or social studies projects. Students' abilities to make self-assessments of their work on these tasks, and to use such reflective judgments when figuring out how to achieve their goals, are critical metacognitive skills to develop (Black & Wiliam, 1998a, 1998b; Brown, 1987; White & Frederiksen, 1998). They are important skills for facilitating students' future learning, and measures of them are leading indicators of students' future success in learning within a discipline (Bransford & Schwartz, 2001; Campione & Brown, 1990). For these reasons, both formative assessments of students' work in its various stages of development and dynamic assessments of how students make use of resources in learning to complete challenging projects are not only appropriate and important to include within the curriculum as tools for students' learning, they are also important tools for evaluating school accountability.

The issues we face if we are to broaden the information base of accountability systems to incorporate formative assessments are

How can we develop formative assessment practices, both assessment tasks and interpretation methods, that will foster students' learning within the curriculum while, at the same time, provide information about students' performance that is useful for accountability purposes?

How can we ensure that such assessments provide accurate and credible representations of students' performance?

How can such assessments provide information about how students are meeting state and national curricular standards that is comparable across schools and classrooms?

We will begin our discussion by considering issues of fairness, to schools and to their teachers, that we believe point to the necessity of including classroom-based assessments within an accountability system. We will then present a theoretical argument for a set of assessment design principles that allows teachers to analyze students' work in ways that support students' learning while also providing useful and credible information for accountability purposes. We will center our discussion on a consideration of what forms the evaluations of students' performance should take to ensure that characterizations of students' performance in the classroom are credible and comparable without distorting the primary, instructional purpose of the evaluations. In our approach, we consider two forms of evaluation: rich characterization of a student's work, based upon a qualitative analysis guided by cognitive theory (Pellegrino, Chudowsky, & Glaser, 2001), and judgments of the quality of that work in relation to a broader set of standards for student performance. We will argue that validity theory in general, and a focus on the "internal validity" of interpretations of performance in particular, plays a central role in ensuring the credibility and comparability of these judgments. Our hypothesis is that, if the focus of assessment is placed firmly on a full and accurate analysis of each student's work processes and outcomes, the assessment process will provide maximum benefit for student learning while also providing a rich source of information for showing how students are meeting standards for learning that can be used for accountability purposes.

Following our theoretical argument regarding assessment design principles, we will present the results of research we have carried out using a system that we developed for assessing scientific inquiry projects, one that incorporates many of the design concepts we advocate here. We will briefly review the findings of our prior research (White & Frederiksen, 1998), which show how the formative use of this system benefits students' learning of scientific inquiry. We will then describe the scoring system and software we developed and used in support of this system, and we will present evidence showing that, with guidance and support from an analytic framework, teachers can make accurate and consistent evaluations of students' project work. We will also present evidence illustrating how information gathered from a detailed analysis of students' projects can be used in making overall, standards-based ratings. Finally, we will illustrate how a statistical analysis of the internal consistency of scorers' analyses and ratings can be used to establish their credibility and comparability.

Assessment Design Principles

Fairness within an accountability system requires that evaluations that have consequences for schools and teachers be based on assessments of activities and outcomes that are within the purview of schools' and teachers' instructional opportunities and curricular efforts. Accountability standards and measures should therefore include assessments that directly reflect the goals that schools and teachers have for their students' learning. These goals are demonstrated when students carry out challenging tasks, like research projects, that they prepare for over their course of instruction. Teachers and students see these tasks as a culminating goal for learning: students bringing together the knowledge and skills they have acquired in order to carry out important problem solving, inquiry, or design projects. Such tasks thus address knowledge and skills that schools and teachers have sought to develop through their curricula. These kinds of assessment tasks are very different from those used in most accountability systems, which tend not to reflect the goals of teaching or areas of student investment.

To ensure the usefulness of assessments in instruction and for accountability, teachers need to base their choices of assessment tasks on a common set of goals for students' learning, in particular, those that are represented in state curricular standards. There is no necessary contradiction between meeting this constraint and teachers' goals in fostering their students' learning. State and national standards such as the California standard for scientific inquiry, which states that "students should develop their own questions and perform investigations" (California State Board of Education, 2000), are best assessed using tasks that involve extended student activity. Given the level of time and effort required of students in carrying them out and of teachers and students in assessing performance, such assessment activities can be justified only if they are important components of the curriculum. They must serve an important instructional purpose, acting as culminating challenges for students along with providing information about students' performance that can be used for instructional and accountability purposes. To develop and interpret such tasks, teachers need specifications and examples of the types of tasks that they may use for assessment activities within their curriculum and tools to help them (and their students) analyze students' performances and make standards-based scoring judgments.

The methods for analyzing and evaluating students' work also need to serve both formative and summative goals. The processes of interpreting work need to be accessible to students and open to their participation and use. The characterizations of students' work that result need to provide insights that will help them learn. And these analyses need to be mapped to state standards in order to show how and how well students are meeting the standards. Such characterizations of students' work can involve reflective deliberation on the part of both students and teachers. Having students engage in peer and self-assessments of their work contributes powerfully to learning and teaching (Black & Wiliam, 1998a, 1998b; White & Frederiksen, 1998). Furthermore, relating characterizations of work to state curricular standards makes possible the aggregation of assessment data to provide measures for school accountability purposes that remain true to the learning goals of schools and teachers realized in the classroom.

We believe the fundamental assessment theory that is central to such a vision of assessment is validity theory applied to interpretation (Moss, 1994). Modern validity theory recognizes that claims about the validity of an assessment are claims about the appropriateness of an interpretation of data obtained from a student's performance on an assessment task (Chronbach, 1971; Frederiksen & Collins, 1996; Mislevy, 1994; Mislevy, Steinberg, & Almond, 2003; Pellegrino, Chudowsky, & Glaser, 2001; Moss, 1992, 1994; Shepard, 1993). This entails presenting a logical argument, based upon empirical evidence contained in artifacts of a student's work, that shows how the interpretation is supported. In essence, each interpretation of an assessment has all of the elements of a scientific inquiry, particularly establishing the internal validity and external validity of the knowledge claims that are being made, based on evidence obtained in the assessment. By *internal validity*, Campbell and Stanley (1963) mean a demonstration that all of the available evidence obtained in a research study supports the interpretation of the evidence that is offered, and supports this interpretation better than alternative interpretations. By *external validity*, they refer to a claim that the interpretation generalizes beyond the particular situation studied to other situations that may have different characteristics.

Applied to assessment, internal validity has to do with the consistency and coherence of the argument made by a scorer (who may be a student, teacher, or external scorer) in using a student's work to make judgments about the kind and quality of knowledge and skills that the student has displayed. The analysis and interpretation of classroom assessment performances makes use of a cognitive, interpretive theory to make claims about the character of a student's performance (Pellegrino, Chudowsky, & Glaser, 2001). Two factors may contribute to the accuracy of scoring judgments: the accuracy and appropriateness of observations of students' performance and the reasonableness of the inferences drawn from such observations in assigning scores for particular criteria. We hypothesize that, by adopting systematic approaches to observing and analyzing performance, teachers and students can accurately and consistently code features of students' inquiry. We further hypothesize that carrying out accurate and complete analyses of students' work will enable teachers to develop the evidence needed to make accurate scoring judgments of the quality of the students' work in reference to state curricular standards (or to other dimensions for characterizing students' performance) that are clearly warranted by the student work they have coded (Mislevy, Steinberg, & Almond, 2003).

In an assessment context, external validity has to do with inferences about how generally applicable a student's knowledge and skills are—what is the range of activities and situations over which he or she can apply them? This can be addressed by including a variety of formative assessment activities and analyzing how learning goals have been met through those activities (Frederiksen & Collins, 1996).

Placing the emphasis on internal validity in establishing the credibility of judgments of performance, rather than relying solely on demonstrations of interscorer reliability, has some advantages in the context of classroom assessment that we have explored in an earlier paper (Frederiksen & Collins, 1989). In considering the systemic validity of an assessment, that is, its impact over time within an educational system in improving the learning of the skills that are the subject of the assessment, we were led to posit a number of standards for an assessment system, two of which, *directness* and *transparency*, are particularly pertinent here. Directness requires that assessment tasks explicitly make use of and make visible the cognitive processes and knowledge being assessed as well as provide opportunities for students to demonstrate their use in doing the assessment task. Transparency is related to the processes used for interpreting task performances. If the assessment is to be successful in motivating and directing learning, students must be able to assess themselves and others in the same way that their teachers, or external scorers, do. If students know how to describe the knowledge and cognitive processes they are using in their work, they can help their teacher and others interpret their work. Thus, transparency of criteria for interpretation requires that all participants have a shared basis for recognizing, discussing, and evaluating students' work (Frederiksen & White, 1997).

An important result of assessment transparency is that it makes students aware of goals, motives, and strategies and of the need to monitor their progress by evaluating qualities of their work as it develops. To help others evaluate their work, students learn how to articulate their work processes and products in order to make them available for inspection, appreciation, and evaluation by others. Directness and transparency thus make it possible for both students and teachers to participate in the assessment processes. Students may make reflective, peer, and self-assessments, which teachers may inspect to assure their consistency and accuracy and revise when needed. Discussion of revisions with students provides an opportunity for developing reflective, metacognitive skills. These practices all depend on a shared set of goals and criteria; a public, inspectable source of evidence; and a logical argument leading from evidence to conclusions that is available for audit by external scorers. Our claim is that documenting these efforts within a school or district to ensure the internal validity of such judgments provides a better basis for establishing their credibility than would obtaining measures of interscorer agreement with an external scorer (cf. Moss, 1994).

In the next section of the paper, we will describe the curricular context of our research. We will then present an example of a scoring system that we developed to serve as a formative assessment tool for students to use in reflecting on their own and others' work as they carry out scientific inquiry projects within middle school science classes, as well as for teachers to use in evaluating this work.

Formative Assessment within the ThinkerTools Project

The ThinkerTools Inquiry Curriculum focuses on the development of scientific inquiry strategies and skills and on their use by students in developing an understanding of science (White & Frederiksen, 1998). The curriculum seeks to develop students' metacognitive knowledge related to inquiry, namely, their knowledge about the nature of scientific laws and models, their knowledge about the processes of modeling and inquiry, and their ability to monitor and reflect on these processes. The curriculum centers on inquiry activities that make use of computer-based tools for simulating force-and-motion phenomena as well as hands-on materials for experimentation. Pedagogical strategies include carefully scaffolding students' inquiry process and having students make their conceptual models and inquiry processes explicit. Metacognitive reflection is introduced by having students evaluate their work using a set of criteria that represent high-level cognitive and social goals. These include broad criteria such as Understanding the Science, Understanding the Processes of Inquiry, and Making Connections. They also include more focused criteria, including cognitive criteria, such as Being Inventive, Being Systematic, Using the Representations and Tools of Science, and Reasoning Carefully. They include socially oriented criteria as well, such as Writing and Communicating Well and Teamwork. The students use these criteria in a process we call *reflective assessment*, in which they evaluate their own and one another's research throughout the inquiry curriculum (see also Black & Wiliam, 1998b; Frederiksen & Collins, 1989). When students evaluate the research they have just completed using these criteria, they are asked to give the work a score on a five-point scale for each criterion and to write a justification for each score they give. Our hypothesis was that reflective assessment would help students to better understand the purpose and steps of inquiry, and it would develop metacognitive knowledge and habits of monitoring and reflecting on their work. We also hypothesized that this metacognitive reflection would be especially important for low-achieving students, who may lack these metacognitive skills (Campione, 1987).

Instructional trials of the ThinkerTools Inquiry Curriculum strongly supported these hypotheses (a full account of this research can be found in White & Frederiksen, 1998). We carried out curricular experiments in two urban middle schools in grades 7 through 9. We experimentally varied the introduction of assessment criteria for reflection, along with self-assessment activities that make use of those criteria. We did this by having matched classes for each teacher, with one class in each matched pair using the assessment criteria for reflection and the other (the control class) having, in their place, general discussions about the curriculum. Students carried out two research projects, one about halfway through the curriculum and the other at the end. The projects were scored by teachers using a five-point scoring rubric. For the sake of brevity, we have added the scores for these two projects together in the findings shown in Figure 1. These results show that students in the reflective assessment classes have higher rated research projects than

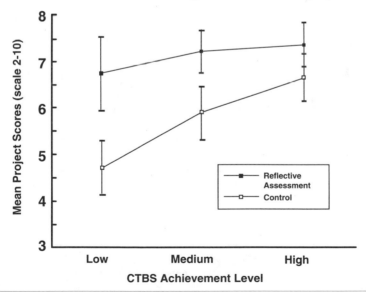

FIGURE 1

Effects of participation in reflective assessment on the quality of students' scientific inquiry projects. Shown are mean scores for two inquiry projects for students in the reflective assessment and control classes.

students in the control classes. The results also show that reflective
assessment is particularly beneficial for the low-achieving students.

 If the reflective assessment criteria are acting as metacognitive tools
to help students in their work, then the quality of their inquiry projects
should depend upon how well they have understood the assessment
criteria. To evaluate their understanding, we rated whether the evidence they cited in justifying their self-assessments was relevant to the
particular criterion they were considering. We compared the quality of
final projects for students who developed an understanding of the set
of assessment criteria with those who had not. The results, shown in
Figure 2, indicate that students who had learned to use the assessment
criteria appropriately in judging their work produced higher quality
projects than students who had not. And again, the benefit of learning
to use the assessment criteria was greatest for the low-achieving students. Thus, there are strong beneficial effects of introducing metacognitive goals, processes, and strategies for students to use in reflecting
on their work, particularly for academically disadvantaged students.

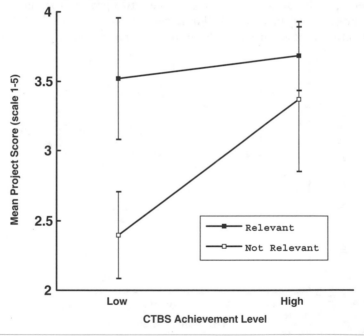

FIGURE 2

Effects of participation in reflective assessment on the quality of students' scientific
inquiry projects. Shown are mean scores on final projects for students who differ in the
relevance of the evidence they provide in writing rationales for their scores.

Supporting Teachers' Assessments of Scientific Inquiry Projects

Based upon our results and those of others showing the value of reflective, formative assessment for classroom learning (see Black & William, 1998b, for an extensive review), we considered ways to link reflection more closely to the processes of inquiry at various stages of an inquiry project. We were interested in increasing students' and teachers' understanding of inquiry as well as in improving the quality of inquiry project assessment for accountability purposes. We decided to add a new layer of analysis to the assessment in which students and teachers would examine detailed aspects of students' work at each stage of an inquiry project. We also sought to link information gathered in this project analysis to the broader criteria, like Reasoning Carefully, that we had found fruitful in the classroom assessment studies described above. These considerations led us to develop a new software tool, called the Inquiry Scorer, to assist students and teachers in evaluating inquiry projects such as ThinkerTools projects and science fair projects. We then carried out a study of teachers' use of this tool to test our hypotheses about the nature and usefulness of this new approach in providing an evidential basis for scoring students' inquiry projects.

In this section we will describe this new approach to assessing inquiry projects, and we will present evidence of how teachers make use of the scoring tool in evaluating students' research projects. We are interested in how easy or difficult such analyses are for teachers to carry out, and how such analyses contribute to teachers' scoring decisions.

The Inquiry Scorer Tool

In this new approach, which we have embedded within a software tool we call the Inquiry Scorer, there are two general parts to assessing a student's scientific inquiry project: 1) a detailed project analysis that covers each section of the inquiry project (Question, Hypothesize, Investigate, Analyze, Model, and Evaluate), and 2) an overall assessment of how important cognitive and social goals, such as Reasoning Carefully and Writing and Communicating Well, have been accomplished in carrying out the research project. Teachers perform the project analysis while reading through the project report, and they make an overall assessment after completing that analysis. The set of screens teachers see when using the Inquiry Scorer are shown in Figures 3 through 5.

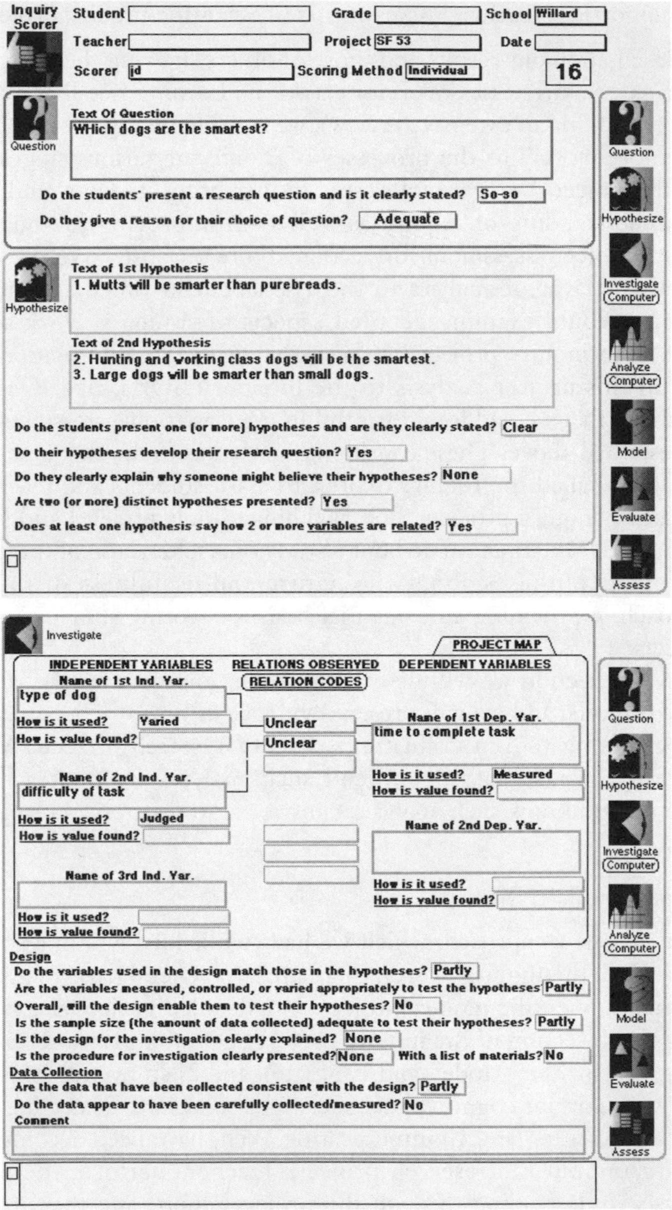

FIGURE 3

Screen shots from the Inquiry Scorer showing the project analysis tools for the Question, Hypothesize, and Investigate steps of a student's inquiry project, with questions about the project answered by a teacher.

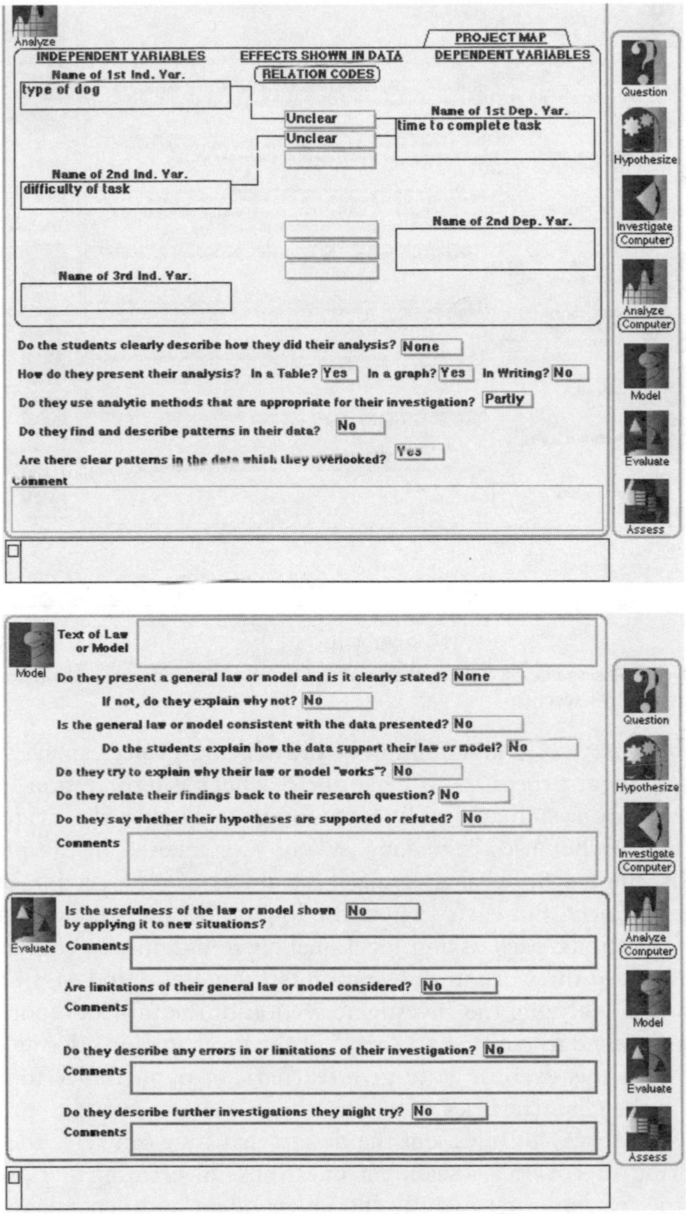

Analyze

PROJECT MAP

INDEPENDENT VARIABLES — EFFECTS SHOWN IN DATA — DEPENDENT VARIABLES

RELATION CODES

Name of 1st Ind. Var.
type of dog

Unclear
Unclear

Name of 1st Dep. Var.
time to complete task

Name of 2nd Ind. Var.
difficulty of task

Name of 2nd Dep. Var.

Name of 3rd Ind. Var.

Do the students clearly describe how they did their analysis? None

How do they present their analysis? In a Table? Yes In a graph? Yes In Writing? No

Do they use analytic methods that are appropriate for their investigation? Partly

Do they find and describe patterns in their data? No

Are there clear patterns in the data which they overlooked? Yes

Comment

Question
Hypothesize
Investigate (Computer)
Analyze (Computer)
Model
Evaluate
Assess

Model

Text of Law or Model

Do they present a general law or model and is it clearly stated? None

If not, do they explain why not? No

Is the general law or model consistent with the data presented? No

Do the students explain how the data support their law or model? No

Do they try to explain why their law or model "works"? No

Do they relate their findings back to their research question? No

Do they say whether their hypotheses are supported or refuted? No

Comments

Evaluate

Is the usefulness of the law or model shown by applying it to new situations? No

Comments

Are limitations of their general law or model considered? No

Comments

Do they describe any errors in or limitations of their investigation? No

Comments

Do they describe further investigations they might try? No

Comments

Question
Hypothesize
Investigate (Computer)
Analyze (Computer)
Model
Evaluate
Assess

FIGURE 4

Screen shots from the Inquiry Scorer showing the project analysis tools for the Analyze, Model, and Evaluate steps of a student's inquiry project, with questions about the project answered by a teacher.

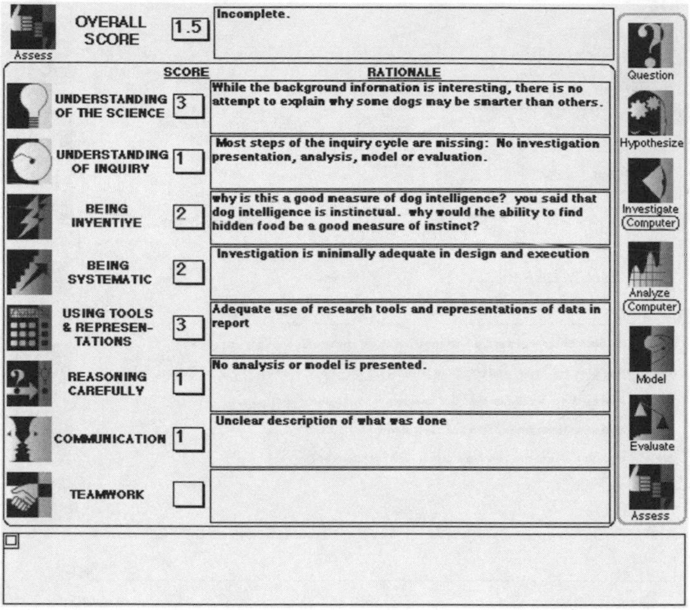

FIGURE 5

The Overall Assessment screen of the Inquiry Scorer, with scores and rationales for a project given by a teacher.

Project analysis. Our intention in introducing project analysis into the assessment process is to make the teacher's interpretation of the project more systematic and, in so doing, to bolster the evidential basis the teacher uses in making overall assessments. In the project analysis, the teacher evaluates specific features of each section of the research project. For each section, the Inquiry Scorer presents a number of questions, each asking for a qualitative judgment about a specific aspect of the work in that section (see Figures 3 and 4). In addition, when analyzing the Investigate section of the project report, the teacher is asked to construct a "map" of the investigation's design. The purpose of this exercise is to give teachers an opportunity to think through the characteristics of the investigation's design and to provide a convenient way to represent the design that they can refer to when answering the overall assessment questions. In creating the project map, the teachers first identify the independent and dependent variables the student used in his or her investigation. They then code how the student used each variable in the research and how they found its value. For instance, a variable may have been manipulated, allowed to freely vary, or purposefully held constant by the investigator. Further, the value or state of a variable may follow directly from its definition (e.g., male or female gender), it may have been judged, or it may have been measured. Finally, the teachers code the salient relations among the independent and dependent variables that they see in the student's data; the software draws lines on the map to connect the variables as the relations between them are coded.[1] An example of a project map is shown in the bottom screen shot in Figure 3. The topic of the project is "Are hunting dogs more intelligent than working dogs?" The student compared several hunting dogs with several working dogs (the type of dog was determined by its breed) and gave them several different kinds of problems that ostensibly differed in difficulty. The student measured the time it took each dog to solve each problem. We suggested to the teachers that they fill out the project map before answering the questions that follow it, which are concerned with the investigation's design and data collection.

Overall assessments. The last section of the Inquiry Scorer (see Figure 5) provides a place for scorers to give their assessments of how well the students have demonstrated their overall understanding (Understanding the Science and Understanding the Processes of Inquiry), how well they have demonstrated valued cognitive competencies in their project work (Being Inventive, Being Systematic, Using the Representations and Tools of Science, and Reasoning Carefully), and also how they have demonstrated two important social goals (Writing and Communicating Well and Teamwork). Definitions for each of these assessment criteria as given in the Inquiry Scorer are shown in Table 1. For each criterion, the teachers are provided with a five-level scoring rubric that describes the performance characteristics at each level. For example, the Being Systematic scoring rubric is as follows:

5 = Investigation is carefully planned and designed, and thoughtfully executed, analyzed, and evaluated

4 = Investigation stands out either as well planned and designed, or as thoughtfully executed and evaluated

3 = Investigation is adequately designed and executed

2 = Investigation is minimally adequate in design and execution

1 = A poorly designed and executed investigation

The teachers are also provided with a place to type a comment for the student, to give feedback about why the particular score was given and perhaps some tips on how the project could be improved.

TABLE 1

Definitions of Criteria for Overall Assessments of Scientific Inquiry Projects

 Understanding the Science. Students show that they understand the relevant science and can apply it in solving problems, in predicting and explaining phenomena, and in carrying out inquiry projects.

 Understanding the Processes of Inquiry. Students are thoughtful and effective in all phases of the inquiry process, including: raising questions for study, developing hypotheses, designing an investigation, collecting and analyzing data, drawing conclusions in the form of laws and models, and reflecting on the limitations of their investigation and their conclusions.

 Being Inventive. Students create innovative investigations through examining multiple possibilities as they develop research questions and hypotheses, design investigations, analyze results, create new laws and models, and evaluate applications of their models in new situations.

 Being Systematic. Students are careful, organized, and logical in planning, carrying out, and evaluating work. When problems come up, they are thoughtful in examining their progress and deciding whether to alter their approach or strategy.

 Using the Representations and Tools of Science. Students understand the representations and tools of science and use them appropriately in their investigations. These may include diagrams, graphs, tables, formulas, calculators, computers, and lab equipment.

 Reasoning Carefully. Students reason appropriately and carefully using scientific concepts and models. They can argue whether or not a prediction or law fits a model. They can show how their observations support or refute a model. And they can evaluate the strengths and limitations of a model.

 Writing and Communicating Well. Students clearly express their ideas to each other or to an audience through writing and speaking so that others will understand their research and how they carried it out.

 Teamwork. Students work together as a team to make progress. They respect each others' contributions and support each others' learning. They divide their work fairly so that everyone has an important part.

Participants in the Study

Six urban middle school teachers participated in the scoring study. Four were experienced science teachers, one was a beginning mathematics teacher, and one was a social studies teacher. Two of the science teachers were involved in the prior ThinkerTools study and had considerable experience in the holistic scoring of inquiry projects (White & Frederiksen, 1998). The teachers participated in an iterative design process in which they tried out an initial design for the Inquiry Scorer and provided feedback to us about the clarity and usefulness of the scoring questions used in the project analysis and the rubrics used in the overall assessments. Then they were each given 16 projects to score using a revised version of the scoring software.[2] They scored the projects individually and then met in small groups to discuss their scoring after every fourth project scored. The amount of time they spent learning to score was very modest when compared with the time the teachers in our earlier study spent learning to judge inquiry projects.

Results of Teachers' Scoring

Project analysis. Our first research question concerned the degree to which a group of teachers, given limited practice in carrying out a project analysis, can make consistent judgments of detailed features of inquiry projects required in carrying out such an analysis. To investigate this question, we first determined the modal response of the teachers for each question on each project they analyzed. Then, for each teacher and question, we calculated the percentage of the projects for which the teacher gave the modal response. This is the rate of exact agreement for that teacher and question. The average rate of exact agreement across all of the project analysis questions was 81%. The agreement rates were the same for the two teachers who had prior experience scoring inquiry projects (79%) and for the four teachers who had no such prior experience (82%). Teachers had lower agreement rates when the questions required making finer distinctions in characterizing the quality of students' accomplishments. This is apparent in the way the agreement rates vary with the number of categories available for answering a question: 90% for two response categories, 78% for three categories, and 72% for four categories; $F_{(2, 15)} = 7.02$, $p < .01$. However, when the teachers' responses for the three- and four-category questions were recoded to two categories, agreement rates for those questions increased to 86% and 90%, respectively. This suggests that the content of the questions is not the source of their difficulty. We also analyzed trends in the degree of agreement as teachers gained experience in coding. Mean rates of agreement increased somewhat (for the first five, middle five, and last six projects, they were 79%, 80%, and 87%, respectively), but these changes were not significant. The overall rates of agreement with the modal response for the six teachers ranged from 64% to 85%. When responses involving three or four categories were recoded to two categories, the range narrowed to 83% to 89%. This suggests that the difficulty experienced by the teachers who had lower levels of agreement has to do with making fine distinctions about qualities of students' accomplishments, rather than making the conceptual distinctions about students' performance required by the questions.

We also looked at the teachers' consistency in identifying and naming the independent and dependent variables when they developed a project map. (Correct coding was determined by the authors after reviewing each project.) We found that independent variables were more difficult (with a mean of 73% correct) than dependent variables (with a mean of 82% correct) for the teachers to code. In coding independent variables, the teachers had some difficulty in choosing names for them. Often they would code particular values of a variable (e.g., "mutts," "hunting dogs") as though they were separate variables rather than giving a name to represent the range of values or states of the variable (e.g., "type of dog"). Nevertheless, the teachers remarked that developing project maps was valuable in helping them to figure out the structure of a student's project and that it made them more efficient in answering questions about the investigation's design and analysis.

Scoring individual criteria. We next looked at the teachers' consistency in assigning ratings for the seven criteria, which were made using a five-point scoring rubric.[3] For each teacher, we calculated the percentage of the projects he or she scored for which the scores agreed with the modal score assigned by the six teachers. The average agreement rate of the teachers in judging criteria was 64%, with a range for individual teachers of 53% to 72%. The agreement rate for the two teachers who had prior experience scoring inquiry projects (68%) was greater than that for the four teachers who had no such prior experience (56%). The overall average agreement rate of 64% can be compared with an estimated agreement rate of 60% for questions requiring five categories of response.[4] This suggests that the difficulty teachers have in assigning scores for the criteria is attributable to the fine distinctions they need to make based on the rubric descriptions for the five levels. On the other hand, making these distinctions can help teachers (and students) more deeply understand the processes of inquiry and can provide more in-depth evaluations of students' capabilities. Learning how to make these distinctions is likely to take more practice than the teachers in our scoring study had.

Teachers' Use of Evidence in Scoring

To further understand the value of a project analysis in improving teachers' use of evidence when scoring higher level cognitive goals, such as Reasoning Carefully and Being Systematic, we investigated the evidence that teachers made use of when scoring each of the criteria. To do this, we analyzed the relationship between the teachers' responses to each of the 33 analysis questions and their ratings for each of the seven scoring criteria. For each of these 33 × 7 relations, we calculated a phi coefficient as a measure of association between the teachers' responses for each question and the scores for each criterion. For these analyses, the teachers' responses to the questions and their criterion scores were recoded into two categories. For the questions, we compared the highest category for that question (e.g., "Clear") with the remaining categories (e.g., "So-so," "Unclear," or "None"). For the criterion scores, we compared "high" scores (4 or 5) with "low" scores (1, 2, or 3). In this analysis, we included data for the five teachers who scored all 16 projects, giving a maximum sample size of 80 (with missing data, the number of judgments analyzed was typically 75, with a range of 69 to 80). As a guide to interpreting the size of phi coefficients, for the lowest sample size of 69, a phi coefficient of .31 is significant at the .01 level, while a phi of .40 is significant at the .001 level.

General relations. First we identified those analytic questions that had the greatest association with teachers' judgments for the set of criteria taken as a whole. To do this, we calculated the average phi coefficient for each question, averaged over the seven criteria (in the following discussion of results, these will be given in parentheses). The questions with the highest average phi coefficients were those in which teachers assess 1) how well students have provided reasons for their decisions and conclusions, 2) how well students have described the relations among different aspects of inquiry in their research, and 3) whether students have created a model that explains their research findings. Giving Reasons for Decisions and Conclusions included these questions: Do they [the students] give a reason for their choice of question (.40)? Do they explain how the data support their law or model (.63)? Do they try to explain why their law or model "works" (.38)? Relating the Different Aspects of the Inquiry Process included these questions: Are the data that have been collected consistent with the design (.40)? Do they relate their results back to their research question (.54)? Do they say whether their research hypotheses are supported or refuted (.38)? Creating and Evaluating a Model included these questions: Do they present a general law or model, and is it clearly stated (.38)? Is the general law or model consistent with the data presented (.56)? Are limitations of their general law or model considered (.36)?

Specific relations. Second, we examined the set of phi coefficients for each of the seven scoring criteria individually to see if there were patterns in the way questions were associated with each criterion that differed from the general pattern reported above. Specifically, for each criterion, we identified those questions with a phi coefficient (presented in parentheses in the following discussion) that differed from the average by .1 or more.

Three of the assessment criteria were intended to be quite broad, asking for overall judgments of understanding of science and inquiry and of the quality of students' written communication. Their associations with coding questions were therefore expected to be broad, although the criteria involve different perspectives in judging the work. For Understanding the Science, the pattern of association with coding questions was similar to the general pattern described above. It included questions about whether students gave reasons for their decisions and conclusions, how they explained the relations among different aspects of inquiry, and whether they presented a law or model to explain their findings. For Understanding Inquiry, the pattern of association with coding questions included in addition two questions that were related to the analysis phase of inquiry: Do they use analytic methods that are appropriate for the investigation (.42)? Do they find and describe patterns in their data (.45)? For Writing and Communicating Well, the pattern of association is similar to the general pattern described above but included two additional questions about students' explanations of their data collection and the model they created: Do the data appear to have been carefully collected/measured (.53)? Did they try to explain why their law or model "works" (.54)?

The remaining four criteria were intended to be more focused, and we expected to find more specific associations with coding questions. For Being Inventive, the pattern of associations with coding questions was similar to the general pattern described above, but there was a particularly strong relation with the question, Do the students explain how the data support their law or model? For this question, the phi coefficient was .86, the highest we observed. This suggests that in scoring this criterion, the teachers were particularly influenced by the students' inventiveness in coming up with a general law or model that was consistent with their findings. For Being Systematic, the pattern of association with coding questions was similar to the general pattern described above but included six additional questions that focus on the investigation phase of the inquiry process: Do the variables used in the design match those in the hypotheses (.39)? Are the variables measured, controlled, or varied appropriately to test the hypotheses (.50)? Overall, will the design enable them to test their hypotheses (.46)? Is the design for the investigation clearly explained (.41)? Is the procedure for investigation clearly presented (.49)? Are the data that have been collected consistent with the design (.50)? This suggests that teachers were particularly influenced by students' care in designing their investigation. The evidence for Using the Representations and Tools of Science appeared to be more specific than the general pattern, focusing on data analysis and how data support their law or model. Questions included: Are the data that have been collected consistent with the design (.41)? Do they use analytic methods that are appropriate for their investigation (.46)? Are there clear patterns in the data which they overlooked (.47, a negative association)? Is the general law or model consistent with the data presented (.47)? Do the students explain how the data support their law or model (.50)? Do they relate their findings back to their research question (.52)? Finally, for Reasoning Carefully, in addition to the general pattern, the evidence included two questions referring to the evaluation phase of the inquiry cycle students were using: Are limitations of their general law or model considered (.45)? Do they describe any errors in or limitations of their investigation (.41)? This was the only criterion that was associated both with the students' reflections on the limitations of their conclusions and the quality of their investigation, which are examples of metacognitive behaviors.

We must bear in mind that the analysis codes are not a direct representation of the teachers' knowledge of the students' project. The codes are assigned at the time the teacher is reading the relevant part of the project report. The analysis questions help the teacher build a model of the project, but the model is not the same as the set of codes. When the teacher scores the project using the criteria, the analysis codes are available within the software for inspection, along with notes the teacher has made, and they may help the teacher recall aspects of the project. But the teachers are most likely reasoning from the rubric level descriptions for each criterion and using their memory of the project with the help of the project map, which teachers report is particularly useful in this regard, rather than inspecting 33 analysis codes and combining them in some way to reach a scoring decision. This criterion scoring process, and the role of the project analysis in supporting it, needs to be studied in more detail in future research.

Understanding how analytic evidence is used in scoring can lead to a better understanding of how the analytic framework questions might be designed to provide better evidence for determining the criterion scores. We note that these relations of coding to scoring also depend on the nature of the criterion one is interested in at the time. In the Inquiry Scorer, we chose criteria for metacognitive purposes—they are ways of reflecting on one's work that are broadly applicable to many things that one does, rather than being evaluations of specific aspects of one's work. Other sorts of criteria, such as those representing state or national performance standards, may make use of difference kinds of evidence from analyses of students' work. Some criteria might even be judged simply by calculating a score based on point values assigned to the individual questions used in the project analysis. As an example, we calculated a set of inquiry scores, one for each phase of the inquiry process (Question, Hypothesize, Investigate, Analyze, Model, and Evaluate). These scores were the sum of values assigned to each question for that phase of inquiry. We then calculated the reliability of these section scores using generalizability analysis (Shavelson & Webb, 1991). The average reliability of these section scores was .67 for a single scorer. This suggests that scores based on totaling the point values of question responses could also be used as a component in the evaluation of students' work. However, a disadvantage in relying only on such scores is that they don't capture or encourage deeper reflection on aspects of work such as reasoning, inventiveness, and systematicity, which cannot be easily decomposed into sets of simpler elements. We have seen in examining the phi coefficients how different sources of evidence appear to be differentially weighed by teachers when making scoring decisions. But their perspectives on the evidence they have observed while answering the analysis questions are likely to be different from the perspectives they have when judging the seven scoring criteria. The use of analytic questions provides a way to open up a deep analysis of students' work, but we do not believe that the pattern of answers to those questions captures the full picture of students' work that teachers develop in the process of answering them. Clearly, more research is needed to understand the best use of analytic questions, scoring criteria, and part scores in evaluating different aspects of students' performance.

Documenting Scoring Accuracy

If scores developed by teachers are to be used as evidence within an accountability system, there needs to be a way of statistically monitoring and reporting their accuracy and comparability. One way to do this would be to have external scorers cross-validate the scoring of a random sample of projects. A potential problem with this approach is that agreeing on a score does not ensure that scorers have the same reasons for inferring the score from their observations (Moss, 1994). An alternative approach is to examine the internal validity of the scores for each of the criteria in relation to the evidence that has been coded in the project analysis. Because the teachers carried out a project analysis and built a project map as they read each project, this information can be used to corroborate their analysis. By characterizing the normative patterns relating coded evidence and scores generated by experienced scorers, we can evaluate whether the pattern of scores generated by a particular scorer in scoring *a particular project* is consistent with the normative model. If the pattern is consistent, we can have confidence that 1) the scorer has applied the interpretive framework correctly in that instance and 2) the framework itself appropriately represents the relations among various features of that project.

Characterizing the Normative Scoring Model

To provide an example, we used multiple regression as a technique for representing the normative relations between project analysis variables and overall assessment scores for each of the seven criteria. Other methods that could be used include MDS (Kruskal, 1964), logit analysis (e.g., Linacre, 1993), Bayesian networks (Pearl, 1988), Latent Semantic Analysis (Landauer, Foltz, & Laham, 1998), and other, AI-based approaches such as PDP models (see Thagard, 1989). Our first task was to characterize the relations among scored characteristics of a project that we should expect when scorers are using a normative scoring model. Because we did not have data for experienced scorers available, in our example we used the scoring data for the five teachers who scored every project. We used the project analysis subscores for each section of the research project (the sum of numerical values assigned to the individual analysis questions for each section) to predict each of the seven criterion scores using multiple regression. The resulting regression coefficients for predicting each of the seven criteria are shown in Table 2. The regression coefficients provide another way of visualizing differences in how the teachers used the evidence they encoded during the project analysis when making overall assessments of different qualities of the project. For instance, judging a student's Understanding of the Science depended mainly on information pertaining to the student's framing of a research question (which includes background information to motivate that choice) and on his or her presentation of a

TABLE 2
REGRESSIONS OF OVERALL ASSESSMENT CRITERIA ON PROJECT ANALYSIS SUBSCORES

Project Analysis Subscores	Overall Assessment Criteria						
	Understanding the Science	Understanding the Processes of Inquiry	Being Inventive	Being Systematic	Using the Representations and Tools of Science	Reasoning Carefully	Writing and Communicating Well
Question	.22**	−.02	.31***	.10	.17	.00	.12
Hypothesize	.13	.24**	.08	.00	.05	.04	−.08
Investigate	.16	.11	.19	.33***	.13	.10	.26**
Analyze	.18	.27*	.11	.32***	.41***	.36***	.21*
Model	.24**	.39***	.15	.31***	.14	.35***	.40***
Evaluate	.06	.02	.12	−.07	−.02	.11	.11
R^2	.74	.83	.71	.84	.72	.77	.80

* $p < .10$, two-tailed. ** $p < .05$, two-tailed. *** $p < .01$, two-tailed.

model to describe and account for the research findings. Judging a student's ability in Using the Representations and Tools of Science was based mainly on information from the Analysis section of the student's report (such as data presented in a table or graph, with trends in the data identified and interpreted). A student's mastery of Writing and Communicating Well was judged on the basis of the parts of the project that were most difficult for students to present and explain, namely, the structure of their investigation and their conclusions.

Evaluating Internal Validity

To evaluate the internal validity of the scores, we used the regression equation for each criterion to calculate a predicted score for each scorer, project, and criterion, and we examined the discrepancy beween the observed and predicted scores (the residual). A lack of agreement means that the way the scorer used evidence gathered during the project analysis to choose a score is not consistent with the methods of the scorers as a group. Our data include a total of 5 scorers evaluating 16 projects, with separate predictions made for each of the seven assessment criteria (a total of 560 cases). To evaluate the credibility of each of the criterion scores, we counted as outliers any cases that deviated from the predicted score by two standard deviations or more in either direction. Using this criterion, the expected number of outliers is 26. We found that there were 32 outliers in the set of analyses.

Lack of consistency in a scorer's use of evidence in judging a project may be due to ambiguity in the evidence presented in the project reports or to differences in the teachers' interpretations of that evidence as compared with the standard method of weighing evidence. If the project is susceptible to multiple interpretations on a particular criterion, we would expect more than one scorer to come up with the same alternative interpretation. We therefore examined the 32 cases that were identified as outliers, looking for instances where at least two scorers had discrepant residuals for the same project and criterion. There were only 4 cases that met this condition. In examining these 4 cases, we found several projects that appeared to raise interpretive issues that need to be considered if we want to improve the accuracy of the scoring system.

For example, in one science fair project, a student was concerned with the question, "How fast do worms speed up the making of compost?" The investigation was very carefully designed and carried out, with precise determinations of the amount and kinds of material (shredded paper and kitchen scraps) placed in each of two composting bins. The control bins had no worms while experimental bins had a fixed number of worms added to them. Although the input variables were carefully measured (grams of food scraps and worms), the observations of composting activity made each day (the dependent variables) were in the form of careful, qualitative descriptions. These were presented in narrative form as a set of detailed notes for days one, two, three, and seven of the investigation.

In scoring this project for Systematicity, scorer S1 showed a strong appreciation for the detailed, qualitative data the student presented, which he thought had been carefully collected. This scorer also thought that the conclusions presented were strongly warranted by the qualitative data. In making his assessment of Systematicity, S1 determined that these features of the student's work warranted a high score of 5. In contrast, scorer S4 did not agree that the data had been carefully collected and measured. Further, this scorer did not think that the student's data supported his conclusion or his model, or even that the student had provided an adequate test of his hypothesis. And in his comments, S4 suggested that the scope of the investigation was too limited, noting that the student hadn't varied the number of worms to see how that would effect the rate of decomposition. Weighing these factors, S4 gave the project a low score of 2 for Systematicity. The two scorers thus strongly disagree about the appropriateness of using qualitative observations as a basis for establishing a scientific generalization. In addition, S4 thought that varying just the presence or absence of worms was not a sufficient test of the hypothesis. These discrepancies in interpretation suggest that, to improve the scoring system, we need to take a stand on how scorers should value the students' use of qualitative information within a research project, in this case, whether students need to quantitatively vary the levels of the independent variables in their experiments. If we were to adopt this position, then we would need to add this as a further specification of the interpretive model for judging research projects and incorporate it within the Inquiry Scorer.

Discussion

We began our argument regarding assessment design principles with considerations of fairness to teachers and schools, and we adopted the principle that teachers and schools should not be judged based on measures of students' performance that are not amenable to improvement through their hard work in seeking the best education for their students.

If they are to find ways of improving learning outcomes, teachers and students need to know the kinds of tasks students are expected to carry out and the ways students' performance will be judged. We have argued that having open standards for tasks and how they are assessed makes possible a merging of classroom assessment goals and goals for creating evidence of students' learning that schools can use in meeting accountability standards. This merger depends on having descriptions of the types of activities or tasks that provide meaningful goals that students and teachers can aim for in learning, and also on having transparent processes for evaluating performance that teachers and students can use in reflecting on students' work. Finally, we have argued that in assessing students' inquiry projects, the most important issue to attend to is the internal validity of each interpretation of a student's performance— mainly, that the interpretation has been properly carried out and that it is accurate in characterizing the student's work. To accomplish this, a thorough assessment is needed, one in which scorers develop multiple sources of evidence for their interpretations and have a principled basis for making scoring inferences based on that evidence.

The key issue we have addressed is how we can scaffold teachers' (and students') interpretations of students' work to ensure that resulting assessments are accurate and comparable. To study how this might be done, we created a software tool, the Inquiry Scorer, for teachers to use as they read and analyze middle school students' science inquiry projects, and we analyzed how teachers made use of this tool in reaching scoring decisions. The Inquiry Scorer scaffolds the scorer in creating a representation (or "map") of the inquiry project and in making a series of analytic judgments of features of a student's work during each phase of the inquiry process. This is followed by the scorer's overall evaluation of the inquiry project using multiple assessment criteria that describe important aspects of the student's performance on the project, some or all of which may be coordinated with state standards for students' learning. The results of our analyses of teachers' use of the scoring software suggest that 1) teachers who have little or no prior experience in analyzing inquiry projects can readily develop skills for accurately and consistently coding important, qualitative features of students' inquiry; 2) they can use this information in a principled way to make judgments of important qualities of students' inquiry and of the cognitive skills students use in carrying out inquiry; and 3) the scoring information contained in their project analysis and the criterion scores they assigned in their overall assessment can provide an evidential basis for evaluating the internal validity of their scoring.

By analyzing statistically the assessment data teachers generated while using the scoring software, we were able to develop a normative scoring model for representing the patterns of evidence that scorers use when they carry out assessments. Then, on a project-by-project basis, we could ascertain whether or not the patterns of evidence each teacher used conformed to the normative model. In this way we were able to verify the internal validity of the performance interpretations. Schools could use methods such as these not only to report their students' performance on classroom assessments, but to provide evidence of the accuracy and credibility of the scores they report by calculating the rates at which scoring judgments have passed a test of internal validity. The analysis of evidence-interpretation patterns on a project-by-project basis is, perhaps, a new area for the application of psychometric methods. In this endeavor, the focus is no longer on estimating values of latent traits; it is on making decisions about the credibility of analysis patterns.

Incorporating such methods for evaluating the internal validity of interpretations can also lead to ongoing improvements in methods of interpretation, enabling them to capture a wider range of ways of demonstrating expertise. Like Moss's (1994) hermeneutical approach to assessment, such an effort reflects a deep concern with the process of interpretation and with documenting it. In the approach we are suggesting, however, the goal is to create a normative interpretive model for scorers to apply, although disagreements with the normative model should be taken seriously and used to inform decisions concerning how to moderate scores assigned using the normative model in cases where it is difficult to apply. Disagreements in interpretations may also lead to attempts to extend the normative model to encompass a wider range of expert performances on the assessment task. Still another possibility that must be considered is the need for alternative interpretive models to represent alternative ways of assessing students' projects. This may be necessary if the strategy or approach a student takes to a task drastically changes how one must go about interpreting his or her actions in carrying out that task. This would mean that scores on a performance task would have to come with a description of the interpretive method employed and why it was used, as in "depth" hermeneutics (Moss, 1994).

An issue that comes up in considering the use of such thorough assessments is the amount of time and effort they require. We found that our teachers were spending in the neighborhood of 15 minutes to score a project after they had had some practice in using the Inquiry

Scorer. They all reported that carrying out the project analysis and creating a project map were the most time consuming tasks, but that these exercises greatly reduced the time it took them to arrive at overall assessments using the set of criteria. They also felt that the value of the knowledge they acquired, of how to analyze students' work and of scientific inquiry itself, has important benefits in helping them support their students' learning.

We have created a paper-and-pencil version of the scoring tool, which is now being used by scientists from local research organizations in scoring more than 300 science fair projects each year in the school district where we are working. The paper-and-pencil version includes most of the questions used in the Inquiry Scorer but omits the project map. We asked six of the scientists who used this scoring framework to fill out a questionnaire evaluating their experience in scoring. The average time they reported for scoring was 10 minutes, and all the scorers we polled said that this was an appropriate and necessary amount of time for reading and judging such projects.

Putting these time considerations aside, we argue that the effort that students put into carrying out extended, authentic assessment tasks needs to be matched by a serious effort to ensure that a rich and valid set of descriptions are derived in interpreting such performances. Such assessment tasks go far beyond conventional tests in that they show how domain knowledge, knowledge of inquiry, and metacognitive skills combine and are integrated in carrying out complex activities. Developing reliable and valid assessments of such knowledge and its use may prove to be important, not only for creating a broader and more accurate portrayal of a student's range of expertise, but also for supporting the teaching and learning of scientific inquiry. This is supported by our teachers' reports that using the Inquiry Scorer gave them a better ability to understand the processes of inquiry and to recognize—and develop—such skills in their students. Further, we have presented evidence that suggests that this understanding leads to a principled analysis and evaluation of students' inquiry projects that can be shown to be credible and consistent and that therefore can be used by schools for accountability purposes.

If assessment frameworks are transparent and accessible to students as well as teachers, it is possible to have students play a collaborative role in assessing their inquiry projects. Students could provisionally encode properties of their own research projects in the course of carrying them out, and the teacher's role could be to verify, correct, and extend the students' self-assessments. This would have the desirable outcome of creating a dialog between students and their teachers about the character of their work, framed by the language of practice represented by the constructs of the assessment (Frederiksen & White, 1997). Based upon our prior research in which we have shown that self-assessment practices are beneficial in helping students learn science and scientific inquiry (White & Frederiksen, 1998), we strongly believe that this sort of metacognitive dialog would be a worthwhile extension to our curricular practices in science education.

NOTES

1. In addition, coding the independent and dependent variables and how they are used are good ways for teachers to learn to recognize the kind of investigation a student has created. Kinds of investigation include 1) controlled experiments, in which the independent variables are purposefully varied (manipulated) in order to see what their effects are on the dependent variables; 2) correlational studies, in which the interest is still in how some variables (the independent variables) influence other variables (the dependent variables), but the independent variables are free to vary and the investigators measure their values rather than control them; and 3) mixed investigations, in which some independent variables are manipulated while others are measured.

2. One of the teachers scored only 6 of the 16 projects.

3. One of the criteria, Teamwork, was omitted because it was difficult for teachers to score from written project reports.

4. The estimated agreement rate is a linear extrapolation of the agreement rates for project analysis questions involving two, three, or four response categories.

REFERENCES

Baker, E.L., Linn, R.L., Herman, J.L., & Koretz, D. (2002). Standards for educational accountability systems (policy brief No. 5). Los Angeles: CRESST.

Black, P., & Wiliam, D. (1998a). Inside the black box: Raising standards through classroom assessment. *Phi Delta Kappan, 80*(2), 139-148.

Black, P., & Wiliam, D. (1998b). Assessment and classroom learning. *Assessment in Education, 5*(1), 7-73.

Bransford, J.D., & Schwartz, D.L. (2001). Rethinking transfer: A simple proposal with multiple implications. *Review of Research in Education, 24*, 61-100.

Brown, A. (1987). Metacognition, executive control, self-regulation, and other more mysterious mechanisms. In F.E. Weinert & R.H. Kluwe (Eds.), *Metacognition, motivation, and understanding* (pp. 60-108). Hillsdale, NJ: Erlbaum.

California State Board of Education. (2000). Science content standards for California public schools: Kindergarten through grade twelve. Sacramento, CA: CDE Press.

Campbell, D.T., & Stanley, J.C. (1963). Experimental designs for research on teaching. In N.L. Gage (Ed.), *Handbook of research on teaching* (pp. 171-246). Chicago: Rand McNally.

Campione, J. (1987). Metacognitive components of instructional research with problem learners. In F.E. Weinert & R.H. Kluwe (Eds.), *Metacognition, motivation, and understanding* (pp. 117-140). Hillsdale, NJ: Erlbaum.

Campione, J.C., & Brown, A.L. (1990). Guided learning and transfer: Implications for approaches to assessment. In N. Frederiksen, R. Glaser, A. Lesgold, & M. Shafto (Eds.), *Diagnostic monitoring of skill and knowledge acquisition* (pp. 141-172). Hillsdale, NJ: Erlbaum.

Chronbach, L.J. (1971). Test validation. In E.L. Thorndike (Ed.), *Educational measurement* (2nd ed., pp. 443-507). Washington, DC: American Council on Education.

Frederiksen, J.R., & Collins, A. (1989). A systems approach to educational testing. *Educational Researcher, 18*(9), 27-32.

Frederiksen, J.R., & Collins, A. (1996). Designing an assessment system for the workplace of the future. In L.B. Resnick, J. Wirt, & D. Jenkins (Eds.). *Linking school and work: Roles for standards and assessment* (pp. 193-221). San Francisco: Jossey-Bass.

Frederiksen, J.R., & White, B.Y. (1997). Cognitive facilitation: A method for promoting reflective collaboration. In *Proceedings of the Second International Conference on Computer Support for Collaborative Learning* (pp. 53-62). Toronto: University of Toronto.

Kruskal, J.B. (1964). Multidimensional scaling by optimizing goodness of fit to a nonmetric hypothesis. *Psychometrika, 29*, 1-27.

Landauer, T.K., Foltz, P.W., & Laham, D. (1998). Introduction to latent semantic analysis. *Discourse Processes, 25*, 259-284.

Linacre, J.M. (1993). *Multi-faceted Rasch measurement.* Chicago, IL: MESA Press.

Linn, R.L. (2000). Assessment and accountability. *Educational Researcher, 29*(2), 4-14.

Mislevy, R.J. (1994). The interplay of evidence and consequences in educational assessment. *Psychometrika, 59*, 439-483.

Mislevy, R.J., Steinberg, L.S., & Almond, R.G. (2003). On the structure of educational assessments. *Measurement: Interdisciplinary Research and Perspectives, 1*(1), 3-62.

Moss, P.A. (1992). Shifting conceptions of validity in educational measurement: Implications for performance assessment. *Review of Educational Research, 62*(3), 229-258.

Moss, P. (1994). Can there be validity without reliability? *Educational Researcher, 23*(2), 5-12.

National Research Council. (1996). *National Science Education Standards.* Washington, DC: National Academy of Sciences.

Pearl, J. (1988). *Probabilistic reasoning in intelligent systems: Networks of plausible inference.* San Mateo, CA: Morgan Kaufmann.

Pellegrino, J., Chudowsky, N., & Glaser, R. (Eds.). (2001). *Knowing what students know: The science and design of educational assessment.* Washington, DC: National Academy Press.

Shavelson, R., & Webb, N. (1991). *Generalizability theory: A primer*. London: Sage.
Shepard, L.A. (1993). Evaluating test validity. *Review of Research in Education, 19*, 405-450.
Shepard, L.A. (2000). The role of assessment in a learning culture. *Educational Researcher, 29*(7), 4-14.
Thagard, P.R. (1989). Explanatory coherence. *Behavioral and Brain Sciences, 12*, 435-502.
White, B., & Frederiksen, J. (1998). Inquiry, modeling, and metacognition: Making science accessible to all students. *Cognition and Instruction, 16*(1), 3-118.
Wiggins, G. (1993). Assessment worthy of the liberal arts; Authenticity, context, and validity. In *Assessing student performance* (pp. 34-71; 206-255). San Francisco: Jossey-Bass.

CHAPTER 5

From Policy to Practice: The Evolution of One Approach to Describing and Using Curriculum Data

JOHN L. SMITHSON AND ANDREW C. PORTER

This chapter traces the development of, and evolving audiences for, a set of research tools developed at the University of Wisconsin–Madison by the authors and others between 1989 and 2003, with roots extending back to work Porter and his colleagues at Michigan State conducted during the 1980s (Porter, Floden, Freeman, Schmidt, & Schwille, 1988). Originally designed for use in investigating questions concerning the effects of policies (e.g., graduation requirements, curriculum standards, high-stakes assessment, and school accountability) on classroom practice, these tools are now just as likely to be used by a state educational agency to examine alignment issues between state content standards and assessments, by school leadership teams to inform curriculum decision making, or by curriculum specialists to plan professional development at the district or school level.

The central requirement for addressing all of these information needs is a systematic, rich, and multidimensional language for describing instructional content. The tools described here provide such a language, based on a two-dimensional model of instructional content consisting of topics and cognitive demand (see Figure 1). Fine-grain topics are organized within coarse-grain content areas. For K-8 mathematics, 103 topics are organized into seven content areas. In the K-8 science

John L. Smithson is a research associate at the Wisconsin Center for Education Research, University of Wisconsin–Madison. Andrew C. Porter is Professor of Public Policy and the Education Director of the Learning Sciences Institute at Vanderbilt University.

Much of the work discussed in this chapter has been supported through grants from the National Science Foundation and the Department of Education and has been conducted with colleagues from the Consortium for Policy Research in Education, the Council of Chief State School Officers, and more recently, the Regional Alliance for Mathematics and Science Education and Learning Point Associates. We especially wish to acknowledge Rolf Blank of the Council of Chief State School Officers, and our ongoing collaboration with participating states as part of CCSSO's State Collaborative on Assessments and Student Standards.

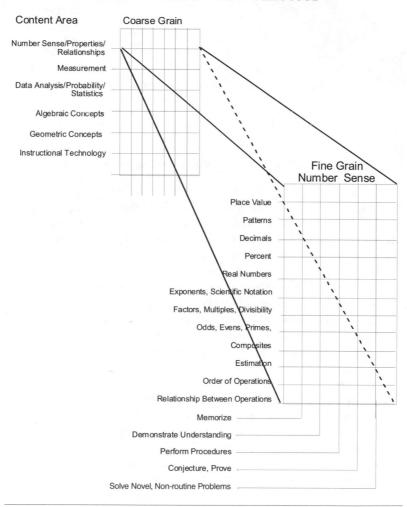

FIGURE 1

Elementary School Mathematics Content Matrix

language, 149 topics are organized into 25 content areas. Relative emphasis is measured at the intersection of topic and cognitive demand.

The content language has several features that make it useful in a broad range of educational applications (Porter, 2002; Porter & Smithson, 2001). It can be employed in a survey format to collect descriptions of instructional content from large numbers of teachers, or it can be employed to conduct content analyses of curriculum-related documents such as assessment instruments, content standards, curriculum frame-works, and a wide assortment of curriculum materials. Each of these descriptions can in turn be compared to one another, both quantita-tively, by calculating an alignment index or correlation, and visually, through content maps and graphs.

Figure 2 shows three content maps (at the coarse-grain level), de-scribing state standards, teacher survey reports, and a state assessment, as well as a content graph displaying the same set of data results as a bar chart. The amount of relative emphasis for a given intersection of topic and cognitive demand is reported by color bands (here repro-duced as shades of gray) that are similar to topographic and weather system maps. Relative emphasis increases as one moves toward the innermost color band on the map. For example, the greatest amount of relative emphasis noted on the seventh grade state mathematics assess-ment test (lower left panel) is found at the intersection of Number Sense/Properties/Relationships and D (Perform Procedures).

The essential purpose of these graphic displays is to provide educa-tors at all levels of the system with a consistent framework for describ-ing and reporting content as expressed by instruction, assessment, con-tent standards, curriculum frameworks, textbooks, and so on. It should be noted that some question the choice of the surface area format to display what are essentially discontinuous data points. However, we find that for teachers and others the maps are powerful tools for visual-izing and comparing descriptions of curriculum content in a manner that does not misrepresent the information. Nonetheless, some may prefer a different means of displaying the content data. The lower right panel in Figure 2 provides an alternate display that is particularly useful for looking at cell-by-cell comparisons across different descrip-tions. Note that this one graphic combines the information displayed in the three content maps included in the figure.

While the topic and cognitive demand dimensions of the language remain constant, the measure of relative emphasis varies depending on what is being described: the instructional content emphasized by state or national standards, reported as the proportion of content strands emphasizing specific topics and cognitive demands; the enacted cur-riculum, reported as a proportion of instructional time; or the content tested, reported as a proportion of test score points.

Figure 3 presents a fine-grain representation of the same standard and teacher data presented in Figure 2. The key difference between the coarse- and fine-grain versions is that the coarse-grain map is con-structed using 30 data points (6 content areas by 5 cognitive demand

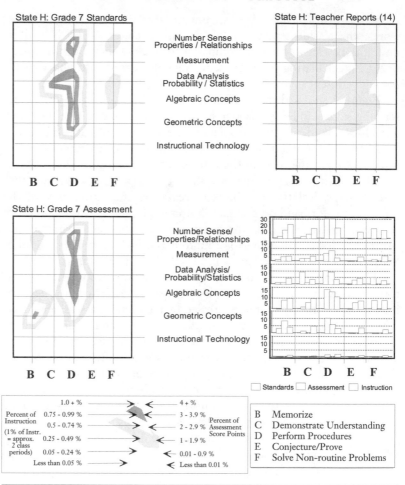

FIGURE 2

Content maps for state standards, teacher survey reports, a state
mathematics assessment and a content graph showing the combined data.

categories), while the maps in Figure 3 were created using 515 data
points (103 topics by 5 categories of cognitive demand). Typically,
individual fine-grain maps are constructed for each content area,
rather than the entire data set, as done for demonstration purposes in
Figure 3. One important characteristic that Figure 3 reveals quite
nicely is the extent to which assessments can only sample a content
area (indicated by the spottiness of the map), while much broader content coverage is indicated for instruction.

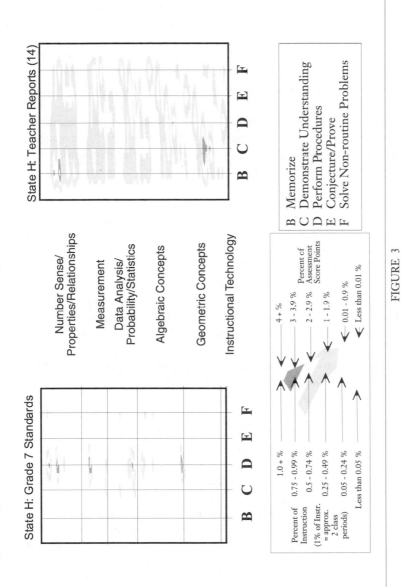

FIGURE 3

Fine-grain content maps for state standards and teacher survey reports.

Situating the Work

The tools discussed here have evolved to their current form through a series of research and development projects undertaken over the course of more than 20 years, but the more general line of work can be situated in the earlier and concurrent work of others. John Carroll (1963) offered a model of school learning that included *opportunity to learn* as a prominent feature. There have been many definitions of opportunity to learn over the years (Porter, 1993, 1995), but the *enacted curriculum*—what students are taught in the classroom—is at the heart of the concept.

The International Association for the Evaluation of Educational Achievement (IEA) has, since the early 1960s, conducted international comparative studies of student achievement. Early in that work, a distinction was drawn between the intended, the enacted, and the achieved curriculum. The *intended curriculum* is defined by national, state, and district content standards, textbooks, and the like; the *enacted curriculum* is defined by what is actually taught; and the *achieved curriculum* is defined by what students learn, usually as measured through student achievement tests. IEA studies were among the first to attempt to quantify measures of the enacted curriculum, or opportunity to learn. Their early approaches were to ask teachers to identify which items on the achievement test the students in their classroom had studied the necessary content for *prior to* the grade, which items they would study the content for *during* the grade, and which items they would likely study the content for *after* the grade. These early crude measures of opportunity to learn were used in some analyses to try to predict student achievement, which they did, but not with the strength one might have imagined.

In the mid- to late 1980s, there was a great deal of interest in education indicators, especially for the academic subjects of mathematics and science (Murnane & Raizen, 1988; Raizen & Jones, 1985; Shavelson, McDonnell, Oakes, Carey, & Picus, 1987). While not at the same high level, interest in indicators has continued (e.g., Porter, 1991; Stecher & Koretz, 1996). A system of education indicators might cover inputs and outputs, but increasingly attention has been called to the need for indicators of school and classroom processes (Porter, 1991). One group tackling this difficult problem is the scholars at the Center for Research on Evaluation, Standards, and Student Testing, at the University of California, Los Angeles (Burstein, et al., 1995; McDonnell, Burstein, Ormseth, Catterall, & Moody, 1990). These researchers have considered a variety of approaches to measuring the enacted curriculum, including collection and content analysis of what they called *artifacts* of the teaching and learning process. At the University of Michigan, a team of researchers has been similarly interested in the content of instruction, emphasizing especially the value of teacher logs (Rowan, Camburn, & Correnti, 2003). As discussed in later sections, the tools described in this chapter grow out of a line of work that has used observations, teachers' logs, and less frequently, teacher surveys to measure the enacted curriculum.

There has also been useful work on the validity of logs and survey data that are based on teacher self-reporting. Teachers may, for example, understand what content is desired, and even believe that they are teaching that content, when in fact they are not (Cohen, 1990). And surveys can suffer from unclear terminology (Scherpenzeel & Saris, 1997; Sudman, Bradburn, & Schwarz, 1996). Generally, what has been found as a result of these investigations is that surveys are quite good at describing quantity, but not so good at describing quality, that is, *what* is taught is better captured in a survey than *how well* it is taught (Burstein et al., 1995; Herman, Klein, & Abedi, 2000; Mayer, 1999; McCaffrey et al., 2001; Spillane & Zeuli, 1999).

Other scholars have tackled the problem of measuring the content of the intended curriculum. Schmidt and his colleagues (Schmidt, McKnight, Houang, Wang, Wiley, Cogan, & Wolfe, 2001) have done substantial work in this area in the context of the Third International Mathematics and Science Study. The conceptual basis for their work has its origins in the work of the content determinants group at Michigan State University in the 1970s, as do the tools described in this chapter. Schmidt and Porter were both members of that research team. Schmidt and his colleagues have also done content analyses of content standards and student textbooks, using a matrix of topics by performance expectations, similar to the matrix of topics by cognitive demand described here.

Another line of work using content analyses addresses the problem of alignment of student achievement tests to content standards. In summarizing that work, the American Educational Research Association (2003) cites the work of Webb (1999), Porter (2002), and Achieve, Inc. (see Rothman, Slattery, Vranek, & Resnick, 2002). The work by Porter is the same work as featured in this chapter. Webb's approach is to use a panel of experts to conduct content analyses of content standards and achievement test items and make judgments on a number of dimensions of possible alignment. Achieve's approach is similar, but more holistic. According to the No Child Left Behind Act of 2001, states must demonstrate that their achievement tests are aligned with their content standards, so measuring this alignment has become a new area of emphasis.

Researchers have been interested in measuring the content of the intended, enacted, and achieved curriculum for at least three decades. What follows is a chronology of one line of work that we are pursuing. As has been noted, this line of work shares, in its conceptual approach, many similarities to the work of Schmidt. It also shares some similarities with Webb's distinctions of depth and breadth, though aspects of Webb's work are unique.

Studying Teachers' Decisions

Initial development of the tools began in the mid-1970s at the Institute for Research on Teaching at Michigan State University. There Porter led a research team in a project called Content Determinants. The purpose of that work was to study influences on teachers' decisions about what to teach students in elementary school mathematics. Teachers' decisions about content included (a) how much time to spend on the subject, (b) what content to cover within that time, (c) which students to teach, and (d) what standards of achievement to use. The working hypothesis of the Content Determinants group was that teachers' content decisions largely determine a student's opportunity to learn mathematics in elementary school. Potential influences on teachers' content decisions are many and varied, but include what the teacher taught the previous year, what teachers in the upper grades would like the teacher to teach, what is in the textbook, and what is on the test. All of these represent independent variables, the effects of which were investigated. The dependent variable was content taught. The researchers developed an initial language for describing content, represented by a three-dimensional taxonomy: general intent (e.g., conceptual understanding, skills, and applications), the nature of material presented to students (e.g., fractions, decimals), and the operation the students must perform (e.g., estimate, multiply). Researchers used this language to describe the content of the enacted curriculum as reported in logs, interviews, and surveys, and to analyze the content of tests and textbooks. Analysis revealed that much of the content tested in elementary mathematics was not widely represented in textbooks, while much of the content contained in elementary mathematics textbooks was not tested. Another finding was that teachers are much more readily influenced to add content to what they have already been teaching than they are to delete content from what they are teaching (Floden, Porter, Schmidt, Freeman, & Schwille, 1981).

This initial use of a multidimensional taxonomy, or language, for describing key elements of curriculum content was substantially expanded in the late 1980s as Porter and a new set of colleagues at the University of Wisconsin-Madison undertook a large-scale investigation into the effects of increased graduation requirements on the mathematics and science content delivered to high school students across six states.

Reform Up Close: Looking Beyond the Classroom Door

By the end of the 1980s, implementations of states' initial policy responses to *A Nation at Risk* were well under way. The policy of choice during this period was to raise the number of mathematics and science courses required for high school graduation. The intent was to provide more challenging mathematics and science content to more students. As these requirements began to be implemented, concerns were raised that the math and science curricula were being compromised by the increased enrollments in higher-level mathematics and science courses (Cohen, 1990; Murnane & Raizen, 1988; Raizen & Jones, 1985).

In 1989, the Consortium for Policy Research in Education (CPRE) at the University of Wisconsin-Madison, with support from the National Science Foundation (NSF), began the study described in *Reform Up Close: An Analysis of High School Mathematics and Science Classrooms* (Porter, Kirst, Osthoff, Smithson, & Schneider, 1993). A key focus of the study was to look for evidence that high school mathematics and science curricula had been watered down. The study also sought to describe the nature of state, district, and school curriculum policymaking as it applied to high school science and mathematics courses and to determine the relationship between these policy characteristics and classroom practice. In order to accomplish this, it was necessary to develop some methodology for looking at the actual, or enacted, curriculum. In order to get a comprehensive picture of the curriculum presented in many, rather than only a handful, of classes, the Reform Up Close research team employed daily logs of instructional practice in target courses for 62 teachers, conducted 116 observations of 75 math and science instructional lessons, interviewed 81 teachers, and surveyed another 312. To this we added 76 school administrator interviews, 44 district interviews, and 18 interviews of state education agency staff. We collected the data from 18 schools in 12 districts across six states.

Study results indicated a positive influence of state, district, and school standard-setting activities on the course-taking patterns of large numbers of high school students. We found that increases in the number of mathematics and science credits required for high school graduation, coupled with increases in university entrance requirements for mathematics and science, as well as district and school efforts toward having all students take at least beginning-level college-preparatory coursework in mathematics and science, led to more high school students receiving more worthwhile math and science instruction than ever before. The study also determined that these increased enrollments did not appear to compromise the traditional curriculum offered in those courses. That was the good news (but note the word *traditional* in the preceding statement).

The bad news was that mathematics and science courses were still some distance from reflecting the type of curricula advocated by the National Council of Teachers of Mathematics (NCTM) in their *Curriculum Standards* (NCTM, 1989) and by the American Association for the Advancement of Science in their *Science for All Americans* (AAAS, 1989). Despite increased enrollment in college-preparatory mathematics courses, arithmetic represented the bulk of the content taught in many remedial and basic courses. This was particularly noticeable in states where basic skills tests served as high school exit exams (e.g., South Carolina and Florida at the time of the study). Statistics, probability, and discrete mathematics, important content areas emphasized in the NCTM *Standards*, received virtually no attention in any of the courses studied, including advanced courses. Math courses reflected a heavy emphasis on exposition and equations and little emphasis on modeling, real-world problems, or data collection. In science, the picture was similar: science courses made little to no use of field work; nearly half of the courses examined allocated less than 5% of instructional time for lab work; and approximately half of the courses allocated less than 10% of instructional time to collecting data. We found the emphasis in science courses to be heavy on memorization and understanding concepts through lecture and textbook presentation.

Such findings were possible only because of the rich description of classroom practices we were able to collect. While the collection of daily logs for a full school year presented the most detailed picture of classroom practice, these descriptions were strengthened by survey and observational data, which were compared with daily reports. Though requiring only 5 to 10 minutes of a teacher's time to complete, the daily logs were a definite burden on teachers (despite the teachers being compensated for their participation) and required a good deal of research staff time spent prodding teachers into submitting their logs in a timely fashion. Having available an overlapping set of observational and survey data that used essentially the same descriptive language provided an opportunity to examine how well teachers' year-end reports compared to the accumulation of teachers' daily reports, and how teachers' daily logs compared to observers' independent reports for a given lesson. The results of those analyses indicated that teachers reported much the same content as observers did, for those lessons where both a teacher log and an observation report were available, and that teachers' year end reports presented a similar picture of practice as the accumulation of their daily logs did (Smithson & Porter, 1994). This was good news methodologically, as it meant we could (and did) focus our data collection strategies increasingly on survey reports, avoiding the labor intensive alternatives of observation and/or teacher logs.

Key to these analyses was our employment of a detailed language for systematically describing practice. Indeed, we were pleased enough with the methodology employed in Reform Up Close to make some comments that, in hindsight, appear to have anticipated the direction in which the methodology has moved over the intervening decade:

Yet a fifth highlight of our work is methodological. The taxonomies we developed for describing high school mathematics and science curricula represent good examples of much needed languages for communicating the content and pedagogy of practice. Teachers need such languages to talk among themselves about their intentions and their successes. Education administrators need such languages for monitoring the enacted curriculum, making sure that instruction is consistent with intentions and equitably distributed. Policy makers need such languages for communicating the intended curriculum. (Porter et. al, 1993, p. A-4)

One regret from the Reform Up Close study was our inability to obtain useful student achievement data with which to compare reports of practice. The study did call for the collection of assessment results, and we did collect some data. Unfortunately the assessment results and methods of reporting available varied considerably from location to location, and useful data were not available in most locations. Thus we reluctantly dropped our plans to analyze the relationship between descriptions of practice and achievement data. This need to connect student achievement gains with classroom practice remained uppermost in our minds as we began considering the next study to undertake.

Upgrading Mathematics: Linking Practice and Outcomes

The Reform Up Close findings regarding the amount of basic, dead-end mathematics and science courses being offered in many high school curricula mirrored the findings of others (Clune, White, Sun, & Patterson, 1991; Firestone, Fuhrman, & Kirst, 1989) and prompted several states to devise various strategies for addressing this problem. The Upgrading Mathematics Project (1994-1997), which we undertook with our CPRE colleagues (again with funding from NSF), looked at competing strategies in order to determine if one approach was more effective than the others in moving students into more challenging mathematics and science courses.

We examined three strategies in particular. One strategy simply eliminated all basic-level math courses from the high school curriculum, requiring all students to take algebra in the ninth grade (unless completed in eighth, in which case the student would take the next course in the college-preparatory series). The second strategy used a variation of the first, with the difference being that, in lieu of offering basic-level math courses, challenging courses were "stretched" to cover in one year what the standard course accomplished in one semester. The third strategy was to offer at-risk students a new kind of alternative math course designed more or less (depending on the particular program) to capture student interest, increase the use of hands-on materials, and promote non-routine problem solving while focusing on real-world applications of mathematical knowledge. The sources of these strategies varied: some were state sponsored programs, such as Math A in California; some were local modifications of state curricula (e.g., Stretch-Regents in New York); and some used curriculum materials developed by the University of Chicago School Mathematics Project (UCSMP). In most cases schools had some choice in which strategy they employed. No single strategy was employed statewide in either of the two states we studied (California and New York).

The first phase of the Upgrading Mathematics Project involved a transcript study of the seven participating schools from four districts across two states. We selected California and New York because both had large populations of students they were trying to move into more challenging course offerings. The selected districts and schools had policies in place that were intended to move at-risk students into more challenging mathematics and science courses. Results indicated that students beginning high school in basic-level math courses (e.g., general math, remedial math, pre-algebra) rarely achieved even one year of college-prep math before graduation. Stretch and alternative courses led to greater completion of college-prep courses, but not as much as the strategy of insisting that all students take college-prep math at the start of high school (White, Gamoran, Smithson, & Porter, 1996).

The second phase of the study combined three components: an assessment (administered three times during the school year), teacher survey reports of instructional content collected at the middle and the end of the school year, and an alignment analysis of the relationship between instructional content, assessment content, and achievement gains. Results indicated that growth in student achievement was significantly lower in general-track classes than in college-preparatory classes, even after controlling for prior achievement and socio-economic status (SES) as measured by the number of students eligible for free and reduced lunch programs. Achievement gains in transition courses (Math A in California, Stretch-Regents and UCSMP in New York) fell between general-track and college-preparatory gains. Further analyses indicated that the content of instruction explained virtually all of the variance in achievement gains noted for the three groups. Indeed our analyses revealed a strong correlation between the alignment we had constructed and student achievement gains (Gamoran, Porter, Smithson, & White, 1997; Porter, 1998).

This result is important and has significant implications for evaluation and research aimed at linking elements of practice to increased student achievement (Porter & Smithson, 2001). At one level, the implication of these findings is not surprising; students score better on assessments that cover material that has been taught than on assessments that cover material that has not been taught. However, correlations of the level we found in these analyses (approaching 0.5) had not previously been reported. The result indicates that while many factors affect student performance in mathematics, an important element often overlooked in studies seeking to connect programmatic and pedagogical strategies to student achievement is the content of instruction delivered to students. The implication for researchers interested in demonstrating the added value of specific curricular programs, pedagogical strategies, or both is that controlling for content is every bit as important as controlling for SES and prior achievement if one wants to succeed in making the connection to student achievement gains. Another implication of these results is that the methodology, which utilizes survey-based teacher reports and the three-dimensional content language described earlier, is sound, demonstrating a valuable psychometric characteristic—predictive validity.

Surveys of Enacted Curriculum

While pursuing research associated with the Upgrading Mathematics Project described above, we began collaborative work with the Council of Chief State School Officers (CCSSO) and a number of member states to develop survey instruments designed to augment and assist in interpreting assessment results. This collaborative work evolved over time into the SEC (Survey of Enacted Curriculum) Collaborative, a member project of the State Collaborative on Assessment and Student Standards program administered and supported by CCSSO.

Initially focused on classroom and student activities, the instruments soon included updated versions of the content languages employed in the Reform Up Close and Upgrading Mathematics studies. Through a series of revision–field study–revision activities, we refined the data collection instruments to focus on measures relevant to the information needs of states, districts, schools, and teachers. As a result of these efforts, a set of survey instruments was packaged as the Surveys of Enacted Curriculum and made available to researchers, state curriculum and assessment departments, and eventually, districts and schools (Blank, Porter, & Smithson, 2001; Smithson, Porter, & Blank, 1995). The set includes mathematics, science, and soon, language arts surveys for teachers and students in grades K-12. The surveys are extensive, focusing on content, pedagogy, teacher and student characteristics, instructional influences, and professional development experiences. Student surveys are limited to classroom activities, and for some grades, courses previously taken (instructional content is not collected from student surveys). For more information on the SEC Collaborative, visit www.ccsso.org/sec.

Content and Alignment Analyses

As part of the work of the SEC Collaborative, member states also assisted in conducting content analyses on a number of state assessment instruments. In 1998, seven states (Kentucky, Minnesota, Missouri, North Carolina, Ohio, South Carolina, West Virginia) participated in an initial content analysis workshop to analyze state mathematics and science assessments (CCSSO, 2000). Over the course of two days, participants conducted content analyses of six state assessments, resulting in quantitative descriptions of mathematics and science assessment content that could be compared with teacher reports of instructional content, either visually (through content maps and graphs) or statistically (by calculating an alignment index describing the degree of overlap between instruction and assessment).

Content analyses were conducted using multiple, independent content experts who were introduced to the process during a half-day training session. After training, raters independently reviewed and coded content-related documents into the content language described above. Raters met as a group periodically during the coding process to discuss issues and questions that arose during independent coding, so that coding conventions and procedures could be updated or reinforced as content analyses proceeded. Typically four reviewers coded a particular document into the language, and the process usually took one or two hours (depending on the length of the document) to complete. Analyses of interrater reliability and generalizability indicated that four raters are generally sufficient to yield a fairly stable description of a document's subject matter content.

Results from these initial content analyses, in addition to demonstrating the feasibility of the process and reliability of the results, suggested that standards-based reform had not yet (in 1998) had a noticeable impact on the content delivered to students, as reported by teachers in the sample of states and schools that participated in both survey data collection and assessment analyses. We reached this conclusion by comparing the alignment between instruction and assessments across participating states and noting that instruction in a given state was no more aligned to the relevant assessment for that state than it was to the assessments of other states. Moreover, instruction tended to be more aligned to the relevant National Assessment of Education Progress (NAEP) test than to a state's own test (see Porter, 2002, for further discussion of these analyses and results).

Some have suggested that a better target for instruction and alignment would be state content and performance standards. While we agree that the broader vision of instruction conveyed by content standards represents a more comprehensive target than the relatively narrow scope of curriculum content represented by state assessments, we were initially skeptical that the content analysis procedures would work well with standards documents. With assessment instruments, the unit of measure is quite clear. Each assessment item contributes some proportion of the potential points to a student's overall score. Moreover, test items tend to be fairly specific in terms of the type and depth of knowledge being assessed. With content standards, the variation in specificity of language and the variety of styles used to convey content standards across all fifty states seemed a more daunting challenge for the language and content analysis procedures. Nonetheless, interest in examining alignment between assessments, instruction, *and* standards led us to attempt content analyses of state standards recently. Somewhat to our surprise, initial efforts in this regard appear to have been successful.

Table 1 displays the alignment analyses of the fine-grain content data displayed in Figures 2 and 3. The alignment index between instruction and assessment in this example is 0.20 (0.21 between instruction and the state content standards). The index functions much like a correlation in that the closer the number is to 1.0 the more instruction is focused on assessed content. There are, however, many reasons why one would not want the number to reach 1.0 for any given classroom. First, the assessment is, by design, merely a sample of some larger domain. Second, the instruction necessary to achieve a particular level of mastery will likely require instructional time focused on types of cognitive demand not assessed but nonetheless important to mastery. That said, our results in the Upgrading Mathematics Project (controlling for prior achievement and SES), indicated that students in classes with relatively high alignment gained more in assessed student achievement than students in classes with relatively low alignment.

TABLE 1
Alignment Analyses of the Fine-Grain Content Data Shown in Figures 2 and 3

State H	Standards	Assessment	Instruction
Standards	1.00		
Assessment	.29	1.00	
Instruction	.21	.20	1.00

Determining just what number represents "good" alignment is at this point difficult to judge. As more assessment content is analyzed and more indices for instruction to assessment alignment are calculated, we should begin to get a better idea of what represents an optimal level of alignment. At the present time, results of alignment between instruction and assessment have ranged from a low of 0.05 to a high of 0.46.

As for the alignment index for instruction and content standards in the example above (0.21), an in-depth review of the data at the fine-grain level would reveal the extent to which misalignment lies in the selection of topics or in the levels of cognitive demand (or both) emphasized in standards compared to those emphasized in instruction. Such data, particularly when examined at the school level, have the potential to provide valuable information about the types of topics and cognitive demand covered during instruction, along with comparable descriptions of assessments and standards.

Data on the Enacted Curriculum

As development of the instruments and the system for reporting results progressed, it became increasingly apparent that the types of information the instruments yielded had great potential to inform local planning and decision making efforts, yet required a professional development model to support interpretation and use of those data results. To meet this professional development need (while simultaneously testing the efficacy of the instrumentation and data in facilitating instructional change), a collaborative partnership was developed between the Council of Chief State School Officers, the Regional Alliance for Mathematics and Science Education, and the Wisconsin Center for Education Research at the University of Wisconsin-Madison, with support from the National Science Foundation, to conduct an experimental study into the effects of data use on instructional planning and practice.

The study, called Data on the Enacted Curriculum (DEC), utilized an experimental design consisting of 40 treatment and 40 control middle schools in five large urban districts that were surveyed at two times (spring 2001 and spring 2003). During the intervening two years, each of the treatment schools received its survey results, along with professional development and technical assistance in interpreting and using those results, as well as assistance in fostering a professional learning community within the school. Data from the two surveys will be compared to determine if any differences between the treatment and control groups can be attributed to the professional development and data-use activities engaged in by schools. After the administration of the SEC data instruments in spring 2003, the design allows for the control schools to receive the professional development training provided to the treatment schools by the Regional Alliance for Mathematics and Science Education, which builds from the work of Nancy Love and others (Love, 2002).

A number of different outcome measures can and will be looked at as part of these analyses. For example, content analyses of relevant assessments and state content standards will permit the calculation of alignment measures for each school (and each classroom) relative to some assessment instrument (in many cases a high-stakes state test) or relevant state content standards. These measures in turn permit investigation into differences in overall alignment, and the pattern of alignment between treatment and control schools. The hypothesis is that treatment schools will move toward closer alignment to state assessments or content standards, or both, than will the control schools during the two-year time frame.

Of course alignment measures focus only on subject matter content, that is, what (mathematics and science) content is taught, what content is tested, and what content is emphasized in state standards. Because the SEC data set was designed in large part by education practitioners looking for a general set of indicators relevant to curriculum and instruction, a variety of other aspects of practice can also be drawn upon to serve as outcome measures. In addition to subject matter content, the SEC data set also collects information about classroom and student activities; teacher readiness, beliefs, and opinions; and on the professional development activities that teachers have engaged in. Any of these measures, depending upon the goals and targets set by school improvement teams, could indicate a relevant outcome for a given treatment school.

As of this writing, the data collection for spring 2003 is just beginning, thus these analyses have not yet begun. Nonetheless, our experiences with the treatment schools over the past two years have provided many insights into data use at the school level. First, our experience convinces us that these tools and supporting procedures and analyses provide a platform for new and innovative approaches to professional development and technical assistance. Second, anecdotal evidence indicates that the data proved useful in several of the treatment schools, providing a focus on instruction, standards, and assessments that has enabled the schools to develop targeted strategies for improving the curriculum and instruction delivered to students. Finally, we have seen the curiosity and interest of teachers piqued as they engage with the data. Teachers quickly begin to engage with each other around issues of instructional content and practice, teacher opinions and beliefs, assessment strategies, instructional influences, and other areas represented by the data set.

Current and Future Developmental Efforts

While the experiences described above have been documented and repeated in numerous workshops associated with the DEC project, they have been largely limited to lead teachers, administrators, and curriculum resource specialists participating in the project as members of school improvement teams. The broader effect of these activities and experiences on classroom practice remains to be demonstrated. Though we are confident that the instruments and design used in the DEC project will permit investigation of this question in some detail, the dissemination of data-based curriculum decision making strategies beyond those personally involved in professional development and technical assistance activities poses a serious challenge to the demonstration of broad-based school-level effects.

Based on our experience in DEC, curriculum data, though necessary, is in most cases insufficient for meeting the data needs of schools. In addition to data, schools require a certain capacity (in terms of resources and skills) to productively engage data of any sort, but especially data concerned with classroom practice. Though we are still processing the second round of survey data, our case study work makes clear that the treatment program had varying effects on schools (CCSSO, 2002). While it is too early to tell if we will see significant differences between the treatment and control groups, within the treatment group it is clear that some schools never fully engaged either the data or the technical assistance offered, while others got very involved, including some that attributed much of their improvement on the state "report card" to participation in the project.

As we begin looking for possible explanations for this variability, we are struck with what appear to be (based on our case study data) important characteristics that identify schools ready to engage SEC-like data. While administrative support at both the school and district levels is important, as is making time available for teachers to work collectively to engage and discuss data, many of the characteristics that seem to be associated with successful data use in the DEC project appear to match many of the characteristics associated with professional learning communities (Loucks-Horsley, Hewson, Love, & Stiles, 1998). These characteristics have less to do with the technical skills of interpreting and using data and more to do with the professional culture of the school and the ability of faculty to engage in collegial discussions about practice. Thus, while curriculum-related data, including information about assessment content and results, can be of benefit to schools, it is important to add that for many schools this must go hand-in-hand with efforts designed to foster professional community and learning.

To meet the challenge of engagement, developers at the Learning Point Associates (LPA) and the Regional Alliance for Mathematics and

Science Education are designing programs and materials to support classroom teachers' use of these data tools, while helping to improve schools' capacity to use the tools and foster professional learning. At the same time, and in concert with these efforts, we at the University of Wisconsin-Madison are working to develop other data tools to support individual teachers in the classroom. For example, SEC surveys can now be accessed and completed online (www.seconline.org). Using the Web-based data collection and reporting system currently under development, teachers can compare their (confidential) individual results to school-, district-, or state-level reports of practice. The online service also provides a means for teachers to review content maps of state standards and assessments (where analyzed) and compare these with their own reports of instructional content.

Our work with schools has led to the realization that classroom teachers could benefit from tools and services designed to provide real-time curriculum data on their own classrooms in order to support their own data-based curriculum decisions. In particular we are interested in exploring how classroom teachers can use content languages to keep track of classroom assessments, assessment results, and the instructional content delivered to students. Toward that end, next steps include development of a CD or Web-based system to support individual teacher data collection and analysis using a logging procedure based largely on the content languages and content analysis procedures already developed. The envisioned tool will be designed for use in conjunction with training in the use of formative assessments aligned to state standards and local goals.

In addition, development of an English/language arts and reading version of the SEC is well underway, with support and assistance from Learning Point Associates and a number of state agencies, including those in Arizona, Indiana, Oklahoma, North Carolina, Michigan, and Wisconsin. Other states continue to work with us in the areas of mathematics and science, and requests from states, school districts, and researchers continue to come in, suggesting the demand for curriculum-based data collection, analysis, and use continues to rise.

Discussion

Over time we have seen the application and use of these tools move steadily from the realm of policy research to practical use by state education agencies, district staff, and now school leaders and teachers. This steady migration from the realm of policy to the realm of practice was not a deliberate goal on our part, but rather a response to a growing interest among educators and administrators to have curriculum information with which to monitor change and to support evaluation of program and policy effects.

We surmise that the interest among educators across various levels of the education system has much to do with two interrelated characteristics of these tools. First, they were designed specifically to describe aspects of the curriculum of particular relevance to teachers (recall that the roots of this work focused on teacher decision making). To accomplish this in a systematic manner, the descriptors had to cover a broad range of instructional practices and content focuses. In short, the language used to describe classroom practice needed to be fairly comprehensive, supporting descriptions of both traditional and innovative approaches to instruction. This in turn required that the instruments/language feature a second critical characteristic—theory neutrality with respect to pedagogical and curricular orientation.

Of course the existence of a theory-neutral tool for collecting descriptions of classroom practice will not necessarily lead to broad use of that tool. For that, there must be a perceived and matching need among potential users. The first such need came with the move toward standards-based reform (SBR) that began in the 1980s. Known best for its use of standards and high-stakes tests in conjunction with some system of accountability, SBR emphasizes an interdependent relationship between standards, assessments, instruction, and outcomes. Content and performance standards provide the vision of quality practice. These standards are linked to assessments that are intended to provide a means for determining success or failure in achieving the standards as set forth. It is important then, within the logic of SBR, that assessments be explicitly aligned to the relevant content and performance standards set by the state.

With the advent of high-stakes tests, a few states, beginning with Florida, found themselves facing litigation (*Debra P. v. Turlington*, 1981) and needing to provide evidence to the courts that students had been given the opportunity to learn the subject material for which they were being held accountable. With time, states also began wondering whether their standards-based reform efforts were actually having an impact on instruction. By the mid-1990s a handful of states, through participation in CCSSO's State Collaborative on Assessments and Student Standards, began working with us to develop indicators of classroom practice to meet these information needs.

As our collaborative work developing the SEC instruments with state education agencies progressed, we began hearing from district-level educators interested in using the SEC instruments. Their motivation for contacting us was typically similar to the interests expressed by state education agencies, that is, they wanted to establish a baseline for current practice, and through subsequent administrations investigate the effects of policies (both state and district) on teacher practice, and ultimately, on student learning. Nonetheless, many of the educators we worked with, particularly those with strong curricular backgrounds and typically many years of classroom experience, advocated use of the data tools at the school and teacher level to serve the data-driven decision-making needs of the school and classroom. As researchers we were somewhat reluctant to pursue this avenue of work, lacking both a professional development model and experience for assisting schools with data use. It was not until becoming familiar with the work of Nancy Love and her colleagues (Love, 2002) that we began to seriously consider delivering data results to schools, which eventually led to our collaboration with the Regional Alliance for Mathematics and Science Education and CCSSO in the DEC study described above.

It is important to note (and we quickly learned) that, in the move from state and district use to school and teacher use, the tools sometimes serve quite different needs. While schools are typically concerned with many of the same issues as states and districts (e.g., alignment of instruction to standards and performance of students on high-stakes tests), schools and teachers have other, sometimes more immediate needs that the data tools also help with. These include questions about scope and sequence, grade-to-grade articulation, and curriculum coherence, but may also include discussions about teacher beliefs and instructional readiness. In some cases the data needs of schools extend beyond the SEC data set. One particularly successful DEC school even developed and administered their own surveys to teachers, students, and parents in order to collect information that the school improvement team felt important to one or another curriculum-related decision. Though at present the evidence is largely anecdotal, we have seen that under the right conditions curriculum data serve as an important focal point for bringing teachers together to better understand their instructional practice and generate ideas about how instructional practice might be strengthened (CCSSO, 2002).

Conclusion

In his introduction to this volume Mark Wilson notes the National Research Council's call for coherence in state assessment systems, and he identifies three challenges to such a system: the challenge to make state assessments relevant and useful for classroom practice; the challenge to make classroom assessments consistent with and supportive of the curriculum, efficient, and useful; and the challenge to create valid accountability systems that draw upon teachers' professional knowledge in a manner that encourages their use of assessment frameworks and styles that are consistent with good practice.

Of these three we consider the third by far the greatest of the challenges faced, and the data tools discussed in this chapter have little to offer in meeting that challenge. With regard to the other two, the data tools and procedures highlighted herein offer some potential value. Content analyses of standards and assessments yield content maps and graphs that provide teachers with a well-defined picture of the instructional content intended and assessed by state policy tools. These descriptions in turn assist teachers and others in reflecting upon the practice necessary to achieve instructional goals that are consistent with both standards and assessments. Through training and systematic analysis of classroom-based assessments, in conjunction with an informed review of student work and relevant content descriptions of both classroom and state assessments, teachers can be better equipped to make informed decisions regarding instructional practice.

We share the belief that classroom assessments play a central role in the education of our children, and we applaud efforts to provide teachers with the skills and tools necessary to employ assessments in ways that help to maximize learning. We also agree that assessments represent an important, yet largely unmined source of information for teachers' curriculum-based decision making. As Wilson points out (p. 4), state assessment results and information are rarely returned to the classroom in a form that makes them especially useful. Teachers find out if their students did well or not on the state test, but they have only limited (if any) information on *what* students did well on, and even less on *why* students may have answered particular items incorrectly. These are important elements of assessment data that state assessment results often lack.

Though state assessments do indeed represent a mere drop in the assessment bucket, a better job could be done of providing teachers more useful information about these high-stakes tests. One level of information that would be valuable to teachers and others is a description of assessment results in terms of subject matter content. For example, we have toyed with constructing content maps utilizing item-level p values in conjunction with content descriptions of assessment items in order to display/identify the topic and cognitive demand areas that students do poorly (or well) on for a given test (see Figure 3). Though such content maps of the learned curriculum could be constructed from state assessment results, their primary value will more likely come from use with classroom or school-based formative assessments, thereby providing teachers a clear picture of the content areas that students have mastered and those they have not.

Classroom assessments have great potential for driving/informing curriculum decision making at the classroom level. In the collaborative work we've undertaken with organizations like TERC and Learning Point Associates, our professional development colleagues have pointed out that our content analysis process is a potentially powerful tool for helping teachers explore and reflect upon what is being assessed and provides a method for comparing assessment content (whether off the shelf, or teacher constructed) to what has been taught and what has been learned. Another valuable feature of classroom assessments is the availability of actual student work. Though requiring some training and a notable amount of teacher time, review of student work can not only help to determine what items a student missed, but also provide clues about *why* the student answered an item incorrectly or insufficiently. This is another feature of classroom assessments that would be difficult if not impossible to mirror in large-scale assessment.

With regard to the flow of assessment information *out* of the classroom, to be used as an input to the larger accountability system, we find ourselves somewhat skeptical. The challenges to building such a system in a way that guarantees some standardization of results across classrooms and teachers seem insurmountable to us. That said, we vigorously agree that the entire assessment system, formative and summative, high-stakes and low-stakes, state-sponsored and classroom-based, stands to benefit enormously from various efforts to bring these component parts into a coherent whole that highlights the interdependent goals of standards, assessments, and instruction.

REFERENCES

American Association for the Advancement of Science. (1989). *Science for All Americans* (Project 2061 Rep. on literacy goals in science, mathematics, and technology). Washington, DC: Author.

American Educational Research Association. (2003). *Standards and tests: Keeping them aligned* (Research Points, Vol. 1, No. 1). Washington, DC: Author.

Blank, R.K., Porter, A.C., & Smithson, J.L. (2001). *New tools for analyzing teaching, curriculum and standards in mathematics and science.* (Rep. from the Survey of Enacted Curriculum Project, National Science Foundation REC98-03080). Washington, DC: Council of Chief State School Officers.

Burstein, L., McDonnell, L., Van Winkle, J., Ormseth, T., Mirocha, J., & Guiton, G. (1995). *Validating national curriculum indicators.* Santa Monica, CA: RAND.

Carroll, J. (1963). A model for school learning. *Teachers College Record, 64*, 723-733.

Clune, W., White, P., Sun, S., & Patterson, J. (1991). *Changes in high school course-taking, 1982-88: A study of transcript data from selected schools and states.* New Brunswick, NJ: Consortium for Policy Research in Education, Eagleton Institute of Politics, Rutgers University.

Cohen, D.K. (1990). A revolution in one classroom: The case of Mrs. Oublier. *Educational Evaluation and Policy Analysis, 12*(3), 327-345.

Council of Chief State School Officers. (2000). *Using data on enacted curriculum in mathematics and science: Sample results from a study of classroom practices and subject content.* (Summary Rep. of the Survey of Enacted Curriculum, with Wisconsin Center for Education Research and 11 States). Washington, DC: Author.

Council of Chief State School Officers. (2002). *Experimental design to measure effects of assisting teachers in using data on enacted curriculum to improve effectiveness of instruction in mathematics and science education* (DEC Project: Year 2 Rep. to the National Science Foundation on Grant REC No. 0087562). Washington, DC: Author.

Debra P. v. Turlington. 474 F. Supp 244 (M.D. Fla. 1979); aff'd in part 644 F.2d 397 (5th Cir., 1981).

Firestone, W.A., Fuhrman, S.H., & Kirst, M.W. (1989). *The progress of reform: An appraisal of state educational initiatives.* New Brunswick, NJ: Rutgers University, Center for Policy Research in Education.

Floden, R.E., Porter, A.C., Schmidt, W.H., Freeman, D.J., & Schwille, J.R. (1981). Responses to curriculum pressures: A policy capturing study of teacher decisions about content. *Journal of Educational Psychology, 73*, 129-141.

Gamoran, A., Porter, A.C., Smithson, J.L., & White, P.A. (1997). Upgrading mathematics instruction: Improving learning opportunities for low-achieving, low-income youth. *Educational Evaluation and Policy Analysis, 19*(4), 325-338.

Herman, J.L., Klein, D.C.D., & Abedi, J. (2000). Assessing students' opportunity to learn: Teacher and student perspectives. *Educational Measurement: Issues and Practice, 19*(4), 16-24.

Loucks-Horsley, S., Hewson, P.W., Love, N., & Stiles, K.E. (1998). *Designing professional development for teachers of science and mathematics.* Thousand Oaks, CA: Corwin.

Love, N. (2000). *Using data getting results.* Norwood, MA: Christopher Gordon.

Mayer, D.P. (1999). Measuring instructional practice: Can policymakers trust survey data? *Educational Evaluation and Policy Analysis, 21*(1), 29-45.

McCaffrey, D.F., Hamilton, L.S., Stecher, B.M., Klein, S.P., Bugliari, D., & Robyn, A. (2001). Interactions among instructional practices, curriculum, and student achievement: The case of standards-based high school mathematics. *Journal for Research in Mathematics Education, 22*(5), 493-517.

McDonnell, L.M., Burstein, L., Ormseth, T., Catterall, J.M., & Moody, D. (1990). *Discovering what schools really teach.* Santa Monica, CA: RAND.

Murnane, R.J., & Raizen, S.A. (Eds.). (1988). *Improving indicators of the quality of science and mathematics education in grades K-12.* Washington, DC: National Academy Press.

National Council of Teachers of Mathematics. (1989). *Curriculum and evaluation standards for school mathematics*. Reston, VA: Author.

Porter, A.C. (1991). Creating a system of school process indicators. *Educational Evaluation and Policy Analysis, 13*(1), 13-29.

Porter, A.C. (1993). School delivery standards. *Educational Researcher, 22*(4), 24-30.

Porter, A.C. (1995). The uses and misuses of opportunity-to-learn standards. *Educational Researcher, 24*(1), 21-27.

Porter, A.C. (1998). The effects of upgrading policies on high school mathematics and science. In D. Ravitch (Ed.), *Brookings papers on education policy* (pp. 123-172). Washington, DC: Brookings Institution Press.

Porter, A.C. (2002). Measuring the content of instruction: Uses in research and practice. *Educational Researcher, 31*(7), 3-14.

Porter, A.C., Floden, R., Freeman, D., Schmidt, W., & Schwille, J. (1988). Content determinants in elementary school mathematics. In D.A. Grouws & T.J. Cooney (Eds.) *Perspectives on research on effective mathematics teaching* (pp. 96-113). Hillsdale, NJ: Erlbaum; (Research Series 179). East Lansing: Michigan State University, Institute for Research on Teaching.

Porter, A.C., Kirst, M.W., Osthoff, E.J., Smithson, J.L., & Schneider, S.A. (1993). *Reform Up Close: An analysis of high school mathematics and science classrooms*. (Final Rep. to the National Science Foundation on Grant No. SAP-8953446 to the Consortium for Policy Research in Education). Madison: University of Wisconsin-Madison, Consortium for Policy Research in Education.

Porter, A.C., & Smithson, J.L. (2001). Are content standards being implemented in the classroom? A methodology and some tentative answers. In S.H. Fuhrman (Ed.), *From the Capitol to the classroom: Standards-based reform in the states. The One Hundredth Yearbook of the National Society for the Study of Education*, Part II (pp. 60-80) Chicago: National Society for the Study of Education.

Raizen, S.A., & Jones, L.V. (Eds.). (1985). *Indicators of precollege education in science and mathematics*. Washington, DC: National Academy Press.

Rothman, R., Slattery, J.B., Vranek, J.L., & Resnick, L.B. (2002). *Benchmarking and alignment of standards and testing* (CSE Tech. Rep. 566). Los Angeles: University of California, Los Angeles, Center for the Study of Evaluation, National Center for Research on Evaluation, Standards, and Student Teaching.

Rowan, B., Camburn, E., & Correnti, R. (2002, April). *Using teacher logs to measure the enacted curriculum in large-scale surveys: Insights from the Study of Instructional Improvement*. Paper presented at the annual meeting of the American Educational Research Association, New Orleans, LA.

Scherpenzeel, A., & Saris, W.E. (1997). The validity and reliability of survey questions: A meta-analysis of MTMM studies. *Sociological Methods and Research, 25*(3), 341-383.

Schmidt, W.H., McKnight, C.C., Houang, R.T., Wang, H.C., Wiley, D.E., Cogan, L.S., & Wolfe, R.G. (2001). *Why schools matter: A cross-national comparison of curriculum and learning*. San Francisco: Jossey-Bass.

Shavelson, R., McDonnell, L., Oakes, J., Carey, N., & Picus, L. (1987). *Indicator systems for monitoring mathematics and science education*. Santa Monica, CA: RAND.

Smithson, J.L., & Porter, A.C. (1994). *Measuring classroom practice: Lessons learned from efforts to describe the enacted curriculum*. New Brunswick, NJ: Rutgers University, Consortium for Policy Research in Education.

Smithson, J.L., Porter, A.C., & Blank, R.K. (1995). *Describing the enacted curriculum: Development and dissemination of opportunity of learn indicators in science education*. Washington, DC: Council of Chief State School Officers.

Spillane, J.P., & Zeuli, J.S. (1999). Reform and teaching: Exploring patterns of practice in the context of national and state mathematics reforms. *Educational Evaluation and Policy Analysis, 21*(1), 1-27.

Stecher, B.M., & Koretz, D.M. (1996). *Issues in building an indicator system for mathematics and science education*. Santa Monica, CA: RAND.

Sudman, S., Bradburn, N.M., & Schwarz, N. (1996). *Thinking about answers: The application of cognitive processes to survey methodology.* San Francisco: Jossey-Bass.

Webb, N.L. (1999). *Alignment of science and mathematics standards and assessments in four states* (Research Monograph No.18). Madison: University of Wisconsin-Madison, National Institute for Science Education.

White, P., Gamoran, A., Smithson, J.L., & Porter, A.C. (1996). Upgrading the high school mathematics curriculum: Math course-taking patterns in seven high schools in California and New York. *Educational Evaluation and Policy Analysis, 18*, 285-307.

CHAPTER 6

Some Links Between Large-Scale and Classroom Assessments: The Case of the BEAR Assessment System

MARK WILSON AND KAREN DRANEY

The purposes of large-scale assessment and classroom assessment are often seen as distinct: Large-scale assessments, including school district, state, and national assessments, are directed at the formative and summative assessments of educational programs, while classroom assessments are focused primarily on the educational status or progress of individual students. Looking beyond this superficial view, however, it is apparent that some very important links between the two need to exist in order that they constitute a *coordinated system* of assessments.

First, educational advancement at either level is dependent on the educational progress of the individual students, thus, achieving improved educational attainment in any program will ultimately depend on the progress of the individual students. As a result, the constructs being assessed at both levels need to be consistent, although in practice, the constructs may be more differentiated at the classroom level than at the large-scale level. This is a characteristic that a recent National Research Council (NRC) report (Pellegrino, Chudowsky, & Glaser, 2001) has termed *coherence*.

Second, a coordinated system of assessments must cover the full range of ways of measuring those constructs that are reflective of classroom instruction, a characteristic termed *comprehensiveness* in the NRC

Mark Wilson is a Professor of Education at the University of California, Berkeley. He specializes in measurement and assessment, particularly in education, and also in educational statistics. Karen Draney completed her dissertation in 1995; she is currently a research coordinator for the Berkeley Evaluation and Assessment Research Center at the University of California, Berkeley.

This presentation is based in part on work by the University of California, Berkeley, Evaluation and Assessment Research Center in collaboration with the Science Education for Public Understanding Program (Lawrence Hall of Science), as part of the National Science Foundation-funded project Issues, Evidence, and You, and WestEd, as part of the National Science Foundation-funded project Research in Standards-Based Science Assessment.

report. Again, one might expect more differentiation at the classroom level than at the large-scale level, but the restriction in assessment formats at the higher level must not lead to deformation of the measured constructs in large-scale assessment. Otherwise the lack of fidelity between what is occurring in the classroom and what is being measured from the large-scale perspective will almost invariably lead to erroneous policy decisions.

Third, individual assessments at both levels need to be part of a continuous stream of evidence that tracks the progress of both individual students and educational programs over time, termed *continuity* in the NRC report. Of course, continuity can only be contemplated where there is consistency in the definitions of the constructs over time.

Wilson and Sloane (2000) have developed one such coordinated assessment system, the Berkeley Evaluation and Assessment Research (BEAR) System, in order to frame classroom assessments within a structure that makes explicit the sorts of validity and reliability evidence that have long been a requirement for large-scale assessment. The resulting system can be a basis for both large-scale and classroom assessments and thus forms just the sort of coordinated system called for in the NRC report. Currently, the BEAR Assessment System is in place in the Issues, Evidence, and You (IEY) curriculum, described below, and is in the process of being incorporated into two other science curricula—the Full Option Science System at elementary and middle school levels and the Living by Chemistry curriculum at the high school level, both developed at the Lawrence Hall of Science in Berkeley. An evaluation of the effectiveness of the BEAR system in its initial deployment showed that the assessment system itself was effective in promoting important and statistically significant gains for students (Wilson & Sloane, 2000). In the section that follows, we explain the principles of the BEAR Assessment System and describe their application in the IEY curriculum. We then propose ways to make the BEAR Assessment System more compatible with traditional large-scale assessments. We conclude with a discussion of how to formulate a framework for understanding the relationships between classroom and large-scale assessments.

The BEAR Assessment System:
An Example of a Coordinated Assessment System

A Developmental Perspective

The first principle of the BEAR Assessment System is that an assessment system should be based on a *developmental perspective* of student learning. Assessing the development of students' understanding of particular concepts and skills (as opposed to assessing current status only) requires a model of how student learning develops over a certain period of (instructional) time. A developmental perspective helps researchers move away from "one shot" testing situations—and away from cross-sectional approaches to defining student performance—toward an approach that focuses on the process of learning and on an individual's progress through that process.

Our strategy for addressing this issue is to develop a set of *progress variables* (Masters, Adams, & Wilson, 1990; Wilson, 1990) that mediate between the level of detail that is present in the content of specific curricula and the necessarily less precise descriptions in state standards and curriculum framework documents. Such progress variables can be defined at different levels of detail. At the classroom level, they might specify the intended content of a curriculum up to a level of detail that would allow, say, biweekly tracking of student progress through the curriculum. At a higher level, these might be aggregated into variables that are useful over a longer time span, perhaps over a semester or a year for a whole subject such as science. At the most detailed level, every instructional unit would be seen as contributing in some way to student progress on at least one of these variables, and every assessment would be closely aligned with one (or more) of the variables. This alignment allows the creation of a calibrated scale for mapping and tracking the progress of individual students and groups of students as they undergo instruction. At the higher levels, the progress of a class over a semester or of a school over a whole year might be the target. This idea of a "cross-walk between standards and assessments" has also been suggested by Eva Baker (Land, 1997, p. 6). In addition, these variables create a conceptual basis for relating the curriculum to standards documents, to other curricula, and to assessments that are not specifically related to that curriculum (discussed below). Thus, the progress variable is the underlying means by which the BEAR Assessment System creates coherence among different types of assessments. It also encourages continuity in the assessments.

Some considerations should be taken into account when developing a set of progress variables if it is to be representative of the curriculum. First, a set of progress variables is not equivalent to a curriculum; it is always less, in the sense that it is a summary of the curriculum. Moreover, it is not a summary of the content of the curriculum so much as a summary of the intended effects of the curriculum. These effects must have certain characteristics: they must be important enough to warrant assessment on a regular basis (essentially a political decision); they must be organized into a particular sort of summary—a developmental perspective (which can be based on research); and they must be few enough for a teacher to keep track of easily (a number that will vary greatly depending on the context). We do not yet have the process of developing the progress variables framework worked out in a sufficiently comprehensive way to lay it out step-by-step (although we do now think we can tell when we are succeeding). It takes quite a while to determine the intended effects for a particular curriculum. In the case of the Science Education for Public Understanding Program (SEPUP), it took about six months. As of this writing, the Living by Chemistry curriculum developers are still working on progress variables after three years, although there has been much successful development in that time (see Wilson & Scalise, 2003).

Progress variables in IEY. Issues, Evidence, and You is a yearlong issue-oriented science course for the middle school and junior high grades (SEPUP, 1995). The goal of issue-oriented science is the development of an understanding of the science content and scientific problem-solving approaches related to social issues, without promoting an advocacy position. In particular, the IEY course focuses on environmentally and socially contextualized science content; consequently, the concepts and skills needed to understand the process of societal decision making form the basis of the IEY curriculum. As part of the course, students are regularly required to recognize scientific evidence and weigh it against other community concerns, with the goal of making informed choices about relevant contemporary issues or problems. Following the developmental perspective principle, we, along with the SEPUP curriculum developers, devised a set of five progress variables that embody the learning that students are expected to experience in the IEY year:

Understanding Concepts (UC): Understanding scientific concepts (such as properties and interactions of materials, energy, or thresholds) in order to apply the relevant scientific concepts to the solution of problems. [This variable is the IEY version of the traditional science content, although this content is not just "factoids."]

Designing and Conducting Investigations (DCI): Designing a scientific experiment, carrying out a complete scientific investigation, performing laboratory procedures to collect data, recording and organizing data, and analyzing and interpreting results of an experiment. [This variable is the IEY version of the traditional science process.]

Evidence and Tradeoffs (ET): Identifying objective scientific evidence as well as evaluating the advantages and disadvantages of different possible solutions to a problem based on the available evidence. [This variable and the two following are relatively new.]

Communicating Scientific Information (CSI): Organizing and presenting results in a way that is free of technical errors and effectively communicates with the chosen audience.

Group Interaction (GI): Developing skills in working with teammates to complete a task (such as a lab experiment) and in sharing the work of the activity.

The first three variables—Understanding Concepts, Designing and Conducting Investigations, and Evidence and Tradeoffs—are primary variables and are assessed most frequently. The traditional content of science tests has not been abandoned in this framework—traditional science content, for example, comes under the progress variable Understanding Concepts. Thus, teachers using this system do not lose anything compared to what they would get from a traditional approach. Students' performance in Communicating Scientific Information can be assessed in conjunction with almost any activity or assessment, depending on the teacher's interest in monitoring student progress on this variable. Opportunities for assessing students' skills in this area are indicated in the course materials. The final variable, Group Interaction, is based on the SEPUP 4-2-1 model of instruction (SEPUP, 1995). Under this model, students first carry out guided investigations in groups of 4 (following specific roles within those groups), then write reports in groups of 2, and finally complete additional written work on their own.

A Match Between Instruction and Assessment

The need to integrate assessment into the curriculum and instruction process (i.e., the classroom context) is often emphasized in discussions of current assessment practices. The second principle of the BEAR Assessment System, then, is that there must be a match between what is taught and what is assessed. This principle represents a basic tenet of content validity evidence (AERA, APA, NCME, 2001): The items on a test must be sampled appropriately from a domain that is defined by the content and the level of cognitive processing expected in a given body of instruction. Matching assessment to instruction ensures comprehensiveness in the BEAR Assessment System and is also an aspect of coherence. Traditional testing practices—in "high-stakes" or other standardized tests as well as in teacher-made tests—have long been criticized for over-sampling items that assess only basic levels of knowledge of content topics and ignore more complex levels of understanding.

Concerns about the match between curriculum, instruction, and assessment have been discussed from both the curriculum development and the assessment perspectives. From the curriculum development perspective, efforts to emphasize new approaches to teaching and learning are inhibited by the form and content of accountability tests. Reports abound of teachers interrupting their use of their regular curricular materials in order to teach the material that students will encounter on district- or statewide tests. From an assessment perspective, advocates of assessment-driven reform hope to take advantage of the tendency to "teach to the test" by aligning high-stakes testing procedures to the goals of curricular reform. As Resnick and Resnick (1992) have argued, "Assessments must be designed so that when teachers do the natural thing—that is, prepare their students to perform well—they will exercise the kinds of abilities and develop the kinds of skill and knowledge that are the real goals of educational reform" (p. 59).

The match between instruction and assessment in the BEAR Assessment System is established and maintained through two major parts of the system: the progress variables, described above, and the assessment tasks, described below. As noted, the reason for developing progress variables is that they serve as a framework for the assessments. However, adherence to the second principle requires that the framework for the assessments and the framework for the curriculum and instruction be one and the same. This is not to imply that the needs of assessment must drive the curriculum, but rather that the two, assessment and instruction, must be in step—they must drive one another. Using progress variables to structure both instruction and assessment is one way to make sure that the two are in alignment, at least at the planning level. In order to make this alignment concrete, however, the match must also exist at the level of classroom interaction, and that is where the characteristics of the assessment tasks become so crucial.

Assessment tasks need to reflect the range and styles of the instructional practices in the curriculum. At the classroom level, they must have a place in the "rhythm" of the instruction, occurring at times when it makes instructional sense to include them. These are usually the times when teachers need to see how much progress students have made on a specific topic (see Minstrell, 1998, for an elaboration). One good way to achieve these characteristics is to develop both the instructional materials and the assessment tasks at the same time—adapting good instructional sequences that produce accessible responses and developing assessments into full-blown instructional events. At the higher levels of focus, such as classes or schools, the tasks should be a sampling from those typically used across the range of contexts where the assessments are taking place.

Matching instruction and assessment in the IEY. In the IEY curriculum, both the instructional materials and the assessments were built around the core set of five progress variables—all instructional objectives for each activity and all of the assessment tasks were linked to one (or more) of the variables. The variety of assessment tasks used for assessment in IEY match the variety of instructional events in range, including individual and group "challenges," data processing questions, and questions following student readings. All assessment prompts are open ended, requiring students to fully explain their responses. For the vast majority of assessment tasks, the student responses are in a written format, reflecting the only practical way we had available for teachers to attend to a classroom of student work.

The following assessment prompt appears in "Is Neutralization the Solution to Pollution?" (IEY Activity 19):

You are a public health official who works in the Water Department. Your supervisor has asked you to respond to the public's concern about water chlorination at the next City Council meeting. Prepare a written response explaining the issues raised in the newspaper articles. Be sure to discuss the advantages and disadvantages of chlorinating drinking water in your response, and then explain your recommendation about whether the water should be chlorinated.

This prompt is typical of IEY embedded assessments in that it requires students to integrate information from readings they were assigned in previous activities and labs and also asks them to explain their reasoning. It cannot be fully answered without access to the curricular materials that precede it. This particular prompt is related to the Evidence and Tradeoffs variable. As with most IEY assessments, this prompt has multiple components that students must consider, and it details what the students should include in their responses. There is no right answer; rather, students are required to make a statement or decision, and then justify it with the information and evidence they have learned through the preceding activities and labs. Their responses are judged by the validity of the arguments they present, not simply by the conclusions that they draw.

In order to provide the sort of summative information typical of large-scale assessments, we also developed *link tests*. Link tests are a series of tests given at major transition points in the IEY course. They are composed of fairly traditional-looking short-answer items, each linked to at least one variable, but are not curriculum-embedded like the assessment tasks. Each test contains open-ended items related to the content of the course that further assess students' abilities with the IEY variables. For example, the following link test item is associated with Evidence and Tradeoffs:

You run the shipping department of a company that makes glass kitchenware. You must decide what material to use for packing the glass so that it does not break when shipped to stores. You have narrowed the field to three materials: shredded newspaper, Styrofoam pellets, and cornstarch foam pellets. Styrofoam springs back to its original shape when squeezed, but newspaper and cornstarch foam do not. Both Styrofoam and cornstarch foam float in water. Although Styrofoam can be reused as a packing material, it will not break down in landfills. Newspaper can be recycled easily, and cornstarch easily dissolves in water.

Which material would you use? Discuss the advantages and disadvantages of each material. Be sure to describe the trade-offs made in your decision.

Link tests can also be used as item banks for teachers to draw upon in designing their own end-of-unit tests or other tests to be administered during the year. Teachers can use the link test items as models of variable-linked, open-ended questions, or they may select specific items to include in other teacher-made tests. The link tests are the analogue of large-scale assessment in the IEY context. Other types of assessments may be used where greater efficiency is desired, such as multiple-choice items (as discussed on p. 146).

Management by Teachers

The third principle of the BEAR Assessment System is that teachers must be the classroom managers of the system and therefore must have the tools to run it efficiently and to use the assessment data effectively and appropriately. There are two broad issues involved in this principle. First, it is the teachers who will use the assessment information to inform and guide the teaching and learning process. To do so to full effect, the teachers must be involved in the process of collecting and selecting student work; be able to score and use the results immediately, rather than waiting for scores to be returned several months later; be able to interpret the results in instructional terms; and take a creative role in the way that the assessment system is realized in their classrooms.

Second, issues of teacher professionalism and teacher accountability demand that teachers play a more central and active role in collecting and interpreting evidence of student progress and performance (Tucker, 1991). If they are to be held accountable for their students' performance, teachers need a good understanding of what students are expected to learn *and* of what counts as adequate evidence of student learning. They are then in a better position, and a more central and responsible position, for presenting, explaining, and defending their students' performances and the "outcomes" of their instruction.

Management by teachers in IEY. For the information from assessment tasks and link items to be useful to IEY teachers, it must be couched in terms that are directly interpretable with respect to the instructional goals of the IEY variables. Moreover, this must be done in a way that is intellectually and practically efficient. These two issues are addressed by the IEY scoring guides. IEY scoring guides define the elements of each variable and describe the performance criteria, or characteristics, for each score level of the element. There is one scoring guide for each of the five IEY variables, with each variable having between two and four elements. (The scoring guide is specific to each of these elements.) Teachers determine a student's level of performance on an assessment task by using the scoring guide(s) for the variable(s) being assessed. Teachers use each guide throughout the course for all assessments relating to that particular variable. This means that there will inevitably be a need for interpretation of the scoring guide for any particular assessment. We have found that a uniform scoring guide with exemplars for score levels was much more efficient for teachers than having different scoring guides for each assessment. The scoring guides that teachers use in the classroom can be the same scoring guides raters use in large-scale assessments. The exemplars will vary if differing items are used at the classroom and large-scale levels, but public-release items can be used to share even that level of detail. Commonality of scoring guides is a major element in making coherence a vital and authentic aspect of an assessment system. In different situations, it may be better to have scoring guides that are specific to each item, although they should still be based on a common underlying concept.

Each IEY scoring guide uses a general logic (adapted from the SOLO Taxonomy; Biggs & Collis, 1982) based on discerning what would be under most circumstances, a "complete and correct" response. This response is coded as a 3. A partially correct response that leaves out at least one essential element is coded as a 2. A response that has only one correct aspect to it is coded as a 1. A response that has no relevant aspects is coded as a 0. A response that goes beyond a 3 in some significant way is coded as a 4. All IEY scoring guides share this structure but use specific criteria to adapt them uniquely to individual IEY variables and elements, as shown in the Evidence and Tradeoffs variable scoring guide (Table 1).

Table 1
IEY Evidence and Tradeoffs Variable Scoring Guide

Score	Using Evidence	Using Evidence to Make Tradeoffs
	Response uses objective reason(s) based on relevant evidence to support choice.	Response recognizes multiple perspectives of issue and explains each perspective using objective reasons, supported by evidence, in order to make choice.
4	Response accomplishes Level 3 AND goes beyond in some significant way, such as questioning or justifying the source, validity, and/or quantity of evidence.	Response accomplishes Level 3 AND goes beyond in some significant way, such as suggesting additional evidence beyond the activity that would further influence choices in specific ways, OR questioning the source, validity, and/or quantity of evidence and explaining how it influences choice.
3	Response provides major objective reasons AND supports each with relevant and accurate evidence.	Response discusses *at least two* perspectives of issue AND provides objective reasons, supported by relevant and accurate evidence, for each perspective.
2	Response provides *some* objective reasons AND some supporting evidence, BUT at least one reason is missing and/or part of the evidence is incomplete.	Response states at least one perspective of issue AND provides some objective reasons using some relevant evidence, BUT reasons are incomplete and/or part of the evidence is missing; OR only one complete and accurate perspective has been provided.
1	Response provides only subjective reasons (opinions) for choice and/or uses inaccurate or irrelevant evidence from the activity.	Response states at least one perspective of issue BUT only provides subjective reasons and/or uses inaccurate or irrelevant evidence.
0	No response; illegible response; response offers no reasons AND no evidence to support choice made.	No response; illegible response; response lacks reasons AND offers no evidence to support decision made.
X	Student had no opportunity to respond.	

In order to interpret each scoring guide, teachers need exemplars, concrete examples of what a teacher might expect from students at varying levels of development along each variable. Exemplars also help teachers to understand the rationale of the scoring guides. Actual samples of student work, scored and moderated by teachers who pilot tested the BEAR Assessment System using IEY, are included with the documentation for IEY. These illustrate typical responses for each score level for specific assessment activities. The following sample is a level 3 response for Evidence and Tradeoffs from "The Peru Story" (activity 12):

As an edjucated employee of the Grizzelyville water company, I am well aware of the controversy surrounding the topic of the chlorination of our drinking water. I have read the two articals regarding the pro's and cons of chlorinated water. I have made an informed decision based on the evidence presented the articals entitled "The Peru Story" and "700 Extra People May bet Cancer in the US." It is my recommendation that our towns water be chlorin treated. The risks of infecting our citizens with a bacterial diseease such as cholera would be inevitable if we drink nontreated water. Our town should learn from the country of Peru. The artical "The Peru Story" reads thousands of inocent people die of cholera epidemic. In just months 3,500 people were killed and more infected with the diease. On the other hand if we do in fact chlorine treat our drinking water a risk is posed. An increase in bladder and rectal cancer is directly related to drinking chlorinated water. Specifically 700 more people in the US may get cancer. However, the cholera risk far outweighs the cancer risk for 2 very important reasons. Many more people will be effected by cholera where as the chance of one of our citizens getting cancer due to the water would be very minimal. Also cholera is a spreading diease where as cancer is not. If our town was infected with cholera we could pass it on to millions of others. And so, after careful consideration it is my opion that the citizens of Grizzelyville drink chlorine treated water.

For this variable, level 3 requires that the student "uses relevant and accurate evidence to weigh the advantages and disadvantages of multiple options, and makes a choice supported by the evidence." The above sample qualifies because, according to the scorer's comment, "Both sides of the chlorinating issue have been presented and supported. The choice to chlorinate was made."

Quality Evidence

The technical quality of performance assessments has been explored and debated primarily in the realm of high-stakes testing situations such as statewide assessment systems. For classroom-based alternative assessment procedures to gain currency in the assessment community, issues of technical quality will have to be addressed as well. Despite the plea of Wolf, Bixby, Glenn, and Gardner (1991), the development of practical procedures for establishing the technical quality of classroom-based alternative assessments lags behind that for high-stakes assessment programs.

For classroom-based assessments to be useful in a coordinated system, we contend that these assessments must be held to high standards of fairness in terms of quality control. Teachers will continue to construct their own tests and will rarely take the steps to establish the comparability or validity of these instruments. However, classroom-based assessment procedures can be developed for specific curricula and made available for teachers' use and adaptation. The evidence generated in the assessment process should be judged by its suitability for purposes of individual assessment and for purposes of evaluating student performance, instructional outcomes, and program effectiveness.

To ensure comparability of results across time and contexts, procedures are needed for (a) examining the coherence of information gathered using different formats, (b) mapping student performances onto the progress variables, (c) describing the structural elements of the accountability system—tasks and raters—in terms of the achievement variables, and (d) establishing uniform levels of system functioning, in terms of quality control indices such as reliability.

Apart from traditional quality control indices such as tables of reliability coefficients and standard errors, the BEAR Assessment System incorporates advances from item-response models that can put richer interpretational information into the hands of teachers in the classroom. The central feature is the *progress map*, which provides a criterion-referenced graph of the progress that students are making through the curriculum. Many examples of such maps have been produced for tests over the last 20 or so years (for a large number of examples, see the "Practice" chapters of Engelhard & Wilson, 1996; Wilson, 1992, 1994a; Wilson & Engelhard, 2000; Wilson, Engelhard, & Draney, 1997). Progress maps have been used for both classroom assessments and large-scale assessments (see, e.g., DEETYA, 1997). As a common means of displaying results, they add significantly to the coherence of the assessment system.

Progress maps for quality control in IEY. We have developed a variety of progress maps for the IEY variables. These are graphical representations of the variables, showing how they unfold or evolve over the year in terms of student performance on assessment tasks. The maps are derived from empirical analyses of student data collected from IEY teachers' classrooms. The analyses for these maps were performed using the ConQuest software (Wu, Adams, & Wilson, 1998), which implements an EM algorithm for the estimation of multidimensional Rasch-type models.

Once constructed, maps can be used to record and track student progress and to illustrate the skills a student has mastered as well as those that a student is working on. Figure 1 shows a map of an individual student's performances on the Designing and Conducting Investigations (DCI) variable. By placing students' performances on the continuum defined by the map, teachers can demonstrate students'

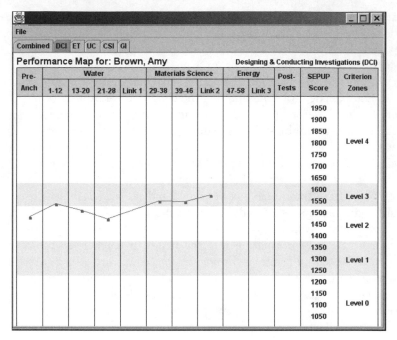

FIGURE 1

A progress map for an individual student's performance on the IEY Designing and Conducting Investigations variable.

progress with respect to the goals and expectations of the course. Teachers can use the maps to provide feedback on how students are progressing in the course, individually and as a class, to students, administrators, and parents.

Because the maps allow teachers to assess both individual and class progress, they can also be used to inform instructional planning. For instance, if the class as a whole has not performed well on a variable tested in a series of assessments, then the teacher might feel the need to go back and readdress those concepts or issues reflected by the assessments. A progress map that reflects the performance of a group of students is shown in Figure 2. Maps can also be used to portray the performances of groups of students in large-scale assessments, showing the whole distribution, not just the mean location. Thus they can convey complex relationships, such as when groups differ in mean, but overlap in range.

In the BEAR system, the traditional indices of quality control for assessments are also available. For example, reliabilities for the link

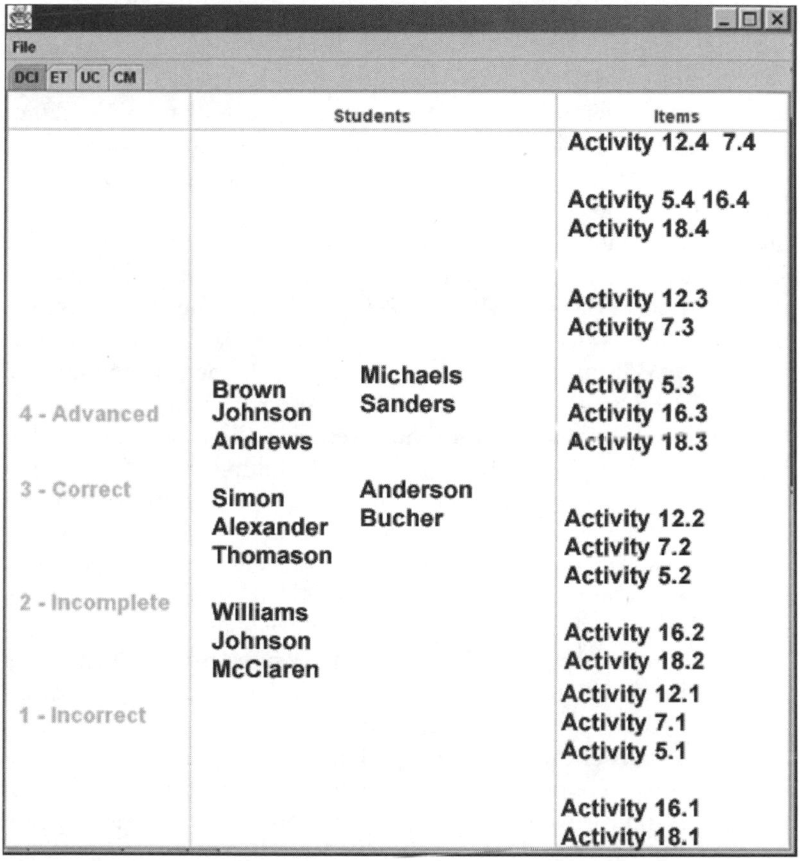

FIGURE 2

A progress map for a group of students' performances on the IEY Designing and Conducting Investigations variable.

test for each part of the assessment system have been calculated and range from .65 to .85; values for the composite across all four dimensions range from .79 to .91. A more useful indicator of quality control for individual assessments is the standard error of measurement, which can be expressed on the IEY maps by indicating 95% confidence intervals directly on the maps themselves.

Making the BEAR Assessment System More "Traditional"

Because the BEAR Assessment System was created with the express idea of incorporating recent innovations in assessment, such as the use of performance assessments, it has been difficult to see how it could be useful in traditional types of large-scale assessments. But the purposes and tradition of large-scale assessment have been developed over a long period, and the familiar types of assessments, such as multiple-choice items, are not only designed to be efficient under the standard set of circumstances; the formats themselves are seen as being important to some constituencies. There is no contradiction between the use of multiple-choice items and a coordinated assessment system such as the BEAR system. Prominent examples are available in both the research literature (e.g., Wilson & Wang, 1995, but see also multiple examples in Engelhard & Wilson, 1996; Wilson, 1992, 1994a; Wilson & Engelhard, 2000; Wilson, Engelhard, & Draney, 1997) and in examples of large-scale assessment (DEETYA, 1997; Wilson & Draney, 2000).

To illustrate the possibilities, however, we will go one step further than showing how to incorporate standard multiple-choice items into this framework. We will describe an alternative form of multiple-choice item that takes advantage of the interpretational possibilities inherent in the idea and structure of a progress variable. Currently we are developing a form of multiple-choice item that uses the levels of the scoring guide (as in Table 1 above) to assist in the development of distractors (i.e., the response options). This not only ensures that the content of the multiple-choice item is well aligned with the variable, it also offers some enhancements at the interpretational step, as is outlined below. The foundations of this work were laid out by the authors of this chapter in the final report to a National Science Foundation (NSF) planning grant, and the work is now being developed under the auspices of two NSF-funded projects, one called Research in Standards-Based Science Assessment (RISSA, at WestEd, in San Francisco) and one called the Full Option Science System (FOSS at the Lawrence Hall of Science, in Berkeley).

As an example, consider the scoring guide for the Forces and Motions variable that is being explored in the RISSA project, shown in Table 2. This scoring guide includes not only increasing levels of sophistication in students' understanding of this variable, but also lists common errors, indications of typical misunderstandings that students at each of these levels tend to exhibit. The levels themselves, and the lists of common errors, are based on an extensive search of the relevant literature. The items shown in Figure 3 have been developed so that the correct distractor reflects a response at the highest level among the distractors (though not necessarily the highest level of the scoring guide).[1] The remaining distractors are designed to reflect responses at lower levels of the scoring guide, sometimes with more than one distractor per level. Note that the common errors and level indicators are included within the items shown here for the reader's information— they would not be included in a real test. The progress maps for this variable are then structured into levels, as for the IEY variables, allowing similar diagnostic interpretations. The results for a set of items in a test for a given variable can also be examined informally to look for consistencies and inconsistencies. In Table 3, the mapping of the different distractors for the items is displayed in a way that emphasizes their allocation into levels. Using such a display, a set of item responses can be quickly examined to see if they display a pattern consistent with particular levels.

TABLE 2

RISSA Forces and Motions Variable Scoring Guide
A continuum for understanding about motions and forces for students
aged 13-14 (8th grade).

Level	Description
5	Student understands that the net force applied to an object is proportional to its resulting *acceleration* (change in speed or direction) and that this force may not be in the direction of motion. Student understands force as an interaction between two objects.
4	Student understands that an object is stationary either because there are no forces acting on it or because there is no *net* force acting on it. However, student may have misconceptions related to a belief that the applied force is proportional to an object's speed or motion (rather than its acceleration). Student can use phrases such as "equal and opposite reaction" to justify the existence of no net forces but may not understand this as an interaction. COMMON ERRORS: Motion is proportional to the force acting. A constant speed results from a constant force. Confusion between speed/velocity and acceleration.
3	Student recognizes that forces are not *contained* within moving objects; however, student believes that motion implies a force in the direction of motion and that non-motion implies no force. COMMON ERRORS: Forces are associated only with movement. Forces are viewed as causing things to move but not causing things to stop. If there is motion, there is a force acting. If there is no motion, then there is no force acting. There cannot be a force without motion. When an object is moving, there is a force in the direction of its motion.
2	Student recognizes that forces can be caused by non-living things; however, student may believe that forces reside within moving objects. COMMON ERRORS: A moving object has a force within it which keeps it going. A moving object stops when its force is used up.
1	Student understands force as a push or pull but believes that only living or supernatural things can cause forces. COMMON ERRORS: Forces are caused by living things. Forces are associated with physical activity or muscular strength. Weight, motion, activity, and strength are important in determining an object's force.
0	No evidence or way off track.

FIGURE 3

Items relating to the RISSA Forces and Motions variable with
common errors and level associations added.

(C039) & (C040)

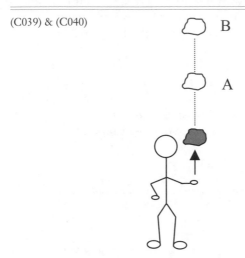

Derek throws a stone straight up into the air. It leaves his hand, goes up through point
A, gets as high as point B and then comes back down through A again.

(C039) When the stone is on its way up through point A, what force(s) are acting on it?

A. Only gravity is acting on the stone. [Level 4]

B. Only the force from Derek's hand is acting on the stone. [Level 3]
   [COMMON ERROR: When an object is moving, there is a force in the direction
   of its motion.]

C. A force inside the stone is keeping it moving upward. [Level 2]
   [COMMON ERROR: A moving object has a force within it which keeps it going.]

D. Both gravity and the force from Derek's hand are acting on the stone,
   but the force of gravity is smaller. [Level 3]
   [COMMON ERROR: When an object is moving, there is a force in the direction
   of its motion.]

E. There are no forces acting on the stone because nothing is touching it. [Level 1]

(C040) Why does the ball come to a stop at point B?

A. There are no forces acting on the stone at point B. [Level 2]
   [COMMON ERROR: If there is no motion, then there is no force acting.]

B. The force of gravity is now equal to the force from Derek's hand. [Level 3]
   [COMMON ERROR: When an object is moving, there is a force in the direction
   of its motion.]

C. There is no more force left from Derek's hand. [Level 2]
   [COMMON ERROR: A moving object stops when its force is used up.]

D. Gravity has slowed the stone until it stops. [Level 4]

E. Gravity is fighting with the force from Derek's hand and neither is winning. [Level 1]

FIGURE 3 (*Continued*)
Some items relating to the RISSA Forces and Motions variable with
common errors and level associations added.

(C036)

The ball sitting on the table is not moving. It is not moving because

A. no forces are pushing or pulling on the ball.   [Level 2]
    [COMMON ERROR: If there is no motion, then there is no force acting.]
B. gravity is pulling down, but the table is in the way.   [Level 3]
    [COMMON ERROR: Forces are associated only with movement.]
    [COMMON ERROR: Forces are viewed as causing things to move but not
        causing things to stop.]
C. the table pushes up with the same force that gravity pulls down.   [Level 4]
D. gravity is holding it onto the table.   [Level 3]
E. there is a force inside the ball keeping it from rolling off the table.   [Level 2]

(C041)

What will happen if a constant force is applied to the block in the direction indicated?
You can assume that there is no friction between the block and the ice.

A. It will start moving faster and faster across the ice.   [Level 5]
B. It will keep moving until the force is taken away.   [Level 3]
    [COMMON ERROR: When an object is moving, there is a force in the direction
        of its motion.]
C. It will move at a constant speed across the ice.   [Level 4]
    [COMMON ERROR: A constant speed results from a constant force.]
    [COMMON ERROR: Confusion between speed/velocity and acceleration.]
D. It will move only if a person is pushing it.   [Level 1]

TABLE 3
A Score Sheet for the RISSA Forces and Motions Items.

Level	Description	C039	C040	C036	C041
5	Student understands that the net force applied to an object is proportional to its resulting *acceleration* (change in speed or direction) and that this force may not be in the direction of motion. Student understands force as an interaction between two objects.				A
4	Student understands that an object is stationary either because there are no forces acting on it or because there is no *net* force acting on it. However, student may have misconceptions related to a belief that the applied force is proportional to an object's speed or motion (rather than its acceleration). Student can use phrases such as "equal and opposite reaction" to justify the existence of no net force but may not understand this as an interaction.	A	D	C	C
3	Student recognizes that forces are not *contained* within moving objects; however, student believes that motion implies a force in the direction of motion and that non-motion implies no force.	B D	B	B D	B
2	Student recognizes that forces can be caused by non-living things; however, student may believe that forces reside within moving objects.	C	A C	A E	
1	Student understands force as a push or pull but believes that only living or supernatural things can cause force.	E	E		D
0	No evidence or way off track.				

Further work on this new multiple-choice item format includes evaluation of its contribution to test reliability, its usefulness for diagnostic interpretations, and its value to teachers. Such items may be particularly helpful in combination with performance items when the performance items are also based on the progress variable idea. This type of development offers ways to enhance the utility of large-scale assessments for classroom applications, as well as making it easier to develop coherent assessments at the two different levels.

Discussion

Standardized tests are usually considered to be relevant in two general ways. First, the total on the test is considered a general indicator of the student's understanding of the test topic. For the most part, the validity and reliability of the test is reported only for this usage. Second, many standardized tests also feature subscores for subsets of the total item set, which are intended to be used for diagnostic purposes. In the main, individual items are separated into subsets in the test blueprint. Unfortunately, these diagnostic purposes are usually not the basis on which items were developed. We propose that the combination of progress variables and scoring guides described in this chapter provides a much more useful way to select items for these diagnostic purposes. The items themselves are sampled on the premise that they correspond to important curriculum distinctions, and the responses have already been classified into the levels of the variables.

However, even with an approach like that illustrated in the BEAR Assessment System, there are serious limitations to the usefulness of subtest results. The essential problem is that standardized test schedules are not aligned with the schedule of the classroom curriculum. Consequently, a large-scale test may be given in fall, long before the class will turn to the specific topic embodied in the specific items in the subtest. In order to address this problem, we need to examine the possible relationships between information potentially available from large-scale assessments and the information needs of the classroom.

One approach is to consider three types of relevance that a large-scale assessment can have. The first type, *micro-relevance*, occurs when the specific subsets of items on the large-scale assessment correspond directly to the topics of the curriculum that are being learned at the time that the teacher receives the test results. This is not very useful in general because of the low probability that this will be true for the specific elements of the curriculum under study (at either testing time or results time). Yet micro-relevance is what most teachers would find useful and what they and others, such as policymakers, generally have in mind when they think of "instructional relevance."

The second type, *macro-relevance*, occurs over an extended period when the test results are organized into progress variables that recur throughout the curriculum. Thus, when progress variables are designed to have this characteristic, the results can be much more directly useful in the classroom. This would indeed be the case for the variables used in the IEY example, where the variables recur on a regular basis throughout the yearlong curriculum. It would also be the case where variables are based on concepts such as the "strands" or "unifying themes" built into the national science standards.

A third type of relevance, *meta-relevance*, can be identified where teacher training in the use of information from large-scale assessments involves learning how items are designed and scored. Such teacher professional development transcends the immediate curriculum content of the items, including both micro and macro levels. The aim is to give teachers experience with exemplary models of a coordinated assessment system, especially how the items, because they are related to the variables, can be usefully interpreted. For example, for the RISSA Forces and Motions items in Figure 3, teachers would debate how to map the distractors onto the variable's scoring guide and discuss how the scoring guide is relevant to their instruction. This is helpful beyond the immediate test results in that teachers can use their resulting familiarity to better interpret standardized tests in general and can improve their own test development activities.

Conclusion

We have shown that the concepts of coherence, comprehensiveness, and continuity form a background to the principles of the BEAR Assessment System and similarly to any such coordinated assessment system. Moreover, the different levels of instructional relevance articulate different ways that the results from large-scale assessments could be useful in the classroom. A topic not directly addressed in this paper is relevance in the other direction—how classroom assessments can be useful in large-scale assessments. This is a large topic, beyond the scope of the current paper, but some possible directions have been explored in Wilson and Adams (1996) and Wilson (1994b).

NOTES

1. The items in Figure 3 are copyright WestEd and were developed under NSF Grant #REC-0087848. The contents do not necessarily reflect the views or policies of NSF or any other agencies of the U.S. government.

REFERENCES

American Educational Research Association (AERA), American Psychological Association (APA), & National Council for Measurement in Education (NCME). (1999). *Standards for psychological and educational testing.* Washington, DC: Authors.

Biggs, J., & Collis, K. (1982). *Evaluating the quality of learning: The SOLO taxonomy.* New York: Academic Press.

Department of Employment, Education, and Youth Affairs (DEETYA). (1997). *National school English literacy survey.* Canberra, Australia: Author.

Engelhard, G., & Wilson, M. (Eds.). (1996). *Objective measurement III: Theory into practice.* Norwood, NJ: Ablex.

Land, R. (1997). Moving up to complex assessment systems. *Evaluation Comment, 7*(1), 1-21.

Masters, G.N., Adams, R.A., & Wilson, M. (1990). Charting student progress. In T. Husen & T.N. Postlethwaite (Eds.), *International encyclopedia of education: Research and studies* (Supplementary Volume 2, pp. 628-634). Oxford: Pergamon Press.

Minstrell, J. (1998, October). Student thinking and related instruction: Creating a facet-based learning environment. Paper presented at the meeting of the Committee on Foundations of Assessment, Woods Hole, MA.

Pellegrino, J., Chudowsky, N., & Glaser, R. (Eds.). (2001). *Knowing what students know: The science and design of educational assessment.* Washington, DC: National Academy Press.

Resnick, L.B., & Resnick, D.P. (1992). Assessing the thinking curriculum: New tools for educational reform. In B.R. Gifford & M.C. O'Connor (Eds.), *Changing assessments* (pp. 37-76). Boston: Kluwer Academic.

Science Education for Public Understanding Program (SEPUP). (1995). *Issues, evidence and you: Teacher's guide.* Berkeley: University of California, Berkeley, Lawrence Hall of Science [Distributed by Sargent-Welch Inc.].

Tucker, M. (1991). Why assessment is now issue number one. In G. Kulm & S. Malcom (Eds.), *Science assessment in the service of reform* (pp. 3-16). Washington, DC: American Association for the Advancement of Science.

Wilson, M. (1990). Measurement of developmental levels. In T. Husen & T.N. Postlethwaite (Eds.), *International encyclopedia of education: Research and studies* (Supplementary Volume 2, pp. 152-158). Oxford: Pergamon Press.

Wilson, M. (Ed.). (1992). *Objective measurement: Theory into practice.* Norwood, NJ: Ablex.

Wilson, M. (Ed.). (1994a). *Objective measurement II: Theory into practice.* Norwood, NJ: Ablex.

Wilson, M. (1994b). Community of judgment: A teacher-centered approach to educational accountability. In Office of Technology Assessment (Ed.), *Issues in educational accountability.* Washington, DC: Office of Technology Assessment, United States Congress.

Wilson, M., & Adams R.J. (1996). Evaluating progress with alternative assessments: A model for Title 1. In M.B. Kane (Ed.), *Implementing performance assessment: Promise, problems and challenges.* Hillsdale, NJ: Erlbaum.

Wilson, M., & Engelhard, G. (2000). *Objective measurement V: Theory into practice.* Stanford, CT: Ablex.

Wilson, M., Engelhard, G., & Draney, K. (Eds.). (1997). *Objective measurement IV: Theory into practice.* Norwood, NJ: Ablex.

Wilson, M., & Scalise, K. (2003). Reporting progress to parents and others: Beyond grades. In J.M. Atkin & J.E. Coffey (Eds.), *Everyday assessment in the science classroom* (pp. 89-108). Arlington, VA: National Science Teachers Association Press.

Wilson, M., & Sloane, K. (2000). From principles to practice: An embedded assessment system. *Applied Measurement in Education, 13*(2), 181-208.

Wilson, M., & Wang, W. (1995). Complex composites: Issues that arise in combining different modes of assessment. *Applied Psychological Measurement, 19*(1), 51-72.

Wolf, D., Bixby, J., Glenn, J., III, & Gardner, H. (1991). To use their minds well: Investigating new forms of student assessment. *Review of Research in Education, 17,* 31-74.
Wu, M., Adams, R.J., & Wilson, M. (1998). ACER *ConQuest* [Computer software]. Melbourne, Australia: ACER Press.

Part Three
COMMENTARY CHAPTERS

CHAPTER 7

The Data Club: Helping Schools
Use Accountability Data

HELEN WILDY

This chapter gives an account of a project known in Western Australia as the Data Club. The origins of the Data Club can be traced to the national assessment project conducted by the Australian Council for Educational Research (ACER) reported by Forster and Masters. In their chapter they argue for a conceptual bridge between a program for system-wide monitoring of student achievement (NSELS) and a classroom assessment resource (DART). The Data Club provides a practical bridge between statewide, system-level data used for national accountability purposes and school-level use of the same data.

Before giving an account of the Data Club, however, I comment on each of the five chapters. In particular I examine the extent to which each set of authors supports the possibility of conceptual or practical linkage between accountability and classroom assessment. My analyses draw attention to arguments that resonate, or contrast, with the conceptual bridge notion of Forster and Masters. I understand that the goal of both classroom assessment and system-wide accountability is to improve students' learning. For this reason, I highlight some of the research findings described in the five chapters that appear useful to improving student learning outcomes, even though the strategies may not link accountability and classroom assessment.

Conceptual Bridge: Developmental Assessment

Forster and Masters (Chapter 3) argue that it is possible to bring classroom and large-scale assessments together conceptually in support

Helen Wildy, PhD, The University of Western Australia, is Associate Professor of Educational Leadership in the School of Education, Murdoch University, Australia.

of student learning. The contribution of the Australian team at ACER is to start with a common concept, the developmental "progress map" of achievement, which links simultaneously to system accountability and classroom assessment.

The key to the approach lies in the involvement of classroom teachers in assessing student performance that is used to inform large-scale accountability. Here teachers play a central role in the data collection process. Indeed, this role became an extensive professional development opportunity for the participating teachers. Materials developed for the DART project helped teachers embed standardized assessment tasks into their everyday teaching. Teachers used a kit focusing on a single theme and including assessment tasks, detailed scoring guides and rating scales, examples of student work, diagnostic information, and report forms exemplifying, both numerically and descriptively, students' levels of achievement. In addition, and most importantly, the tasks themselves were explicitly linked to learning outcomes in a national curriculum framework, against whose outcomes state educational jurisdictions are required to account. This framework is constructed around sequences of developing knowledge, skill, and understanding in a number of learning areas of the school curriculum.

When the time came for states to assess students against the national statements and profiles of the national curriculum developed in the early 1990s, teachers in many jurisdictions were already familiar with the DART materials and subsequent resources designed to help them understand assessment principles and practice. These materials are known collectively as the Assessment Resource Kit (ARK). The recurring and central element of these resource materials is the progress map, the metaphor representing the concept of a variable or latent trait. All the ARK materials build teachers' understanding of this central idea: for example, by helping teachers to select the appropriate assessment method to obtain evidence of students' achievement along a particular progress map; or by estimating a student's location on a progress map; or by using graphical, numerical, and descriptive interpretations of achievement measures against a progress map.

The consequence of this early preparatory work at the classroom level meant that many teachers were already skilled in the use of those assessment tasks that would inform the large-scale assessment program. Additional efforts were put in place to ensure comparability of teacher judgments across the nation: for example, a cascade model of "train the trainer" was used to prepare 900 participating teachers as assessors. Extended training sessions were supplemented by involving the participating teachers in developing some of the assessments.

In the event, a sample survey of one of the learning areas, literacy, was introduced in 1996. Forster and Masters describe in their chapter two of the most challenging elements of literacy—viewing and speaking—as well as reading, by providing examples of tasks, student responses, marking rubrics, and the relevant scales showing indicators at each of five levels (or standards) of achievement. Both for standardized tests and for regular classroom work, classroom teachers were judges of student performance. This was possible because both standardized tests and classroom assessments were built on the same central concept—the progress map.

The strength of the Australian approach using developmental assessment, according to Forster and Masters, lies in a common set of principles that guide the work of both classroom teachers and education systems. These principles involve monitoring student growth against learning outcomes of a progress map; selecting an appropriate method for the outcomes to be addressed from a range of assessment methods; judging and recording student performance on assessment tasks; estimating students' levels of achievement against a progress map; and reporting achievement in terms of the progress map. This process can be applied to individual students in the classroom and also to groups of students. Hence the process can be used to monitor performance over time, which is at the heart of accountability.

Working from the Classroom Outward

In contrast, Smithson and Porter (Chapter 5) are less optimistic about linking accountability systems and teachers' classroom assessments within the U.S. context. The tools they describe in their chapter have important uses, but they are not useful for providing such a bridge, the authors claim. The tools developed by Porter and his colleagues use content mapping processes to highlight for teachers what is being assessed and to compare the taught content with the assessed content and the learned content. In addition, the tools are used by state educational authorities to review the match between state content standards and assessment. Further, the tools are useful at the school level to guide curriculum decision making and to plan professional development programs.

It is not surprising that this group of researchers is skeptical about the links between classroom assessment and large-scale accountability systems. Their research using content analysis tools is designed to show variation between and within schools. This focus on variation leads to a conclusion that building a system that guarantees standardization of results across classrooms is fraught with insurmountable challenges. It is a method that builds *outward* from the classroom.

One of the strengths of the content analysis tools, though, is that they provide teachers, school leaders, and state educational agencies with a common language—"a systematic, rich, and multidimensional language," according to Smithson and Porter (p. 105)—to talk about the content of teaching, learning, and assessment. This is no small contribution to the field of school improvement, particularly as school leaders become increasingly engaged in management and leadership and further removed from curricular matters.

Another strength of the content analysis tools is in helping teachers to understand why some groups of students fail to achieve as well as others. Smithson and Porter demonstrate that content is every bit as important as student background and prior achievement. Some groups of students are failing to score well on assessments simply because the content on which the assessment is based is not part of what is taught. Notwithstanding the importance of these contributions of the content analysis tools, linking with large-scale accountability programs is not within their scope.

Formative Assessment and Teacher Change

Like Smithson and Porter, Black and Wiliam (Chapter 2) in their chapter also conceptualize the theme of this volume from the classroom level outward. And, like Smithson and Porter, these authors find that working from the classroom outward does not seem to deliver effective links between classroom assessment and large-scale monitoring of student achievement.

Nevertheless, their work with teachers in the U.K. on their formative assessment practices has important consequences for improving student learning. Where these researchers intersect with the work of Forster and Masters is in their discussion of recognition, support, and development of teachers' professional knowledge and practice. When Black and Wiliam began the KMOFAP in 1999, working first with mathematics and science teachers and then with English teachers, their study was to improve formative assessment practices. Their interest was stimulated by their earlier international research review. Evidence from this review pointed strongly to a tension between, on the one hand, the capacity of formative assessment to improve student performance and, on the other hand, the reality that most teachers' assessment practices do not promote good learning. Indeed, many practices were found to have a negative impact on learning, particularly among those students with the greatest need for support and encouragement.

The KMOFAP encouraged teachers to experiment with strategies suggested by the research on improving formative assessment. The strategies were rich questioning, comment-only marking, sharing criteria with learners, and student-peer and self-assessment. The consequences for teaching practice were quite dramatic. After beginning with small changes—for example, increasing wait time in questioning—teachers in this study then reviewed the kinds of questions they were asking, their purposes, and indeed the role of questions in the learning process. More powerful, though, was that the KMOFAP teachers began to reflect on their own role in students' learning and to move from being "presenters of content" to being "leaders of exploration."

The teachers began to move from traditional roles of covering content toward more constructivist approaches to learning. They noticed they were using more small-group work, where students had increased opportunities to talk about their work. Students were taking responsibility for the pace of learning, and students were applying quality criteria in making judgments about their own and others' work.

That the project gave teachers the opportunity and stimulus to achieve "very significant, often radical" (p. 46) changes to their practice was the source of enthusiasm to the participating teachers, according to Black and Wiliam. Like the work described by Forster and Masters, we see here a rich and unexpected opportunity for personal and professional development among those involved in the project.

Shifting toward student-centered classroom practice is challenging for teachers, especially in the face of high-stakes external assessment regimes. My own work with physics teachers in schools in Western Australia illustrated for me and my colleagues how teachers struggled with a newly imposed "constructivist" curriculum (Wildy & Wallace, 1995). We noticed how hard it was for teachers to give up practices that had worked for them in the past and which were expected of them by students and their parents (Wildy, Louden, & Wallace, 1998).

There is an unexpected outcome of the work of Black and Wiliam reported in their chapter. Their study suggests that bringing about large-scale change to teaching practice is probably more effectively tackled indirectly by focusing on one small element of teaching, such as changing questioning or marking practices, than by expecting teachers to change all of their practices. This latter approach seems to me to have had limited impact in the Western Australian context.

More significantly, though, is how the KMOFAP students changed. When teachers reviewed their questioning techniques and purposes, students took responsibility for what they needed to know, for how they presented information, and generally for seeing the classroom as a place for learning. Furthermore, their test scores seemed to improve. Black and Wiliam report, cautiously, that compared with control groups, those students whose teachers experimented with improved formative assessment practices—and the changes that followed—gained higher scores in national tests, national school leaving examinations, or scores from school assessments.

Too rarely are studies of changes to teaching practices associated with changes in student learning. For example, one of our studies of physics teachers indicated that when constructivist principles were applied, some students dropped out of the subject because their test results decreased (Wildy & Wallace, 1995). In another study, physics teachers in low socioeconomic status schools where students did not have high achievement expectations felt less constrained from experimenting with practices that allowed students to take responsibility for their learning than did teachers in high socioeconomic status schools where both the school and the parents had high expectations of their students' performance in tertiary entrance examinations (Wildy, Louden, & Wallace, 1998).

Notwithstanding the evidence that improving formative assessment practices can improve student learning, Black and Wiliam do not link classroom-level assessment practices with external accountability. For example, they report that the aim of the KMOFAP was to focus only on formative assessment. However, teachers were unable to resist applying their new strategies to help students prepare for summative assessment. Here, though, in the face of "the alliance of external tests [where] the armies of accountability and public certification are firmly entrenched" (p. 42), classroom teachers seemed powerless. Black and Wiliam report that teachers felt they could only do the best they could in the time available. And the most they could do was to improve the interface between formative and summative assessment so that students were more thoroughly prepared. So, like Smithson and Porter, these authors see little hope for much in the way of conceptual or practical linkage between classroom assessment and system-wide accountability processes.

Credible and Comparable Interpretive Judgments

Frederiksen and White (Chapter 4), however, adopt quite the opposite view. Just as Forster and Masters describe how teachers in multiple jurisdictions can be supported to use developmental assessment to make fair and valid judgments that inform accountability processes, Frederiksen and White also find links between classroom and large-scale assessments. These authors argue that, within the U.S., assessments of students' classroom work can be used to evaluate the school's effectiveness within an accountability framework.

Their study focuses on the scientific inquiry project—an example of the kind of work that students work on and think about for an extended period of time. The science fair project is an example entailing rich, open-ended tasks involving higher order cognitive skills. Assessment of such projects involves interpretive judgment, similar to the assessment of speaking and viewing performance described by Forster and Masters. And the challenge is to judge these projects in ways that both encourage student learning and also generate credible and comparable information to account for performance against state and national curricular standards, just as was described in the Australian example.

Using the concept of internal validity, Frederiksen and White argue that when the assessment attends to full and accurate analysis of both student outcomes and the processes used to obtain those outcomes, there are consequences at the student level and at the accountability level. They apply two key constructs: directness and transparency. Directness focuses on the assessment tasks themselves: they must explicate the cognitive processes to be assessed and give students opportunities to demonstrate them. Transparency focuses on the assessment processes: they must be amenable to use by students in relation to their own work, as well as by teachers. Here Frederiksen and White go beyond what is proposed by Forster and Masters, whose work is with teachers, rather than with students. The vehicle Frederiksen and White describe, the ThinkerTools Inquiry Curriculum, supports students in evaluating their own and others' research projects. The goal is to help students understand the purpose and steps of inquiry and therefore "develop metacognitive knowledge and habits of monitoring and reflecting on their work" (p. 81). Evidence seems to indicate that this strategy is effective, and particularly so for low-achieving students.

In contrast with the view of Smithson and Porter, Frederiksen and White claim that it is possible to generate consistent evaluations that can be used to make standards-based ratings. By scaffolding teachers' and students' interpretations of students' rich, open-ended tasks, judgments can be made that are both accurate and comparable. Hence they claim that the internal consistency of judgments establishes the credibility and comparability of these judgments. And, like Black and Wiliam, they build on the formative assessment practices of teachers. However, unlike Black and Wiliam, they are more optimistic about linking classroom assessment with national accountability.

Coordinating Classroom and Large-Scale Assessment

Wilson and Draney (Chapter 6) argue for a coordinated system of assessments that meet standards of coherence, comprehensiveness, and continuity. They illustrate such a system with the BEAR Assessment System. Underpinning this system is the concept of developmental assessment central to the assessments described by Forster and Masters. The vehicle used here is the progress variable, and its depiction as a progress map. At issue is the relationship between progress variables and a curriculum. Unlike the work of Smithson and Porter, which directs attention to the content of what is taught, assessed, and learned, Wilson and Draney focus on the outcomes or effects of the curriculum. Hence, the focus is not on what is covered, but on what students know and can do as a consequence of their exposure to a particular set of learning opportunities.

There are a number of key principles underlying this approach. First is that there is a match between instruction and assessment. Progress variables, the basis for the assessment tasks and also for classroom interaction, provide the vehicle for such alignment. The second key principle is the central role of teachers. Collecting and selecting student work, scoring this work, making sense of the results in relation to their teaching programs, and using the results to plan their programs are some of the ways teachers are involved. Wilson and Draney argue that if teachers are to be accountable for student learning, then they must understand what students are expected to learn and also know what such learning looks like. Here we see, as we have seen in each of the other chapters, an emphasis on supporting and enhancing the professional role of teachers. In this instance, Wilson and Draney illustrate the role of teachers in using scoring rubrics and exemplars for each score level, similar to the kinds of materials described by Forster and Masters. Similarly, the scoring processes used in the classroom are also used in large-scale assessments.

The third key principle of coordinated assessment systems, according to Wilson and Draney, is quality evidence, both in the classroom and at the large-scale level. Again, as with Forster and Masters, the progress map—a criterion-referenced graph of the progress that students make through the curriculum—provides the conceptual link.

The progress map can be used to map individual student performance, to map the progress of groups of students, and also as evidence for teachers to account to parents and administrators about students' individual and group progress over time. Progress maps show the performance of students not only in classroom assessments but also in large-scale assessments.

It appears that those jurisdictions that use developmental assessment and the associated tools of progress variables and progress maps, namely Australia and some authorities in the state of California, are having some success in making links between classroom assessment and large-scale accountability. Without such a conceptual bridge, or "cross-walk," between standards and assessments, there is little to bring coherence to the plethora of classroom assessment activity that characterizes most educational jurisdictions. Working from the classroom outward, despite research activity that generates abundant worthwhile local improvement to professional practice, offers little in the way of coherent and systematic linkage with large-scale external assessment regimes.

The Data Club

While developmental assessment and the concepts of progress variables and progress maps offer a conceptual bridge between classroom assessment and large-scale assessment, the Data Club provides another, more practical link.

Background

The origins of the Data Club lie in a pilot partnership between Edith Cowan University and the Education Department of Western Australia funded in 2000 by the Australian Commonwealth Department of Education, Training, and Youth Affairs (DETYA). The pilot project sought to identify and document best practice in supporting teachers and parents in making judgments about performance in relation to benchmark standards within the National Literacy and Numeracy Plan (Louden & Wildy, 2001). However, although the pilot was intended to focus on teachers and parents, in the event, focusing on school leaders provided sufficient challenge in what was intended to be a one-year timeframe. This focus alone brought the project to the attention of educational jurisdictions across the nation.

Targeting teachers and parents is the subject of current activity, funded locally and federally. A project that focuses on teachers is being piloted by the state education authority in Western Australia. Research into best practice in reporting to parents was commissioned by the federal government late in 2002 (Butorac, Figgis, Wildy, & Zubrick, 2002).

The pilot project was titled Developing Schools' Capacity to Performance Judgments. Very early in its history, this project became known as the Data Club. Subsequently, the Data Club was funded solely by the W.A. Department of Education, and in 2003 the project has been retained—managed and funded—within the (now) W.A. Department of Education and Training.

In Western Australia there are 612 government schools whose students take the statewide literacy and numeracy tests on which national benchmarks are set. These tests are known locally as W.A. Literacy and Numeracy Assessments (WALNA). In its pilot phase, the project involved three people—Bill Louden, me, and a statistician—with Web design support from Edith Cowan University staff.

The success of the project can be attributed to four principles:

- School data is the focus of the workshop.
- Participation is voluntary.
- More than one school leader attends the workshop.
- Presenters are specialists and independent of the employer.

School Data is the Focus of the Workshop

When schools nominated themselves for the Data Club, we asked them to send their WALNA data report so that we could re-present it in ways that might help them to make use of it. The typical response was, What data report? In 2000, not only were schools not using their data report, they were not even keeping it. We arranged for schools to obtain replacement data reports, and to pay for this service.

Once we received the school WALNA data (which initially took nearly six months), we could proceed to the next two stages: data analysis and workshops. WALNA data were reanalyzed to provide schools with box- and whisker-representations of school-level performance on each of the four strands (Reading, Writing, Spelling, and Numeracy), over time. Comparisons could be made over the years, as the data accumulated. Regression analysis was used to show expected growth—value added—in school performance in a given strand over time. Standardized residuals were used to indicate the relative amount of change.

The workshops—a total of 30 half-day sessions—were conducted in districts across the state. Louden and I each conducted half of these.

The session consisted of two sections: first, participants were introduced to the box- and whisker-method of representing data, as well as regression analysis, standardized residuals, confidence limits, and examples of valid and invalid inference. Next, participants were given envelopes containing their reprocessed data and were supported as they worked through tasks designed to explore their data. Participants liked receiving their data in this way: *It's like Christmas*, they'd say, as they opened the package. Although all schools had previously received their WALNA data, participants were now keen to examine the data with new enthusiasm.

We encouraged schools to keep from year to year not only their data reports, but also records detailing the particular conditions under which the assessments were conducted and other factors likely to help in interpreting the data. We drew attention to factors such as which students took the tests, who supervised the tests, and what changes had occurred in classroom arrangements, teaching programs, and staffing allocations. We challenged participants to think about the data in relation to what was happening in their schools. Most importantly, we urged caution in interpreting the data, stressing that most variation was chance variation, rather than real upward or downward change, unless some pattern over time was evident.

Participation is Voluntary

When we invited schools to nominate themselves for the pilot, we expected to deal with 20 or so schools. However, when 200 schools responded, we decided to work with all of them. Over the following three years, the number of participating schools increased to 508 schools in 2002.

Some participants travelled long distances to attend Data Club workshops. One principal said to me, *I have driven five hours to attend Data Club, and I will get in my car and drive home when we finish today. I did it last year, and I'll do it again next year.* It seems that when participation is voluntary and people take responsibility for their choices, they value what they do and sometimes make extraordinary commitments.

More Than One School Leader Attends the Workshop

We invited schools to send to the workshop the principal and one other person with curriculum responsibility. Except for small schools, this is what happened. We believe that learning occurs when people talk together about their data. The workshop provided the time and space to sit together and explore the data, in a supported setting and without interruption. We also understand that such interactions promote commitment to taking action when participants return to their school.

Presenters are Specialists and Independent of the Employer

Both Louden and I had experience as facilitators and years of experience in the school sector. Louden was an English Head of Department and had worked for many years in the central office of the state education authority, in curriculum innovation and policy development. I was a secondary mathematics teacher and in recent years had worked with school principals in leadership development. We were both known to participants, and we had relevant expertise. These factors allowed us to build relationships with principals as they learned techniques of statistical analysis and interpretation. More importantly, though, we were employed outside the Department of Education. This allowed us to work with participants as coaches rather than being seen as judges.

The Impact of the Data Club

To meet our obligation to the funding agent, we commissioned an independent evaluation of the Data Club's impact at the end of the first year of its operation. We provided a randomly generated set of names of school principals and system-level personnel to an independent consultant, AAAJ Consulting Group. The following are excerpts from the report they submitted to the Commonwealth Government.

The Data Club evaluation suggests that the data, analysis, skills and understanding developed through participation in the Data Club are being applied extensively. A significant observation is that, as a consequence of the Data Club, schools have been making much more use of the data emerging from the WALNA tests. The principals are looking their school data squarely in the eye, accepting that it has something important and relevant to say. While it was the principals who were the Data Club's target audience, the analyses have been used at the whole school level for school planning and for annual reports.

A significant number of principals made the point that even talking about the Data Club and WALNA data at the whole staff level was making a major contribution to individual teachers' thinking. Test data and individual professional judgements do not always match and many teachers are taking this external reference point as a fact that needs to be considered. (Figgis & Butorac, 2001)

In summing up their investigation into the impact of the Data Club after its first year of operation, the consultants concluded:

The survey of principals suggests that the Data Club approach to analysis is being applied extensively. What has been of most immediate value is the potential provided by the data for schools to see their achievements in context—like schools in the same band or more broadly schools across the School District and the State. This has generated school-level discussions on a wide scale, which raised concerns about the relevance of the data for very small schools or schools with transient populations, time lags in delivery of data, and further scope for professional development. Nonetheless, what emerged was an extremely positive view of the usefulness of Data Club data analysis, and most schools are clearly taking it very seriously. In some schools there is already evidence of significant school change being undertaken to address weaknesses highlighted by the data.

Perhaps it is that the graphs are seductively (and indisputably) clear—there seems less argument with the data, less wish to hide from these facts. Of course there is a danger that schools may become too accepting and uncritical of the numbers. After all, the principals all pointed out to us that the WALNA data is one small bit of information to add to all the other sources of insight about their students and their school. However, an important impact of the Data Club is that in their involvement, principals are no longer defensive if their school is not performing as well as they expected. And this is a starting point for improvement in schools. (Figgis & Butorac, 2001)

Beyond the Data Club

Schools need support to understand the data they generate, beyond manuals and printed guides. There is evidence that the best support for interpreting data is a combination of information about data analysis and representation strategies together with application of this information to participants' own data.

Schools need guidance about how to use the information, particularly for whole school decision making in relation to planning, resource allocation, and performance reporting. In its initial phase, the Data Club provided the beginnings of such guidance. However, if schools are to benefit so that student learning can improve, then assistance in using data will need to be central to all schools' continuing professional learning programs.

REFERENCES

Butorac, A., Figgis, J., Wildy, H., & Zubrick, A. (2002). Reporting benchmark information to parents. Report prepared for the Performance Measurement and Reporting Taskforce of the Australian Commonwealth Ministerial Council on Education, Employment, Training and Youth Affairs (MCEETYA): AAAJ Consulting Group, Perth, Western Australia.

Figgis, J., & Butorac, A. (2001). The Data Club: Its impact on WA primary schools. Report prepared for the Australian Commonwealth Department of Education, Employment, Training and Youth Affairs (DETYA): AAAJ Consulting Group, Perth, Western Australia.

Louden, W., & Wildy, H. (2001). Developing schools' capacity to make performance judgements: Final report. Report prepared for Australian Commonwealth Department of Education, Employment, Training and Youth Affairs (DETYA): Edith Cowan University, Perth, Western Australia.

Wildy, H., Louden, W., & Wallace, J. (1998). School physics and the construction of educational inequality. *The Australian Educational Researcher*, 25(2), 39-59.

Wildy, H., & Wallace, J. (1995). Understanding teaching or teaching for understanding: Alternative frameworks for science classrooms. *Journal of Research in Science Teaching*, 32(2), 143-156.

CHAPTER 8

Tools for Two Masters: Classroom Assessment and School System Assessment

LARRY E. SUTER

The contributors to this volume have sought to make large-scale (usually national) assessments more useful to the daily classroom practices of elementary and secondary school teachers. They ask whether it is possible to modify the existing testing instruments in ways that could provide information that teachers could use to inform their instruction. The conversation is relevant for those who develop policy regarding the use of test scores and other forms of student assessment in classrooms. The issues on national and classroom assessment raised in this volume are also relevant for those who prepare future teachers, and the lessons learned here should be added to the training they provide. Each chapter provides a perspective on classroom assessment that comes from a separate research project carried out over a number of years; thus, the chapters were not initiated around a common framework nor around a common perspective or model of teaching and instruction or of assessment. But the contributors were asked to use the concepts of cognition, observation, and interpretation from the book *Knowing What Students Know* (Pellegrino, Chudowsky, & Glaser, 2001) as a guide to their discussion. Another common feature is that several of the projects in this volume were supported by funds from the mathematics and science education research programs of the National Science Foundation and thus represent highly regarded current research efforts recognized by reviewers of research projects.

The examples in this volume of how to think about assessment as a part of classroom learning are a worthy change in emphasis from the

Larry E. Suter is a program director for the Division of Research, Evaluation, and Communication of the National Science Foundation. He received his Ph.D. in sociology from Duke University and has worked for U.S. government statistical agencies, and NSF, since 1969.

The opinions, finding, and conclusions or recommendations expressed in this publication are those of the author and do not necessarily reflect the views of the National Science Foundation.

frequent national practice of using test scores on national student assessments only to increase the accountability of school systems. Such an emphasis is represented in national legislation (No Child Left Behind Act of 2001) and in state education agency policies regarding large-scale assessments. Some of the chapters discuss whether or not the needs of classroom teachers can be addressed by any of the information provided by the national assessments.

As a set, these chapters represent various attempts to develop guidance for teachers on how to better integrate curriculum and assessment practices to improve student learning. Two are based on broad views of the organization of curriculum and assessment (Forster & Masters, Smithson & Porter) and three are based on micro studies of teachers (Black & Wiliam, Frederiksen & White, Wilson & Draney). I will first comment on how each chapter contributes a research basis for applying assessment methods to classroom-level instruction, and then I will provide summary comments on the set.

Smithson and Porter

Smithson and Porter (Chapter 5) take a macroeducational approach toward understanding the relationship between policies about the content of the curriculum and what students learn in the classroom. Their chapter is an example of how research experiences contribute to the development of accountability measures (tools) for evaluating the top-down implementation of standards-based reform. It provides a partial history of the development of "opportunity to learn" (OTL) measures, spearheaded largely by Porter, and examines various conceptual frameworks of the opportunities for students to be exposed to substantive content areas while in school.

One of the important issues about OTL that grew out of the education reforms of the 1960s was whether classrooms watered down the mathematics curriculum to accommodate a greater number of students. As school enrollment rates increased greatly during the 1950s and 1960s, eventually reaching a nearly 100 percent increase for those up to age 15, it was feared that schools were reducing the emphasis on important content areas such as mathematics. (The Coleman report of 1966, however, brought attention to the fact that student achievement was less associated with classroom characteristics than it was with family background; Coleman et al., 1966.)

Smithson and Porter credit the first international comparative studies of student achievement with making the first attempts to measure classroom content coverage through surveys of teacher practices (Husen, 1967; Schmidt et al., 1996; Suter, 2001; Travers & Westbury, 1990). A significant contribution to the creation of manageable frameworks of the content areas of mathematics and science has been made by the international comparative studies of student assessment and by Porter and his colleagues. The measures that can be created from these frameworks allow analysis of strings of content areas to be followed through the education system from the national and state established standards (intended curriculum) to the classroom (enacted curriculum) and then to student performance (achieved curriculum) (Schmidt et al., 1999; Travers & Westbury, 1990). Smithson and Porter have treated subject matter content areas of the implemented curriculum as though they were elements in a compound that needed to be explicated, measured, and compared. This approach easily demonstrates how the issues of alignment between the intended curriculum and student achievement can be defined as reaching agreement on what specific content areas of mathematics and science should be covered in schools. Not all topics can be covered in every year. Smithson and Porter's charts, which teachers can use for reflection and analysis, show just how the schools organize the subject matter to increase student learning.

The authors created a data collection system to measure the connection between system-level policies about curricular coverage and classroom decisions. While most of the chapters in this volume discuss learning and assessment tools to measure learning, Smithson and Porter focus on the curriculum itself. They also show empirically (even pictorially) the extent to which various topics are presented in a classroom and the extent to which these topics are sampled by the assessment instruments of the state- and school-level tests. The statistical relationships are positive (that is, classrooms that have a greater emphasis on one content area in the state standards are more likely to also have a greater emphasis in classroom coverage; see figure 2 of their chapter), but the association is not very high. Their statistical analysis demonstrates that school systems practice a great deal of individual choice about the content areas covered.

The size of the observed correlation between standards and classroom coverage provides a useful basis for speculation about the possible effects of standards-based reform. These correlations are merely descriptive of the current status of schools and cannot be considered evidence that a causal path exists between increasing state standards and increasing classroom emphases on specific topics. Yet they provide some evidence for believing that the top-down approach to changing curricula may have resulted in some adoption of higher standards by teachers. But the evidence Smithson and Porter present, although somewhat minimal, suggests that the relationship between national intentions and classroom behavior is very loose. Therefore policymakers should not exaggerate the strength of top-down policies for changing teacher behavior regarding content area coverage in their classrooms.

Porter's most recent research, briefly touched on in Smithson and Porter's chapter, takes the analysis of these relationships another step toward action and perhaps toward developing stronger evidence for a causal chain. He has created a tool to intervene in the classroom decision making process about curriculum coverage. This tool collects information from teachers about their curriculum practices and displays graphs that show how these practices differ from the standards and from other teachers' practices in the coverage of specific topics. The new study seeks to use a model of content specification to gather information from teachers, to encourage them to reflect more on their decisions and ultimately to change their behavior in order to achieve greater alignment with state standards as the school year proceeds. The results of this experiment have not yet been reported but are consistent with results from the other efforts reported in this volume that have sought to provide teachers with real-time basic information about their performance in the classroom in an attempt to modify and improve their teaching practices. That study will help address the question of whether a significant causal connection exists between intended and implemented curriculum coverage.

Wilson and Draney

The BEAR Assessment System study presented by Wilson and Draney (Chapter 6) demonstrates an attempt to examine the link between large-scale and classroom assessments by creating a classroom assessment that reflects the same results as large-scale assessments do. The researchers suggest that by applying psychometric standards of reliability and validity to a classroom assessment, they will be able to assist teachers in better describing the status of their students. Thereby, the same information can be produced by both classroom and large-scale assessments.

Like Smithson and Porter, Wilson and Draney are attempting to create reliable data that are useful for describing the performance of a classroom rather than larger systems such as states. Rather than merely providing a comparative description of the current status of classes, as most national assessments do, they seek to assess the development of student understanding. So, at the start of this project, the investigators introduced a new purpose for assessment: measuring changes in performance. This project used the curriculum of a very specific program (SEPUP) rather than the framework of existing national assessments such as the National Assessment of Education Progress or of one of the state assessments.

Wilson and Draney are more concerned with policies of high-stakes testing—which are designed to create a match between curriculum and instruction by having teachers teach to the test—than they are with policies of the standards-based reform that Smithson and Porter describe. Wilson and Draney assert that their assessment system solves the problem of obtaining content validity by selecting test items chosen from a domain defined by both content and cognitive processing. Their assessment is intended to be integrated into the rhythm of daily instructional practices, thus instructional materials and assessment methods are designed together.

Like Smithson and Porter, whose system depicts classroom curriculum emphases on a graph, Wilson and Draney have created a series of "progress maps," which provide a criterion-referenced graph of student progress though the curriculum. Each student is provided with a copy of the maps to track their own progress. Teachers use these maps for giving feedback to students. The authors point out that classroom assessments should be created to be as reliable and valid as large-scale tests. They also enhance the information that is provided by applying Rasch-type models to the student responses. These statistical models help ensure that the scale points are more consistent throughout the scale.

Unlike other projects described in this volume, the BEAR model begins with a specific textbook or curriculum guide in a subject area and then adds more sophisticated measurement models to the analysis of student responses. The test items used in the approach are not multiple choice, thus the student responses must be coded and rated by experts. Wilson and Draney argue that this approach conforms to the principles of coherence, comprehensiveness, and continuity (derived from Pellegrino, Chudowsky, & Glaser, 2001) by providing measures of student progress on topics that are presented in class. This approach is unlike the national assessments, which are based on a national framework that may or may not include specific items that cover topics taught in the specific science class being assessed. The authors acknowledge that this approach is of more utility for teachers than it is for creating national large-scale assessments.

Wilson and Draney's approach might be described as a curriculum-centered assessment that relies on statistical models (multivariate Rasch) and psychometric principles of measurement to improve the application of tests to measurement of change in student performance. This model is not based on any particular psychological theory of learning. It focuses on teacher educational practices in the classroom. Assessments are written around science learning experiences that are expected to occur during specific instructional periods on a particular curriculum (such as SEPUP). These understandings are measured by student responses to written items scored by experts and scaled by Rasch models. Wilson and Draney present results to teachers to show the degree that students have grown in sophistication and understanding for those topics. While this scale does not give the detailed instructional practice suggestions that are discussed in the chapter by Black and Wiliam, it is a step toward a more relevant scale than that used in large-scale assessments, which are only suitable for general ranking.

The BEAR assessment method does not yet reach the originally specified goals of merging results of large-scale assessment with classroom assessment. While many of the methods that have been applied to large-scale assessments are being applied to classrooms in this project, only a few concept areas have been developed, and the study shows that this approach would require many more years of effort to map detailed classroom assessments to national frameworks.

The BEAR study demonstrates some of the reasons why attempting to create a single assessment of student learning that can be applied to national as well as classroom purposes is so difficult. The needs of the teacher and the administrator, or policy wonk, are simply too disparate. Is it possible to completely identify the skills that schools transmit to students in sufficiently clear ways that can be measured by a paper and pencil test? Wilson and Draney show that sophisticated scaling methods can provide somewhat useful scales, but they do not present convincing evidence that they will ever identify completely all the skills that schools are expected to provide to students or that those skills can be measured by a paper and pencil test with the validity and reliability the authors seek.

Frederiksen and White

The chapter by Frederiksen and White (Chapter 4) asserts that formative assessments that attempt full analysis of student work processes will provide the most benefit for student learning as well as provide the best indicators of how students are meeting standards. Thus, they seek assessments that serve both accountability and instruction.

Frederiksen and White report on their long-term project to develop software that assists students in learning the processes of scientific inquiry. The emphasis on inquiry is interesting because inquiry is included in the national science standards (NRC). But because the process of inquiry might be carried out in many areas of science, Frederiksen and White present it as a topic to be taught separately from specific science content areas. Their aim is to create an assessment tool that is more closely associated with the purposes of teaching students to gain these skills. They point out that assessments need to measure the quality of student work on consequential tasks, measure student abilities to make self-assessments of their tasks, and encourage the use of reflective judgments and the development of metacognitive skills. They seek to create a tool that is formative, in that it engages students in self- and peer assessment (emphasizing the process and outcome of student work), and summative, in that it can be aggregated for schools to provide a source of information for accountability with the state curricular standards. They expect that the tool would be of use to low-achieving students who lack metacognitive skills.

They have chosen to test their hypothesis that such a multipurpose tool can be developed with a most difficult curricular goal: to prepare students to ask their own questions and perform scientific investigations. The authors assert that making the teaching of scientific inquiry an important component of the curriculum requires assistance for teachers in developing extended activities for students. The teachers also need assistance in interpreting assessment tools like theirs, which Frederiksen and White hope can be applied generally.

The standard of internal validity that the authors apply to their assessment is different from most psychometric studies. In fact, Wilson and Draney make a very different argument in this volume about the use of psychometric models to improve the quality of the assessments used in classrooms. Frederiksen and White believe that internal validity can be judged by creating a logical framework for scorers to use in judging the quality of student skill and the coherence of an argument. They say that they seek "transparency" of the processes used for interpreting task performances so that students will understand all the criteria of success and thus be motivated to learn. They claim that the efforts within a school to ensure internal validity of teacher and student judgments about the quality of work provide "a better basis for establishing their credibility than would obtaining measures of inter-scorer agreement" (p. 80). While this argument has merit if the aim of the project is strictly to provide classroom teachers with guidelines on how to incorporate science inquiry into their classes, it does not lead to empirical evidence that students would be consistently judged. Logic is a necessary but not sufficient aspect of the validity of assessments.

The authors note that their larger project seeks to show how to merge a large-scale assessment program for schools with classroom assessment. But the body of the chapter in this volume describes only one aspect of that problem: how to achieve reliability and internal validity of a classroom exercise in science inquiry. The chapter discusses how classroom assessments can improve teacher understanding of student performance. The application to school-level accountability is never made obvious. The assessment tool is chosen to represent the greater values of the curriculum, such as state standards, but the chapter does not makes a sufficiently direct connection between the intended curriculum and the implemented curriculum in the classroom.

The tool is still in development and apparently has not been used outside a single school laboratory. The main evidence presented in the chapter is a demonstration that a normative interpretative model and scoring rubrics could be developed for assessment tools that rate student performances in science inquiry. Prior to having these rubrics, the teachers participating in the project had no knowledge of how to consistently rate student performance on inquiry. The chapter provides no evidence that someone else can successfully replicate the scoring techniques they used for student science projects using the rubrics developed by the investigators. The authors provide a logical argument for integrating classroom assessment with system accountability, but no strong empirical evidence that these scores can be aggregated to higher levels and interpreted with equal meaning. But the approach is intriguing, in that the authors have created a framework for training both teachers and students in how to use and understand, and evaluate, one of the most elusive concepts in science learning: inquiry.

Forster and Masters

The Australian Council for Educational Research (ACER) has developed a set of materials to support classroom teachers in their assessment of reading and writing that was later used in a national survey. A unique aspect of their project is that they developed a scoring form that provides a (Guttman-like) scale of scores with interpretative statements that describe what kind of knowledge a student is expected to achieve at that level. Chapter 3 is an operational description of how their assessment system evolved from a classroom-developed assessment into a broader system for administrators. The system includes a progress map, a range of assessment methods, teacher development activities in the assessment methods, tools for teachers to assess student work, procedures for system-wide data collection, and methods of monitoring and reporting school- and system-level achievement over time.

The logic of their system begins with the idea that there is a normal path of development, or progress, within an area of learning (students' knowledge, skills, attitudes, and understandings). They assume that there is a normal direction of student progress that can be identified and represented on a progress map. Both teachers and administrators can use the same map, they assert.

The conceptual development of the progress maps is not described in the chapter, although a thorough example of a map for speaking is provided. The project is a good demonstration of a model of understanding the subject matter (in this case, English language) as a progressively more complex set of concepts. The purpose of the assessment is to provide a measure of the position of the student, or the whole class, along that progression. While the approach appears worthwhile, Forster and Masters do not describe the complex process of arriving at the standards that define the progress maps. It is impossible to evaluate the usefulness of their approach from the material provided in the chapter.

The general approach Forster and Masters describe requires the development of a scale that is both meaningful to the teacher and faithful to the underlying concept, which in this case is the speaking of English. This approach has some similarity to the intent of the work reported by Wilson and Draney in this volume. In their chapter, Wilson and Draney seek to create a scale that has known psychometric properties but which also has easily interpretable meanings that classroom teachers can use to explain the most significant strengths and weaknesses of the subject being studied. While neither of these approaches is in full practice yet, they represent good examples of the use of assessment instruments to create teacher-friendly scales of knowledge. The problem is to create these scales in a way that suits both content specialist and practicing teacher. That such a scale exists has not been demonstrated in this volume. But the general outline of how it could be created is presented.

Black and Wiliam

Black and Wiliam (Chapter 2) have already established in their prior research that classroom learning can be improved by formative assessment. They find that the assessment methods teachers use most often are not effective in promoting learning because they tend to create competition rather than personal improvement among students. Feedback to students is better when it is positive and instructive, rather than leading students to believe that they lack ability, as happens when test scores are assigned without discussion.

Black and Wiliam are concerned with how to develop good formative assessment practices among teachers, but along the way they provide a deep philosophical and practical examination of the purpose and use of assessments in elementary and secondary classrooms. The primary purpose of formative assessment, they say, is to promote learning. Accountability, the ranking or certification of competence, is not the purpose of formative assessment but of summative assessment. They point out that frequent assessment—for example, weekly tests—are summative in nature, not formative, unless the results are used to improve student performance.

Their exploratory research on developing teachers to use formative assessment as a continuing part of their practice was carried out in three English schools with which they had had previous experiences and which they knew would participate in their experiment. The unique aspect of this study is that no specific formative assessment model was imposed, but rather a general problem was introduced to the teachers and then the investigators supported the teachers in their efforts to use assessments in their classrooms. They were able to collect some quantitative measures of achievement by using the local test and comparing the experiment classrooms with other classrooms. While this design would not have passed the test of rigorous experimental design, it does provide some useful evidence about the likely impact of their approach. The results show that there is some evidence to conclude that frequent use of formative methods was associated with greater levels of achievement on the school tests by about one quarter of a standard deviation.

The beautiful aspect of the chapter by Black and Wiliam is that it includes useful descriptions of their experience in changing the daily routine of classroom teachers in their effort to encourage them to use various methods to assess students. The chapter contains a number of general principles that were extracted from the experiment. Some examples of their recommendations about how to improve teacher awareness of student understanding include: aiming lessons to guide students toward greater engagement with the material being presented; using long wait times after questions; asking questions to initiate a lesson; providing better feedback in response to student work; using both self- and peer assessment; and taking ownership of learning. Each of these principles is elaborated with examples from the teachers in the study.

The authors were able to address the central question of this volume, the connection between classroom assessment and large-scale assessment, through an accident of design. Some teachers in their study conducted the in-class study of formative assessment in classes that were taking the national tests (summative assessment). The authors observed that, although an emphasis on narrow summative tests can have a harmful influence on learning, separate preparation for formative and summative tests is unrealistic, and schools need to "achieve a more positive relationship between the two" (p. 42).

Black and Wiliam provide an intriguing description of the thoughts of the participating teachers regarding the use of summative tests. Since these opinions and experiences are drawn from a specialized sample, the authors do not attempt to argue for generalizability. But the variety of comments and practices in schools that show how test scores are created and used for reporting student performance is valuable to have on record. Teachers' concern with the validity of national tests was apparent and seemed to undermine the purpose of assessment, because teachers were often unable to prepare students effectively for such tests.

The authors anticipate that although teachers may continue to "teach to the test," they may also "teach for understanding" by using some of the principles described in the chapter to improve student learning, such as helping pupils to use revision, to pay attention to the intention of test questions, and to anticipate the criteria by which answers might be judged. The main result of this study is that the authors found that once teachers understood the use of formative test practices, the practices had a broad impact on their teaching methods. Black and Wiliam note that their study and others like it have found that "learning requires active and frequent interaction between teachers and learners" (p. 47).

Black and Wiliam have made a number of instructive observations about the connection between teaching and assessment that should inform policymakers and teachers about what to expect from the various policies that are being carried out in the United States regarding the use of school tests as a way of measuring school success. Their chapter is really a lesson in how teachers can be more constructive in communicating with pupils, either by asking good questions during a lecture, or by marking comments on written work or on assessments. They encourage creating a culture of learning by providing students with constant feedback on strengths and weaknesses and next steps.

Their observations on page 45 about how summative assessments affect what is taught in class and how it is taught are especially valuable to current policymakers who are intent on using national assessments exclusively. Teachers said that they had to teach to the test even though the test was not valid in relation to the national curriculum specifications. The pressures to provide a summative assessment inhibited linking test topics to other topics. Each lesson was restricted in style and imagination. Tying lessons to specific national curriculum statements restricted pupil involvement and enjoyment.

The authors' interviews with teachers pointed out the difficulties with developing a valid measure. If the validity could be improved, overall validity would still require some independent assessment by teachers as a complementary source of evidence. The formative use of summative tests helped them increase achievement for their students, but it limited their ability to make interesting connections to other material. Thus, more than any other in this volume, this chapter nicely outlines many of the pitfalls in creating assessments that seek to serve two masters: administrators, who want rankings for accountability purposes, and teachers, who want formative assessments that they can use to increase student attention to the topic and thereby improve student understanding of their subjects.

Conclusion

The chapters in this volume represent a set of research studies that are still in progress. None of the studies has been completed on a large scale nor have all of the hypotheses that drive the studies yet been sufficiently tested. Each of the chapters contributes new knowledge about the difficulties in helping teachers improve their instruction within the current emphasis on national assessments.

Each researcher approached the development of specific examples of classroom assessment from a different set of experiences. Smithson and Porter sought to find ways of measuring whether the adoption of national standards by the nation's professional associations in mathematics and science led to the adoption of new topics in the classroom.

Thus their interest in teachers' classroom behavior followed efforts to establish a nationally recognized framework of content areas. Wilson and Draney created an assessment that grew from their association with helping teachers teach a particular science curriculum (SEPUP), and so they sought to establish useful indicators that might guide teachers through the presentation and learning of the science material in a classroom. Frederiksen and White came to assessment after years of exploring how to teach students about scientific inquiry. Their research ideas are steeped in the theory of educational psychology and experience with the learning of science. Their assessment efforts were created late in their research project, after they had developed both a theory and a practice of teaching scientific inquiry. They present a nonpsychometric argument for establishing the validity of their measures that is of value. The chapter by Forster and Masters of the Australian Council for Education Research describes an example of creating assessment tools for instruction because of a perceived opportunity by researchers who were engaged in developing survey instruments for another purpose. ACER, in attempting to create new test instruments and teaching materials for classrooms, found a way to integrate their instruments into a single tool with a scale that is intended to be instructive for classroom teachers. Black and Wiliam are strong advocates for improving teaching practices through the principles of formative assessment. After years of studying large-scale assessment techniques in England, they appear to have little good to say about the value of summative assessments. Their chapter contains a very readable and instructive dialogue about their experience with creating classroom practices that might actually lead to improvements in student learning. They have shown that the type of instrument used for assessment affects the style of teaching and often, therefore, the reaction of the students. Thus, their chapter provides valuable insights for policymakers at all levels of assessment development.

All of these chapters are written by researchers with recent experience in improving classroom teaching. Assessment projects, such as those conducted by large-scale testing organizations, state education agencies, the National Assessment of Education Progress, and the Third International Mathematics and Science Study, provide summative achievement scores that stimulate discussion and debate about the status of an entire school system. Just as economic indicators such as the gross national product inform businesses about the rate of growth for the national economy (not for a local grocery store), the indicators from large-scale assessments describe the status of things that were already known with a level of precision that permits the measurement of change and of differences within the community. They do not provide a prescription for what needs to be done to fix the observed educational problems. The purposes of national and classroom assessment are different, and the efforts described here to integrate them so that these separate purposes do not compete for student or teacher time have not yet accomplished their aim. Yet, we have learned a significant amount about the integration of assessment and classroom teaching processes.

REFERENCES

Coleman, J., Campbell, E., Hobson, C., McPartland, J., Mood, A., Weinfeld, F.D., & York, R. (1966). *Equality of educational opportunity*. Washington, DC: U.S. Department of Health, Education, and Welfare.

Husen, T. (Ed.). (1967). *International study of achievement in mathematics* (Vol. 1). New York: Wiley.

No Child Left Behind Act of 2001. Reauthorization of the Elementary and Secondary Education Act Legislation and Policies. Public Law 107-110.

Pellegrino, J., Chudowsky, N., & Glaser, R. (Eds.). (2001). *Knowing what students know: The science and design of educational assessment*. Washington, DC: National Research Council.

Schmidt, W.H., Jorde, D., Cogan, L., Barrier, E., Gonzalo, I., Moser, U., et al. (1996). *Characterizing pedagogical flow: An investigation of mathematics and science teaching in six countries*. Dordrecht, the Netherlands: Kluwer.

Schmidt, W., McKnight, C., Cogan, L., Jakwerth, P., & Houang, R. (1999). *Facing the consequences: Using TIMSS for a closer look at U.S. mathematics and science education*. Dordrecht, the Netherlands: Kluwer.

Suter, L. (2001). Is student achievement immutable? Evidence from international studies on schooling and student achievement. *Review of Educational Research (RER)* 70(4), 529-545.

Travers, K.J., & Westbury, I. (1990). *The IEA study of mathematics I: Analysis of mathematics curricula*. Oxford, England: Pergamon Press.

CHAPTER 9

Classroom Assessment Is Not (Necessarily) Formative Assessment (and Vice-versa)

PAUL BLACK AND DYLAN WILIAM

The terms classroom assessment and formative assessment are often used synonymously, but as the chapters in this collection show, the fact that an assessment happens in the classroom, as opposed to elsewhere, says very little about either the nature of the assessment or the functions that it can serve. Classroom assessments may provide a sound basis for summative assessments, and those conducted outside the classroom may provide valuable insights into how to move learning forward. As well as the locus of the assessment, we think that it is also important to attend to the issues of authority, resources, interactivity, and scoring. Each of these is discussed in turn below.

Authority

The assessments may be generated by the teacher, by outside agencies, or by someone between these two extremes. In many European countries assessments are proposed by the teacher, and approved (or not!) by an external agency, such as a regional inspector. Whether it is fair to assess students in different regions, or even students in different schools in the same region, on a different basis is, of course, problematic (see below).

Resources

The conditions under which students respond can be more or less controlled. At one extreme, typified by the traditional written examination, students may be required to respond alone, without any additional

Paul Black is Professor Emeritus of Science Education in the Department of Education and Professional Studies, King's College, University of London. Dylan Wiliam is formerly Professor of Educational Assessment and Assistant Principal of King's College, University of London. He is now Senior Research Director of the Learning and Teaching Research Centre at Educational Testing Service, Princeton, NJ.

materials. In other assessments, they may be able to consult specified textual resources (as in an open-book examination), a wider range of materials (e.g., the Internet), or even, with group projects, other students.

Interactivity

In the traditional test or examination, there is a stimulus to which the student makes a response, which is then judged. There is no scope for the student to ask for clarification of the meaning of the stimulus, and the rater is required to make a judgment of the response as it stands. In this context, it should be noted that the majority of tests or quizzes that teachers employ in their classrooms as part of their normal classroom practice are of this sort. In an oral examination, however, the student can seek clarification of the meaning of the stimulus, and the rater can ask the student to clarify or elucidate his or her response. Furthermore, the oral examination allows for in-depth exploration of issues, although this necessarily compromises the extent to which all students are examined on the same basis. In some examination systems, the ability to interact with candidates is regarded as essential for valid assessment. Of course, although face-to-face oral examinations have been the traditional way of providing interaction between student and rater, modern technologies allow a much greater range of options, including the possibility of having computers, rather than humans, conducting the assessments.

Scoring

Where the results from the assessments are expected to serve summative or evaluative purposes, it is essential that the grades, marks, or scores awarded depend as little as possible on who is doing the assessment—in other words, that the assessments are *objective*. This is generally achieved through the use of machines, or by employing human scorers who have no knowledge of the student. At the other extreme, where assessments are intended to serve only a formative function, consistency of meanings across different raters is less important. What is more important is whether the assessments lead to improved instruction. But just as teachers can author assessments for summative purposes, they can also be involved in the scoring of their own students' work for summative purposes. One way that the necessary consistency of scoring across teachers has been achieved in the past is through scrutiny of the assessors' judgments, which amounts to a kind of quality control process. Marks, grades, or scores are generated, and at the end of the process, the quality of the assessing is inspected and, if necessary, adjusted (a process frequently termed moderation). What is important here is that although the assessment may be conducted by the teacher, it is done so in a way that is intersubjective—reliant on the shared understanding of a community of teachers—so that the judgments are objective in the sense that they are free from individual subjectivity. Furthermore, the assessment is against a set of standards that are determined by the community rather than the teacher, so that even though the teacher is involved in scoring the student's work, the teacher is, in a very real sense, the student's ally rather than his or her enemy (e.g., "I'd love to give you an A for this, but you just haven't reached the required standard yet").

A key theme running through several of the issues raised above is the extent to which all students are assessed on the same basis. Traditional wisdom dictates that fair assessment can be attained only if all students are assessed on the same basis; this is the notion of "fairness" used in traditional tests. However, it is also routinely acknowledged in the same breath that it is essential to make adjustments to assessments for particular populations, such as students with visual impairments, specific learning disabilities (such as dyslexia), or motor impairments. At the higher levels of the educational system, it is routinely accepted that at least part of the purpose of the assessment is to provide candidates with an opportunity to show what they can do, through non-uniform assessments such as coursework, projects, and theses. Of course, it could be argued that the requirement for non-uniform assessment at these higher levels arises from the complexity of the judgments that are necessary, but then the same also applies to earlier stages of the learning process—recent research has shown convincingly that the state of anyone's learning is a complex schema that defies simplistic analysis. Failure to recognize this (or, perhaps even worse, recognition with failure to acknowledge its importance) has resulted in a simplistic approach to assessment that leads to an emphasis on low-level aims, which weakens validity. If more complex notions of fairness than simply making sure that all students are asked the same question are felt to be necessary for certain populations, then why not for all?

The chapter by Smithson and Porter (Chapter 5) provides a useful framework for beginning the process of examining the extent to which the (often noble) aims of standards are mirrored in classrooms and in what is assessed. Given the prevalence of high-stakes assessment, we must accept that assessment may drive instruction, and therefore, there can be little hope of aligning instruction with standards unless the assessment is also aligned with the standards. The tools Smithson and Porter provide can be used to illustrate, in a very convincing way, the extent to which these three aspects are aligned, and they will frequently point to the need to improve the validity of the assessment being used.

In any well-designed system, the judgments of teachers will inform the summative function, and external ideas about what to assess will inform instruction. This is particularly notable in the chapters by Forster and Masters (FM, Chapter 3), Frederiksen and White (FW, Chapter 4), and Wilson and Draney (WD, Chapter 6). What is at issue is the quality of the instruments and of the inferences made from them.

The approaches outlined by FW and FM signal a move away from a traditional quality control orientation toward one of quality *assurance*. The major effort goes not into correcting marks that are wrong but into improving the ability of the assessors to get it right the first time. It is also noteworthy that both FW and FM focus on securing consensus, not through getting teachers to agree on some lowest common denominator, but through beginning to address explicitly the features that are likely to be present in good responses. The notion of "community of practice" is a useful idea for thinking about how teachers can come to consensus over the marks, grades, or scores to be awarded to students' work, but it can serve to disguise what they have come to agree *on*. After all, the requirements of reliability are met if teachers' judgments are consistent, even if they have no idea what they are doing or how they are doing it. The result of this can often be that teachers can accurately judge the standard of students' work, but have little idea about how to improve it.

Our own work with teachers and students suggests that when teachers take pains to share with their students the criteria for success, students are able to internalize these criteria quickly (often more quickly than the teachers would have thought possible). As Royce Sadler (1989) notes, this is a necessary but insufficient condition for improvement. For progress to be possible, in addition to having a notion of quality, it is necessary for either the teacher or the learner to have an *anatomy* of quality. In other words, it must be possible to break down the path from the current position to the goal, into a series of steps that the learner can take. While this may be possible for learners to do for themselves, more often it will be the responsibility of the teacher, and our experience is that many teachers do not have very clear models for progression. As one teacher in an in-service program remarked in the context of the National Curriculum for English, "I know he's a level 4, but I don't know what to do to get him to level 5." This is why the developmental models inherent in the assessments described in FW, FM, and WD are so important. As well as grounding assessment in developmental principles, they provide models that help teachers understand the nature of progression in the domain, thus supporting them in identifying next steps for students.

In discussions of assessment, it is commonplace to distinguish between assessment *of* learning and assessment *for* learning. However, the rich tasks proposed by FM, FW, and WD demonstrate an intermediate possibility—assessment *as* learning. While the tasks proposed in these three chapters have as their primary goal the rendering of accurate, meaningful judgments of students' achievements, the tasks themselves are valuable learning activities. The extended nature of these tasks enhances reliability, but the extra time that these tasks take is justifiable only because students are learning while they undertake them. These activities therefore assess not what the students know at the beginning of the assessment, but what they know at the end.

For assessment to function formatively, we need accurate information about where students really are in their learning, but this is also what we want for summative assessments. It may be, therefore, that we can find synergy rather than tension in the relationship between formative and summative. For example, consider the following item:

> Give an algebraic expression for the nth term in the sequence 5, 8, 11, 14...
>
> A) $n + 3$
> B) $5 + n$
> C) $3n + 2$
> D) $2n + 3$

This item is designed to support both summative and formative inferences. The distractors here are derived from well-known difficulties that students encounter in this domain. Distractor A is attractive to students who have established the term-to-term rule (i.e., add 3) rather than the position-to-term rule that is required. Distractor B is also based on a recursive approach, but focuses on the idea of adding a number to the initial term. The key (C) and the last distractor (D) permute the parameters.

Thus in putting this question before a student, the teacher will have in mind a tentative judgment of the pupil's understanding and will be able to confirm or amend this judgment in light of the response. In addition, choices such as A or B will serve to pinpoint different types of error. A student choosing A may have misunderstood the question's requirement for a general term rather than just a rule for generating the sequence. The student who chooses B is likely to believe (as they have been repeatedly told!) that "n can be any number," and this misconception will need to be addressed (note, it is important that this distractor is expressed as $5 + n$ rather than the more usual $n + 5$). This item could therefore serve both formative and summative functions well. The diagnostic potential of this item could be improved further by replacing distractor D with "$n3 + 2$." Then, where formative functions are paramount, all of the distractors will be useful. Many would argue, however, that "$n3 + 2$" is an unfair distractor in the context of a high-stakes assessment—especially if it were to be scored as incorrect.

All of the chapters embrace, explicitly or implicitly, the idea that we must find ways of integrating the formative and summative functions of assessment, but more work needs to be done in order to fully understand the nature of the relationship between the two. If such an integration is to be found, it certainly will not rest on a simple equation of external assessment for summative purposes on the one hand and classroom assessment for formative purposes on the other.

REFERENCE

Sadler, R. (1989). Formative assessment and the design of instructional systems. *Instructional Science, 18*, 119-144.

CHAPTER 10

Systems of Coherence and Resonance: Assessment for Education and Assessment of Education

PAUL G. LeMAHIEU AND ELIZABETH C. REILLY

The source chapters in this volume raise issues that collectively address the question of coherence within systems of assessment and accountability: what dimensions define coherence such that practical development efforts can hope to realize it; to what extent can assessments designed to address the needs of classroom practitioners serve the interests of those who work some distance from the classroom; and what design elements need to be addressed (and how should they be addressed) to maximize utility across levels of the system?

There is a lengthy history to this discussion. Nearly twenty years ago, LeMahieu and Wallace (1986) explored the conditions that best enabled assessments for what they termed *clinical* uses in contrast to those that addressed *evaluative* ones. Cole (1984) similarly explored whether assessments constructed for accountability purposes could ever be appropriate and effective for instructional uses. More recently, Black and Wiliam (1998), Shepard (2000), and Chappuis and Stiggins (2002) all examined similar questions. They explored what has variously been termed clinical versus evaluative assessment, instructional versus accountability testing, classroom versus large-scale assessment, or in its most contemporary form, assessment *for* education versus assessment *of* education. Whatever the terminology, the issue concerns the coherence and compatibility of assessments intended to inform intervention on behalf of the growth and development of students as opposed to assessments that inform judgments about the accomplishment or status of individuals, programs, schools, or systems.

While each of these researchers examines this issue from a different perspective and thus illuminates a portion of the considerations

Paul G. LeMahieu is the Director of Research, Evaluation and Information Systems for the National Writing Project and was formerly the State Superintendent of Education in Hawai'i. Elizabeth C. Reilly is Academic Coordinator for the Joint Doctoral Program in Leadership for Educational Equity in the Graduate School of Education at University of California, Berkeley and a former K-12 school administrator.

inherent in it, there emerges a general consensus across authors and across the years. Most have only modest hopes that the same assessment devices can serve both purposes, instead recognizing the legitimate need for each type of information and counseling that we establish systems made up of elements that address each purpose. These sentiments echo throughout a recent NRC report (Pellegrino, Chudowsky, & Glaser, 2001) in its call for coherence in terms of the integration of assessment frameworks and methods across all levels of the assessment system.

Guided by such sentiments, researchers and practitioners alike are struggling to conceive of such systems of assessment that realize genuine coherence across its various elements and, to the extent possible, integration of those various elements. This means developing assessment strategies that potentially can serve multiple purposes to achieve coherence and resonance across disparate elements. Resonance occurs when separate elements of a complex system actively reinforce each other for their mutual benefit. While many of the authors' efforts are very thoughtful and successful in realizing whatever forms of coherence serve as a focus for their work, few approach being coherent in any broad sense. Simply stated, they lack a comprehensive exposition of this idea of coherence in assessment systems.

Each of the source chapters treats one or more dimensions of this idea of systemic coherence in the work that it describes. Some dimensions are addressed explicitly; many more are addressed implicitly throughout the chapters. It is possible to examine these chapters with an eye to synthesizing a much more elaborate view of coherence and, in doing so, articulate a reasonably comprehensive framework that can guide development efforts pursuing coherence and resonance.

In this chapter, we will first examine each of the projects described in this volume to explore the elements of coherence that it manifests, how the elements are defined, and the manner in which the elements are addressed in the assessment program described. Following that review, we will augment those elements with others that seem necessary and organize them into a framework that can guide efforts at developing coherent and resonant systems of assessment. We will conclude with reflections on the application of the framework and advice to educational leaders and assessment practitioners seeking to use it.

Elements of Coherence

The work of Black and Wiliam, Forster and Masters, Frederiksen and White, Smithson and Porter, and Wilson and Draney addresses a number of the elements of coherence and resonance between class-room and system assessment. Three projects point out the importance of consonance in the larger goals and purposes of assessment by look-ing for common elements that should make up classroom and large-scale assessment systems. Wilson and Draney (Chapter 6) frame the discussion within the principles derived from the National Research Council's report, *Knowing what students know: The science and design of educational assessment* (Pellegrino, Chudowsky, & Glaser, 2001). Coherence between classroom and large-scale assessment is essential, as is a comprehensive system—one that offers a full range of ways to assess progress. Finally, the principle of continuity provides evidence over time of individual student development and of educational pro-grams' progress.

In their efforts to bridge the potential conceptual gap between sys-tem accountability and classroom assessment, Forster and Masters (Chapter 3) draw upon their decade of experience in Australian schools working on literacy achievement. They provide greater detail to the Wilson and Draney hallmarks of a comprehensive assessment system by presenting six components of an ideal system: 1) a progress map with a conceptual framework; 2) multiple assessment methods; 3) opportunities for professional development; 4) tools to help teachers assess student work; 5) procedures for collecting system-wide data; and 6) processes for reporting and monitoring achievement over time at the school and system levels.

Frederiksen and White (Chapter 4) add to the discussion of assess-ment system standards two additional factors: directness and trans-parency. By directness, they refer to the tasks that students perform in assessments, asserting a preference for direct assessment. Tasks must require the explicit application of the cognitive processes and knowl-edge that one wants to assess with the opportunity for students to demonstrate this visibly. Transparency refers to providing access to the processes used for interpreting the data so that "all participants have a shared basis for recognizing, discussing, and evaluating stu-dents' work" (p. 79). Black and Wiliam (Chapter 2) support the asser-tion that transparency is an essential component of assessment that must extend not only to the teachers (Wilson & Draney) through pro-fessional development, but also to the students.

In their discussion of the content that becomes the basis of assess-ments, Smithson and Porter (Chapter 5) begin with a detailed and extensive description of the history of instances wherein the interpre-tation of assessment information with reference to content coverage has proved useful. They assert that in the end few things are quite so important as thoughtfulness about and understanding of what is being assessed. Early on, principally researchers attended to these matters. Over time policymakers and educational managers joined the researchers, and at present, the constellation of interested parties extends into offices of school districts and state capitals as well as into the classroom.

Forster and Masters present a way to describe areas of student learning—frequently called "outcomes" or "indicators"—that they term a "progress map." The use of these progress maps is the centerpiece of their notion of "developmental assessment," which becomes the principal means of summarizing and describing students' achievements and group trends over time. Progress maps present students' typical development from year to year in the form of outcomes for achievement. These maps serve both system accountability and individual classroom teachers. Wilson and Draney further explicate the concept of a progress map with descriptions of the progress variables that define the specifics of the progress maps. Weighing in on the discussion of what is assessed as an important element of coherence, Frederiksen and White emphasize measuring "significant work that students are undertaking in the classroom" (p. 74).

Three of the chapters—those by Frederiksen and White, Smithson and Porter, and Wilson and Draney—address the technical quality of assessment, namely, that matters of validity and reliability must be attended to. Smithson and Porter state that "the challenge to create valid accountability systems that draw upon teachers' professional knowledge in a manner that encourages their use of assessment frameworks and styles that are consistent with good practice" are "by far the greatest of the challenges faced" (p. 127). Frederiksen and White augment qualitative analysis by asserting the need to establish "the internal validity and external validity of the knowledge claims that are being made, based on evidence obtained in the assessment" (p. 78).

Most of the authors address in some fashion the matter of how data should be analyzed and interpreted. Wilson and Draney and Forster and Masters speak of the nature of evidence as generated by the assessment, and that this evidence in the form of feedback is presented as quantitative data, numerical, simplified, and summarized through the analytic technology that is applied. Because the data are highly reduced, scores then are compared to other information to give them meaning, raising the issue of score referencing. Black and Wiliam enlarge the discussion with a call for more narrative data, as do Frederiksen and White. Such narrative data would then, for the purposes of system assessment, need to be distilled and generalized in the form of trends, themes, and so on. Some form of scoring guide accompanies any classroom assessment, and according to Frederiksen and White, they must provide "a principled basis for making scoring inferences based on that evidence [to address] how we can scaffold teachers' (and students') interpretations of students' work to ensure that resulting assessments are accurate and comparable" (p. 99).

A number of the projects address the role of students as active participants in assessment. While Frederiksen and White call this form of analysis "reflective assessment," in which students evaluate their own and other students' projects, Black and Wiliam refer to it as "self- and peer assessment." Both point out the value of student involvement in the assessment process. The benefits of this involvement are many, including the integration of assessment as an extension of the learning process rather than an add-on endeavor.

Collectively and individually the authors have identified many elements of assessment and offered examples of very practical means of addressing them to achieve coherence. We list and define a number of them here and describe the manner in which each is addressed by the authors:

- *Goals and Purposes—the functions served by the assessment.* The development of assessments must be guided by principles of coherence, continuity, and comprehensiveness (Wilson & Draney) with at least the six specific elements delineated (Forster & Masters).
- *Locus of Authority—who defines content and standards for assessments.* A locus of authority must be established, through curricular and content specialists (Forster & Masters) or through the use of curriculum standards (Wilson & Draney) or through standards documents, curriculum frameworks, textbooks, and teacher choice (Smithson & Porter).
- *Content Assessed—what is measured.* The definition of content and assessments can be guided by progress maps and progress variables (Forster & Masters, Wilson & Draney). Assessments should measure "significant" work that is happening in classrooms (Frederiksen & White) and measure the overlap with standards documents, curriculum frameworks, or instructional content as appropriate (Smithson & Porter).

- *Nature of Evidence/Data—the type of data used to support inferences of various sorts.* Evidence can be quantitative, simplified, organized, and presented in relational terms to give meaning (Forster & Masters, Frederiksen & White, Wilson & Draney). However, to maximize instructional utility, it should be expository, narrative, and descriptive (Black & Wiliam, Frederiksen & White).
- *Technical Quality—the applicable hallmarks and standards of quality and fairness.* Researchers should apply validity theory to both large-scale and classroom assessment (Wilson & Draney) and use it to augment qualitative interpretations that are undergirded by cognitive theory (Frederiksen & White).
- *Score Reference—the comparison of derived scores with other information to imbue them with meaning.* Scores can be compared with those of other students in the class (or other appropriate reference groups), with the student's individual performance over time (Black & Wiliam, Forster & Masters, Frederiksen & White, Wilson & Draney), or with identified content domains (Smithson & Porter).
- *Analysis and Interpretation—procedures for deriving meaning from the evidence.* Cognitive theory can bolster the use of scoring guides (Black & Wiliam, Forster & Masters, Wilson & Draney) and normative or modal response patterns (Frederiksen & White).

A Framework for Systems of Coherence and Resonance

Based on the preceding review, we turn now to a more detailed explication and illustration of the dimensions of coherence and resonance between classroom and large-scale assessment design. We have synthesized the preceding discussion into a framework of elements along which coherence and resonance must be pursued (Table 1). The framework presents the seven elements listed above, augmented by nine others taken from the literature and from the authors' experiences in developing assessment systems that aspire to serve classroom practitioners as well as program managers, system leaders, and policy makers. Table 1 also offers very brief descriptions of desiderata for each element, in terms of both assessment *for* learning and assessment *of* learning. Before exploring particular entries in the table, a few general comments about the framework are in order.

First, the presentation is referenced to both assessment *for* and assessment *of* education. This is in keeping with the distinction offered by Black and Wiliam (1998), in which assessment intended to inform

TABLE 1

Elements of Coherence and Resonance
Between Large-Scale and Classroom Assessment Design

Domain	Element	Qualities in assessment *of* education	Qualities in assessment *for* education
Conceptual			
	Goals / Purposes	Evaluation, certification, summary judgments, higher stakes; desire to establish long-term trends of student learning	Diagnosis, intervention, formative information, lower stakes; desire to make immediate changes in student learning
	Nature / Effect of motivation	Generate best possible scores; high stakes vis-à-vis rewards and sanctions; risk taking discouraged as potentially damaging to the demonstration of accomplishment	Improve teaching and increase learning; low stakes vis-à-vis rewards and sanctions; risk taking encouraged as useful to the revelation of the learner
	Epistemological frame of reference	Positivism, logical empiricism	Relativism, social constructivism
	Relationship of assessment to learners	Short term, distant, circumscribed, observer, "-etic"	Long term, involved, participatory, "-emic"
	Consequential validity / Desired impact	Distant impact on resource allocation, program-level goals, and designs; minimal impact *in situ* to control potential narrowing of educational experience	Immediate and profound shaping of educational experience *in situ*
Substantive			
	Locus of authority / Control over form and content	Macro level—external to classroom; experts in field and boards, "the public" as expressed through political structures determines content, benchmarks, and goals	Micro level—involving teachers and students in classroom; teachers determine content, benchmarks, and goals often using state or national standards
	Content assessed	Knowledge, skills, behaviors based on global, industrial, or societal learning outcomes external to classroom; emphasis on breadth	Knowledge, skills, behaviors based on local, individual, class, or course learning outcomes; emphasis on depth

TABLE 1 (*Continued*)

Elements of Coherence and Resonance
Between Large-Scale and Classroom Assessment Design

Domain	Element	Qualities in assessment *of* education	Qualities in assessment *for* education
Substantive (cont.)			
	Methods / Instruments	Tests, scales, surveys generally added to class work; efficiency and economy highly prized	Observations, interviews, personal documents derived from class work
Technical			
	Nature of evidence / Data	Reduced, often quantitative, standardized, emphasis on comparability and aggregation	Narrative, extensive, "thick," "rich," potentially idiosyncratic
	Technical quality	Usually privileges reliability as well as content and concurrent validity	Usually privileges consequential and hermeneutical notions of validity
	Score reference	Normative; standards referenced	Standards referenced; criterion referenced; ipsitive
	Unit of analysis / Sample size	Groups of individuals, relatively large sample	Individual, relatively small sample
Procedural/ Logistical			
	Data generation plan	Structured, predetermined, standardized, detailed plan of operation; replication and generalizability desired	Evolving, flexible, authentic conditions desired; replication and generalizability not necessary
	Timing / Frequency of data collection	Infrequent, periodic, or even ad hoc; often collected and stored over long time	Frequent, even ongoing; often collected and stored for short time
	Timeliness of feedback / Data analysis	Delayed	Immediate
	Primary audiences and users	External: policymakers, education leaders and managers, the public	Internal: teachers, students, and parents

decisions about educational opportunities offered to students for the purpose of strengthening their instruction and learning is referred to as assessment *for* learning, and assessment that informs decisions about the accomplishments of programs, schools, and systems is referred to as assessment *of* learning. This distinction roughly parallels that between classroom and large-scale (or clinical and evaluative, or instructional and accountability) testing.

Second, the depictions of assessment *for* and assessment *of* learning that are offered for each element are admittedly exaggerated. Few assessments fully realize these extreme portrayals on many of the elements and none exemplifies them for all sixteen of the elements. The framework is best understood as a template for ideal practice. Any single assessment will exhibit a profile consisting of its positions on each of the continua, positions that will be closer to the assessment *for* education ideal for some elements and farther away from it for others. It is in the analysis of this multidimensional profile that one can judge the suitability of an assessment for one or the other purpose.

The framework presents many elements in terms by which the attributes of assessments *for* learning and *of* learning can be characterized. They are organized into four broad domains: those pertaining to the conceptual framing of the assessments; those describing its form and substance; those qualifying its technical attributes; and those concerned with its procedural and logistical administration. Within each domain exists a number of particular elements. The descriptions of the qualities of each element in terms of assessment *for* and *of* learning are not intended to be exhaustive or exceptionally detailed. Rather, they are framed so as to highlight distinctions between the two types of assessment as they relate to each element.

Upon first examination, the characterizations of ideal qualities with respect to many of the elements seem incompatible. For example, assessment *for* learning calls for very frequent (even ongoing) measurements, while assessment *of* learning requires much less frequent measures. Similarly, the timeliness of feedback must be immediate (or as close to it as is possible) in the case of assessment *for* learning and can typically be much more delayed in assessments *of* learning.

The application of the framework to an existing assessment system (a type of system with which most are familiar) is very illuminating. With this in mind, we turn to the typical state-implemented large-scale assessment system used for evaluative and accountability purposes. An exhaustive and extremely detailed characterization, however, is beyond the scope of this chapter (and probably not interesting or helpful apart from taking up a close examination of a particular state's program). While there are certainly differences from state to state, it is nonetheless possible to characterize such assessments generally and for the most part in a fair manner. Here we will describe the typical state assessment system in terms of the elements presented in the framework. However, for illustrative purposes we will examine only selected elements from each of the domains (i.e., Conceptual, Substantive, Technical, and Procedural/Logistical).

In the typical state assessment system, the element *relationship of assessment to learner* differs between classroom and large-scale assessment. Large-scale assessments tend to minimize this relationship in order to lessen the amount of instructional time given over to the assessment, or to maintain standard testing conditions across students. On the other hand, classroom assessment perspectives permit, and in the ideal, encourage a long-term, involved, and in some instances even participatory (in terms of defining the assessment itself) relationship.

The *consequential validity/desired impact* of the assessment is another element along which interesting differences arise. Both assessment types may lay legitimate claim to improving education, as each provides information that can conceivably be used for its betterment, whether directly or indirectly. Large-scale state assessment does so through more distant mechanisms: the identification of needs (and the required or desired responses to those needs), the allocation of resources, and most recently, the application of accountability influences, so as to increase and focus effort with the goal of improving performance. The consequential impact of classroom assessment is (to the teacher and learner at least) much more immediate and much more profound. It shapes the choice of curricular and instructional approaches; it contributes to the grouping and regrouping of students for instruction; and it directly influences the learning experience.

A third element in the Conceptual domain is *nature/effect of motivation*. Typically in large-scale assessments the test taker is singularly motivated to demonstrate accomplishment by generating the highest scores. This is certainly true as the political and most recently even material salience of those scores increases. Classroom assessment, on the other hand, ideally encourages risk taking and with it the occasional misstep, and it values the demonstration of current and future needs alongside the demonstration of accomplishment.

Additional similarities and differences exist across the other domains as well. For example, in the Substantive domain there are generally differences between these two types of assessment with respect to *locus of authority/control over form and content.* A state's large-scale assessment *of* learning typically vests such authority external to the classroom to maintain common standards across settings and to ensure the validity and credibility of accountability processes. By contrast, classroom assessment *for* learning places authority with teachers and students in the classroom, with interesting (some would say beneficial, some not) social, political, and educational consequences. With respect to *nature of evidence/data*, in the Technical domain, there are typically differences as well. Large-scale assessments have an obligation to serve individuals and groups who work at some distance from the classroom. Therefore, they typically prize highly reduced information. Classroom assessments designed to inform and drive instruction seem to do so best when they deliver thick, rich, descriptive narratives of performance, needs, and means of addressing them.

Reflections and Considerations

Even just this brief application of the framework to a typical state assessment system in contrast to a typical classroom assessment reveals much about the framework itself and the assessments that it describes. First, the very idea of coherence is a complex matter. More than attending to similarities of content, coherence is best understood as requiring critical analysis and effort across a number of elements. Second, while there are clearly differences between large-scale and classroom assessment across these many elements, many are by no means intractable. Innovative thinking coupled with hard work in expanding the science of assessment development opens up the possibility of coherence (or, beyond coherence, resonance in the form of mutual support and benefit), far surpassing anything that we have achieved to date.

Thus the framework raises the question of whether assessments can be designed, constructed, and implemented in ways that serve both ends. While this is an important question to confront, the answers are not as unambiguous as first examination of the framework might suggest. Three factors open up possibilities for coherence and genuine resonance, and within them, mutual benefit across assessment types.

First, the characterizations of the elements must be regarded as a mixture of descriptive and prescriptive statements. Thus, while it is clearly a prescription that assessment *for* learning involves immediate feedback (as much of the research on feedback in the learning process supports this view), it is by no means a prescription that there be delays in the reporting of results in accountability systems. This is rather a descriptive statement of typical practice. Subject only to technological and practical exigencies, assessments *of* learning could serve classroom purposes better if they could be implemented in ways that provided feedback much more quickly. Here the framework challenges assessment developers to use innovations in practice that would greatly enhance the utility of the assessments. Not all of the elements are as clearly or easily determined to be prescriptive or descriptive. Only extensive efforts at innovative development and attendant research and reflection (such as those described in the source chapters of this volume) will reveal the limits and possibilities.

A second factor enhancing the potential for coherence and resonance across these elements is that they are by their nature interdependent and to some extent compensatory. Thus, while the statements about the consequential validity and desired impacts of accountability assessments may lead to problematic and troubling consequences in the classroom (as so many authors have pointed out), the extent to which they necessarily do so depends upon the profile of the assessment across many of the other elements. To the extent that an assessment *of* learning assesses domains of genuine interest in the classroom or does so using item types that are reflective of desired practice there, it may be less troubling to see somewhat more direct impact upon classroom practice. The only way to speculate with confidence (as guidance for development efforts) is through analyses guided by the framework; the only way to know with certainty is through empirical investigation.

A third factor revealed through close analysis of these elements is that thoughtful and clever design can enable an assessment intended primarily for one purpose to provide evidence serving the other. The timing and frequency of assessments discussed above is a good example. While the assessments that serve classroom decisions and practice should be administered frequently (much more so than those for accountability), it is possible to design for classroom purposes with respect to this element and occasionally cull evidence for accountability purposes as appropriate.

Similarly, ample research (including several of the source chapters in this volume) demonstrates the nature of evidence that serves each purpose best. Assessment *for* learning requires descriptive, narrative feedback—what some have termed thick, rich, or extensive. By contrast, most of the evidence found useful by those who work at a great distance from the classroom is highly reduced. Clever design might permit generation of evidence useful in the classroom before subsequent analyses reduce and summarize that evidence in ways appropriate to accountability systems. Similar treatment could well address nearly all of the elements listed in the Technical and Procedural/ Logistical domains of the framework.

It is interesting to note that in many cases there is a directionality or asymmetry to the flow or processing of evidence. In every regard, assessment *for* learning requires evidence that is more complex, detailed, persistently gathered, and timely. This framework and the authors' personal experience in assessment development suggest that to the extent that there is interest in expanding the purposes to which assessment information is appropriately put, synchronicity is most likely found in developing assessments to serve classroom purposes first, and then processing the evidence in ways that make it appropriate to and useful for accountability purposes. (See, for example, LeMahieu, Eresh, & Wallace, 1992; LeMahieu, Gitomer, & Eresh, 1995; LeMahieu & Eresh, 1996 for other examples of assessment development guided by these principles to serve expanded purposes.)

The initiatives described in the source chapters of this volume explore the extent to which assessments can be pushed to serve multiple purposes. From these descriptions, we have distilled a framework that enumerates and organizes the elements to which efforts at coherence must attend. These initiatives begin to illustrate in practical terms the ways in which such coherence can be pursued. There is much more that can be done. Each case that seeks to expand the utility of classroom assessment in service of accountability does so with the well-intended goal of rendering accountability contingent upon assessments that are coherent with classroom goals and practices. However, a certain cautionary tone in the authors' writing betrays a reluctance to commit to the position that one assessment can serve both purposes wholly.

It would seem that classroom assessments pressed into the service of accountability (especially when made politically charged by systems that involve rewards and sanctions) might be rendered useless as assessments for the classroom context. Many have written of the potential for content choices that distort the curriculum, particularly as the political salience of the assessed content is heightened. At the very least, the accountability motives would seem to militate against the risk taking necessary to reveal completely the students' learning needs.

In the face of such potentially disturbing consequences, it would seem that the best accountability assessment is one that describes the status or accomplishment of its focus while not influencing what is measured at all. However, there is ample evidence that the act of measuring educational outcomes most often does, in fact, influence them. Moreover, policymakers who invoke accountability as an essential element of reform rather hope that it will exert such influence.

One outcome of the application of the framework presented here is to expand the range of utility for both kinds of assessment. It instructs and guides the design of assessments that remain true to their first purpose while being expansive along the sixteen elements in ways that define those assessments as more appropriate to certain purposes. The framework also challenges our development of assessments to move beyond mere coherence, defined as noninterference, and to achieve a resonance in complex systems in which the parts are mutually supportive and beneficial.

References

Black, P.J., & Wiliam, D. (1998). *Inside the black box: Raising standards through classroom assessment.* London: King's College School of Education.

Chappuis, S., & Stiggins, R. (2002). Classroom assessment for learning. *Educational Leadership, 60*(1), 40-43.

Cole, N.S. (1984). Testing and the "crisis" in education. *Educational Measurement: Issues and Practice, 3*(3), 4-8.

LeMahieu, P.G., & Wallace, R.C., Jr. (1986). Up against the wall: Psychometrics meets praxis. *Educational Measurement, 5*(1), 12-16.

LeMahieu, P.G., Eresh, J.T., & Wallace, Jr., R.C. (1992). Using student portfolios for public accounting. *The School Administrator: Journal of the American Association of School Administrators, 49*(11), 8-15.

LeMahieu, P.G., Gitomer, D.A., & Eresh, J.T. (1995). Portfolios in large-scale assessment: Difficult but not impossible. *Educational Measurement: Issues and Practice, 13*(3), 11-28.

LeMahieu, P.G., & Eresh, J.T. (1996). Comprehensiveness, coherence and capacity in school district assessment systems. In D.P. Wolf and J.B. Baron (Eds.). *Performance based student assessment: Challenges and possibilities. The Ninety-fifth Yearbook of the National Society for the Study of Education*, Part I (pp. 125-142). Chicago: National Society for the Study of Education.

Pellegrino, J.W., Chudowsky, N., & Glaser, R. (Eds.). (2001). *Knowing what students know: The science and design of educational assessment.* Washington, DC: National Academies Press.

Shepard, L. (2000). The role of assessment in a learning culture. *Educational Researcher, 29*(4), 4-11.

CHAPTER 11

And There Is Much Left To Do

MARGARET A. JORGENSEN

The assessment of learning plays an important role in the instructional process. The effective use of classroom assessments can and does support effective instruction. Further, effective classroom assessments provide a framework for individualized instruction.

This concept is not new. Carroll (1963), Scriven (1967), and Bloom, Hastings, and Madaus (1971) set the stage when they clarified formative versus summative evaluation and advocated for mastery learning. Block (1971), Block, Efthim, and Burns (1989), and Guskey (1997) continued to advocate for the integration of assessment into instruction.

It is time to build an integrated assessment model that includes assessments that diagnose learning strengths and weaknesses, incrementally tracks student progress on critical state content standards, and provides bellwether tools for school administrators to use in identifying potential failing schools. An integral part of the equation would be to provide information from these assessments (e.g., score reports) that helps teachers teach more effectively and helps students understand their own strengths and weaknesses.

In the pages that follow, I offer commentary on select chapters in this volume. I also present a model that extends this work and merges the needs of teachers, students, parents, and administrators so that it becomes more likely that schools improve, teachers are more effective and successful, and students learn what has to be learned. Fueled by the No Child Left Behind Act of 2001, it is time to build this integrated assessment system.

Each of the chapters present part of what is required for such a system. Black and Wiliam (Chapter 2) found that "there is strong and rigorous evidence that improving formative assessment can raise standards

Margaret Jorgensen is the Senior Vice President for Product Research and Innovation at Harcourt Assessment, Inc. She was previously Vice President for Product Development, Psychometrics and Research at Harcourt.

of students' performance" (p. 20). I, too, found this to be the case in research I did in the mid-1990s (Jorgensen, McDevitt, Hensley, & Wolfe, 1998). What isn't clear is the actual cause and effect. Is the change in a pupil's performance the result of improved assessment? Would you get the same effect with frequent assessments of *any* quality? Or can it be that focusing on conversations with teachers about credible evidence of student learning is the key factor in explaining increases in student performance?

I question the feasibility of implementing Black and Wiliam's intervention model. Certainly the ability of teachers to frame thought-provoking questions is key to developing critical thinking in students. This is not assessment; it is the essence of education—leading students to construct meaning. But the question of how teachers gain that ability is not answered in a convincing manner. For instance, take Black and Wiliam's compelling comment that "the only point of asking questions is to raise issues about which the teacher needs information or about which the students need to think" (p. 27). I am hard pressed to think that teaching teachers to frame important questions is simply a function of assessment. Testing professionals can do this work, most assuredly. But this is the heart of teaching, not only assessment.

Black and Wiliam's assertion that a variety of instructional and pedagogical practices is the norm is important to understand. In recent work at Harcourt Assessment, we have identified wide variations in the way teachers use instructional materials. Indeed, the autonomy of the classroom and standards-based instructional practice supports tailored use of textbooks and other instructional materials. In the presence of good teaching, where the particular sequence of materials to be learned is sensitive to the unique needs of individual learners and groups of learners, this defines high-quality instruction. But it also requires a flexible assessment system for use by teachers that reflects with validity what has been taught, as well as when and how. This remains a huge challenge that Black and Wiliam do not address.

Finally, Black and Wiliam cite a fundamental and intolerable situation: when test questions lack validity in relation to the governing set of content standards. Content validity must be obvious and replicable. Any kind of measurement is a waste of time if it is not a valid representation of what should be learned and what is actually taught.

Frederiksen and White's work (Chapter 4) seems very demanding of teachers' time and somewhat contradictory to the U.S. standards-based reform legislated by No Child Left Behind. One can argue the merits of their work, especially the involvement of teachers in the systematic judgment of extended student work. However, as we define and build an integrated assessment system that links classroom assessment to high-stakes tests and ties in curriculum, instruction, and cognitive science at every point, we must be mindful of the realities of teachers' jobs. I find it difficult to imagine a school culture that would support teacher use of a demanding assessment system that did not yield direct results in terms of state content standards and proficiency levels and did not provide useful classroom information.

I do agree that technology can support objective evaluation of student work. However, research shows that teachers do not use most of the technology tools that are available. The interfaces and content knowledge provided with instructional materials are often complicated. In addition, the work required to build tests is often too technical. Both the technology and the technical knowledge required can create a barrier to use.

The notion of standards that cross specific tasks is, of course, compelling, as is the goal of objectively evaluating extended projects. But where is the direct relationship to state-specific content and performance standards?

Forster and Masters (Chapter 3) argue for tools with which teachers can construct high-quality, reliable, and valid assessments. My experience has been the same—with training and tools, teachers can become excellent test developers. But is a teacher's time best spent doing this kind of work? Teachers might instead prefer a variety of published tools, thematic and developmental, that would best meet their own needs as well as the needs of their students. And, if this type of system were available, would teachers embrace it and provide developmentally appropriate instruction for all students? What extra professional development would be required?

The use of videos, magazine-format print materials, and thematic assessments is indicative of where the world of testing will move in the decades ahead. The technology for development and distribution/delivery is already in place in some schools. As bandwidth requirements shrink and T1 lines (or the next generation) become part of every school building's infrastructure, I hope we are able to move to the cutting edge of virtual reality and gaming components to maximize the engagement of students. These technology tools will enable educators to deliver developmentally appropriate curricula in ways that students find challenging, interesting, and rewarding. At the same time, the technology must make these assessments easy to integrate into instruction.

The ultimate composition of such an engaging system is not likely to have modular components such as wall charts, resource kits, videotapes, magazine-style booklets, and workshops unless those components can be seamlessly integrated with a point-and-click delivery tool. However, the conceptual beauty of the progress map is that it becomes the clear and simple way to track an individual student's learning journey.

Wilson and Draney (Chapter 6) extend the work on progress mapping by proposing a common set of variables to link unlike assessments together. This is a very interesting approach. Without a common metric to track achievement across grades and within grades, the value of embedded instructional assessment will be limited. With such a common metric, there would be great power behind the progress maps. This requirement goes beyond a calibration study for the items making up each assessment.

The challenge from a psychometric perspective is to work through what I refer to as the "construct integrity" of this approach. Typically, when tests are equated, those tests are parallel in construction and meaning. The inferences drawn assume equivalent experience for the student and equivalent utility of the score. This approach uses regression analysis to predict a position and confidence band on the common scale score system. This would allow for different types of tests or other scored events to be placed on the common developmental scale without the development of progress variables. With this common frame of reference to describe students' progress, we would give teachers, students, and parents a clear and easy-to-understand picture of achievement growth. Would this approach provide equivalent and equally clear information as would be gained from Wilson and Draney's progress variable mapping?

Within the framework of No Child Left Behind, it is also important to understand the relationship between Wilson and Draney's progress maps and content standards. Can student achievement be mapped on content as well as progress variables? A review of state content standards and high-stakes tests makes it clear that many standards would not routinely be considered cumulative indicators of progress but rather aggregable indicators. Is there a crosswalk between what Wilson and Draney describe as progress variables and the range of content standards driving education reform in the United States today?

If the work of Wilson and Draney generalizes across content areas, and if their definition of progress variables provides the useful and valid information about student growth required under No Child Left

Behind, we would have an elegant yet simple way to understand students' academic progress.

Smithson and Porter (Chapter 5) remind us that development and implementation of content and performance standards is as much a political-social exercise as it is one intended to support teaching and learning. At the same time, these standards must contain enough content to bring policymakers to a level of comfort about educational goals and outcomes so that appropriate decisions can be made about schools, teachers, and students. In the absence of a conceptual framework such as that offered by Smithson and Porter, there is a disconnect between the processes and decisions, creating inequity in use and interpretation.

If instructional and assessment materials, along with the specific content standards each student is expected to learn and be able to do (including those covered in each annual accountability test), were analyzed using this model, what should happen in classrooms would be explicit and consistent within a state. Whether this would cement the narrowing of the curriculum is a question for me. But this type of analysis would surely lead to a rational, coherent, and predictable system of instruction.

In summary, I find the work of Smithson and Porter most powerful in building a rational and coherent system of standards-based education. This methodology, coupled with the potential of the progress maps described so clearly by both Wilson and Draney and Forster and Masters, brings a sharpness and clarity to the principle issues of today's educational reform movement in the United States. Basically, there is a lack of understanding about what content standards mean in terms of enacted curriculum, in terms of instructional materials requirements, and often in terms of test content. There is also a lack of a common metric to describe students' development over the course of their educational experience.

So what is the ideal integrated assessment model? The delivery platform must be online and on paper to meet the needs of all schools and infrastructures. The costs must be reasonable, and the value to teachers, administrators, and students must be high.

Along with this system must come a road map. From the teacher's perspective, an effective assessment system is needed to allow them to pick and choose, from a variety of reliable and valid assessments, exactly the right ones for their classes at specific points in time. The assessments must reflect excellent teaching, fully engage students, and yield information regarding content standards. The scoring must be fast, if not immediate, and the administrative burden must be low.

From the administrator's perspective, an effective assessment system must maximize the likelihood that teachers will be effective. At the same time, the system must identify at-risk students, teachers, and schools relative to high-stakes accountability assessments.

A common metric should be developed and adopted as part of refining the integrated system of classroom and high-stakes testing, which is needed to provide teachers with enough timely information to tailor instruction and thereby maximize learning. This common metric can be articulated across the many progress maps that students would cross as they move from kindergarten to high school graduation. Normative information provides part of the picture, but until and unless the norm-referenced test is fully and completely aligned to state content standards and performance levels on content areas, this, too, will be a disconnect. A common vertical scale that can be used for the calibration of content standards, instructional materials, embedded tests, and high-stakes assessments is a necessity. This common vertical scale would result in multiple and frequent snapshots of student learning throughout each year, all in terms of a common metric.

REFERENCES

Block, J.H. (1971). *Mastery learning: Theory and practice*. New York: Holt, Rinehart & Winston.

Block, J.H., Efthim, H.E., & Burns, R.B. (1989). *Building effective mastery learning schools*. New York: Longman.

Bloom, B.S., Hastings, J.T., & Madaus, G.F. (1971). *Handbook on formative and summative evaluation of student learning*. New York: McGraw-Hill.

Carroll, J.B. (1963). A model of school learning. *Teachers College Record, 64*, 723-733.

Guskey, T.R. (1997). *Implementing mastery learning* (2nd ed.). Belmont, CA: Wadsworth Publishing.

Harcourt Assessment, Inc. (2003). Qualitative research on the use of technology in assessment. San Antonio, TX: Goal Centric.

Jorgensen, M., McDevitt, M., Hensley, T., & Wolfe, S. (Fall 1998). New forms of assessment in reading: Capturing the gist of student performance. *Florida Journal of Educational Research, 38*(1), 1-12.

No Child Left Behind Act of 2001, Pub. L. No. 107-110, 115, Stat. 1425 (2002).

Scriven, M. (1967). The methodology of evaluation. In R.W. Tyler, R.M. Gagné, & M. Scriven (Eds.), *Perspectives of curriculum evaluation* (pp. 39-83). AERA Monograph Series on Curriculum Evaluation, No. 1. Chicago: Rand McNally.

CHAPTER 12

Converging Paths: Common Themes in Making Assessments Useful to Teachers and Systems

JOHN L. SMITHSON

Assessment, accountability, validity, alignment, and fairness are all interrelated terms with particular currency in today's educational environment. The U.S. education system has become particularly preoccupied with issues related to these terms as a result of recent federal legislation. The contributions to this volume from England and Australia indicate, however, that similar issues are being addressed around the world. Indeed, the Third International Mathematics and Science Survey (TIMSS) itself indicates an international interest in the use of assessments to make judgments about educational quality and system efficiency and efficacy. All of which make the collection of work in this volume quite timely.

What strikes me most about the varied contributions presented here is the sense of converging conceptual and strategic frameworks, each arising in one of several different places, for diverse purposes, with unique characteristics; yet each concerned in some way with the careful, systematic, and coherent management of assessment information. In particular, three unifying themes emerge from this set of papers: 1) the value of formative assessment and the need for training and materials to assist teachers in conducting and using formative assessments; 2) the need for a systematic conceptual framework within which to manage a formative-assessment-driven curriculum; and 3) a general agreement (in broad terms) about what such a framework should look like. There is one other theme addressed by several of the authors: the link between classroom assessments and accountability programs. There is less clarity and agreement among the authors on this last theme, however. Each of these themes is worthy of comment.

John L. Smithson is a research associate at the Wisconsin Center for Education Research, University of Wisconsin–Madison.

Formative Assessment: The Value and the Need

Paul Black and Dylan Wiliam (Chapter 2) remind us of the research evidence supporting the positive effects of formative assessment on student performance. They also remind us of the broad territory that formative assessment covers, including such behaviors as the questions posed and answered during classroom discussion and when working with students individually. Indeed, it is formative assessment that distinguishes education from instruction, and educators from content experts. Black and Wiliam's discussion provides some sense of the skill and effort required to conduct quality formative assessment, while making the point that far too many teachers have little familiarity with the skills and knowledge required to use formative assessments effectively. It seems ironic then that high-stakes summative assessments are viewed (and in many ways are) the engine that is supposed to drive educational improvement, while formative assessments are given relatively little (though growing) attention despite their potential to provide the real horsepower necessary to reach the goal that summative assessment and accountability are expected to attain.

While Black and Wiliam go furthest in setting out the argument for the value of quality formative assessments, each of the projects described within these pages is in one way or another concerned with the use of classroom-based formative assessments as a tool for improving student performance on the high-stakes/high-profile summative assessments typically used to hold students, teachers, and schools (and now, in the U.S., districts and states) accountable. Whether talking about the Developmental Assessment Resource for Teachers (DART), the BEAR Assessment System, the ThinkerTools Project or the King's-Medway-Oxfordshire Formative Assessment Project (KMOFAP), formative assessment lies at the heart of each. The authors also appear to agree on the need for training and supplemental materials to assist teachers in making the most of classroom assessments.

Our own work with content languages (Chapter 5) is arguably somewhat removed from formative assessments, since we are not directly involved in the training, development, or use of such tools. Nonetheless, we do provide support, materials, and structure for a number of professional development providers who find the Surveys of Enacted Curriculum (SEC) framework useful for examining student work, managing and analyzing formative assessments, and interpreting assessment results. Though not directly involved in the development and use of formative assessments, we are strong advocates of their potential for increasing student performance.

The Importance of a Systematic Framework for Managing Assessment Data

Formative assessment, by its very nature, is a data-driven process. While a master educator may use elements of formative assessment in a dynamic, moment-to-moment, context-sensitive, and student-centered way, even such skilled practice requires the teacher to collect, analyze, and respond to data regarding the extent of student understanding and ability, albeit in a more fluid and integrated way. The master educator has managed to internalize the data processing required to conduct such formative evaluations "on the fly" as a seamless part of instructional practice. For the rest of us, a more explicit structure is necessary for managing, analyzing, interpreting, and acting upon assessment data.

Each of the projects described in this book includes some sort of conceptual framework for managing, organizing, analyzing, and evaluating assessments, student work, or both. The BEAR assessment system utilizes progress variables, DART uses learning outcomes, substrands, and levels, and both the KMOFAP and ThinkerTools projects use various types of criteria to accomplish much the same goal.

In most cases, the conceptual framework used appears to be designed to serve two, at times competing, purposes. Pedagogically, the framework must provide a means for distinguishing various levels of student accomplishment, reflecting what Wilson and Draney (Chapter 6) describe as a developmental perspective of student learning. At the same time, the structure needs to reflect the performance requirements demanded by the relevant educational authority (facilitating coherence). In some cases these requirements will be stated as performance standards that can be easily embedded within the pedagogical structure of student development that is being employed. As often as not, however, performance requirements will be defined simply (or primarily) in terms of cut scores (the minimum score required on a given assessment for a student to be classified as proficient) on standardized achievement tests.

Whether summative indicators are described as achievement scores or more descriptively in terms of what students should know and be able to do, the danger is that they will supplant rather than supplement the developmental, learning-based structure upon which formative assessments should be based. A good conceptual framework for supporting formative assessment will assist in identifying where a given student is on the developmental path for a given curriculum, while also clearly delineating where along that developmental path performance requirements have been set for different age groups. This can help teachers and even students themselves see where they are in terms of performance relative to some performance standard, thereby inviting consideration of strategies to increase performance. Thus, not only the assessments but also the conceptual framework for structuring and managing assessment data should reflect the characteristics of coherence, comprehensiveness, and continuity described by Wilson and Draney.

Agreement on the General Features of the Conceptual Framework

While each of these projects uses its own unique conceptual framework and terminology, and in some cases does not directly address the characteristics of coherence, comprehensiveness, and continuity, similarities can be discerned from each of the frameworks employed that reflect general agreement on the importance of these characteristics to the successful implementation of an effective assessment system.

A common structural feature for each of the projects described here has been a focus on expectations for student performance. Whether using the term *progress variables, learning outcomes, criteria for high level cognitive and social skills,* or *cognitive demand* all the authors note the importance of paying attention to indicators of students' cognitive abilities in relation to assessments and the curriculum. Even Black and Wiliam's work, with its constructivist orientation and consequent reluctance to force a predetermined structure upon teachers, clearly encourages teachers to employ criteria upon which they and students could base feedback of student performance.

While this focus on expectations/criteria for student performance is clearly emphasized by most of the authors, it is not the only dimension of assessment (whether formative or summative) that is a common feature of the frameworks employed. Attention to the subject matter content itself is a key element for managing, analyzing, and acting upon assessment information. This may seem obvious, but it is a dimension that easily falls into the background of discussions about assessments, perhaps *because* it is so obvious. Nonetheless, if we are serious about tracking student progress over time, and we make formative use of that information to improve learning, it is just as essential that the topics covered be documented and integrated with the information on student performance. In other words, student performance must be measured not only in terms of the cognitive abilities demonstrated but also in terms of the subject matter knowledge assessed. Indeed, both of these elements (or dimensions, as we prefer to say) of teaching and learning are implicit to the characteristics of comprehensiveness, coherence, and continuity described by Wilson and Draney. That these two dimensions of teaching and learning should play central roles in the conceptual frameworks used to monitor and assess learning should, however, come as no surprise. What students should know (i.e., their knowledge of subject matter) and be able to do (i.e., performance indicators or learning outcomes) is the very language most often used to describe content and performance standards.

The Roles of Classroom-Based Assessment and System Accountability

While there appears to be general agreement among the authors on the importance of formative assessments and the need for assessment systems to reflect characteristics of comprehensiveness, coherence, and continuity, there remains one theme in the current work for which there is some diversity of opinion. This concerns the role of formative assessments in educational accountability.

Two issues worthy of comment emerge from discussion on this topic. For convenience, we can summarize these as arguments regarding desirability and issues regarding feasibility. Of these, the argument that classroom-based assessments (presumably, though not necessarily, formative in nature) are feasible for use as contributing data sources for accountability purposes has received the most attention in these pages.

Judging the feasibility of classroom-based assessments as a component of an accountability system hinges in part on the nature of the accountability system in place and in part on the nature of the performance goals being assessed. In the DART program described by Forster and Masters (Chapter 3), we see an apparent (and presumably successful) example of the systematizing of classroom assessment in such a way as to allow the aggregation of classroom assessment data across teachers and schools to serve the informational needs of the larger educational authority. While not entirely familiar with the accountability system of Australia, I presume the focus is on "system-wide monitoring of student achievement." It is important to distinguish this type of accountability from accountability as experienced in the U.S. In the DART example, schools and teachers are presumably not strictly "held accountable" in the sense of rewards and sanctions for meeting or failing to meet specified performance goals. The aggregation of classroom assessment information is collected for "monitoring" purposes, which, though worthwhile and no doubt valuable in identifying problem areas, is not the same as losing funds or facing takeover by external agencies as is the case in the U.S. Teachers participating in DART were not facing specific sanctions based on the scores they gave their students, which is good, since the information fed into the accountability system was based on teacher reports (evaluations) of student progress. If teachers were being held accountable in this way, Forster and Masters would have almost certainly felt compelled to provide evidence concerning the reliability and validity of the teacher evaluations, which is exactly what we see in descriptions of the BEAR and ThinkerTools projects.

Note this is not a criticism of the DART program at all. In our work, concerned with describing instructional content (defined as the intersection of topic and cognitive demand utilizing a two-dimensional taxonomy or language), we frequently aggregate teacher reports in order to get regional and system-wide descriptions of practice. Much like DART, the goal here is to monitor practice and progress. Such information is quite valuable in monitoring system change and diagnosing problem areas. What we are adamant about though, when working with district and state entities, is that the data *not* be used for accountability purposes, precisely because it would bring into question the very teacher reports upon which the monitoring function depends.

The BEAR and ThinkerTools programs address this credibility problem by collecting and reporting information on the reliability ("accuracy and comparability" to use Frederiksen and White's phrase, "technical quality" to use Wilson and Draney's) of teacher scoring. Frederiksen and White (Chapter 4) point out that such data can be used to further analyze the scoring behaviors of teachers (e.g., examining patterns of how teachers use evidence to base their scoring decisions for various outcome criteria). Wilson and Draney, in addition to pointing out the need for "quality control indices such as reliability" (p. 143) to ensure that classroom-based performance assessments "be held to high standards of fairness" (p. 142), incorporate item response models in order to "put richer interpretational information into the hands of teachers" (p. 143). The efforts in these regards are commendable. Classroom-based performance assessments *should* strive for high standards of fairness. Even if the quality indices are not as high as one might like, the mere fact that they are calculated and reported helps the credibility and informative value of classroom assessments. If nothing else, low measures can be analyzed to diagnose problem areas in the scoring procedures, thus providing not only recommendations for improvement but also the means by which to judge the degree of improvement the amended procedures yield.

However, if the goal is to use classroom-based performance assessments for accountability purposes, then these indicators of quality must not only be calculated, they must be acceptably high. While the results reported by Wilson and Draney on scoring quality are good (though not complete), the results reported by Frederiksen and White seem less so, leaving the overall question of scoring quality somewhat murky. In any case, it is one issue to determine just what the "standard" should be for such indicators, and yet another to establish what happens if this quality standard is not met. It would seem that these issues should be addressed before classroom-based performance assessments are used for system accountability (as opposed to system monitoring).

Even if it is feasible to implement an assessment system wherein classroom-based assessments are employed as part of the accountability program (and that remains an open question), it does not make such a system desirable. In judging desirability it is important that we be clear on what is meant by the term *accountability*. Three notions of accountability emerge from the various discussions in this book: monitoring, student accountability, and system accountability.

The weakest form of accountability serves a monitoring function. Here accountability means, literally, "the ability to account for." When the authors argue for a conceptual framework with which to collect and analyze student performance and progress as indicated by formative and summative assessments, that framework serves precisely this accounting function. Like the accountant's ledger, progress maps provide a means for recording, accumulating, and comparing information, that is, information for *monitoring* student progress. This monitoring can (and should) take place at various levels of the system. Teachers monitor individual student progress; schools, departments, and teachers monitor classroom progress; districts monitor school progress; and states monitor regional and district progress. But monitoring is something quite different from those forms of accountability that are used to distribute rewards and sanctions.

While classroom-based performance assessments may be fine for monitoring purposes, they become more difficult to justify as the stakes for students increase. When student advancement hinges on student performance, we have student accountability. This type of accountability raises issues of fairness. These are often discussed in terms of test reliability and validity but also include such concerns as accommodation, equity, and opportunity to learn. Teacher-scored performance assessments may be suitable for determining assignment and course grades, but if the test prevents promotion to the next grade, more concern will be raised about teacher differences and score validity. Use the test to determine whether a student can graduate high school, and the system may find itself having to justify its assessment system in a court of law.

Move to the level of system accountability and the complications are magnified. Now those other than students are held accountable for student performance. Leaving aside the statistical and technical machinations used to set and justify decisions about school-, district-, and now state-level performance, it seems inappropriate and unnecessary to use teacher evaluative judgments (which themselves will be of varying quality) about student performance as evidence upon which to assign rewards and sanctions to states, districts, schools, and ultimately the teachers themselves. Even if classroom-based scoring processes were reliable and valid (no small feat in itself), it is not at all clear that it is either wise or desirable to structure an accountability system with rewards and sanctions that are in part based on the reports of the very teachers that could be negatively affected by those reports. This would likely weaken both the reporting and the pedagogical value of the data gathered from formative classroom-based assessments.

There is sufficient semantic wiggle room among the various authors' comments on accountability that it is not completely clear whether, or to what extent, the authors agree or disagree about the role of classroom-based assessments in an accountability system. Although it is not clear that any of the authors would actually argue that rewards and sanctions for elements of the system should be based on teacher reports of student performance, I would argue against both the feasibility and desirability of such use. If, however, the term accountability is used to reference a monitoring function, then there may be no disagreement at all among the contributors to this volume. Even if classroom-based assessments are intended to serve student accountability, the authors may find room for agreement, assuming adequate measures of scoring reliability are demonstrably attained.

In closing, it is worth repeating that the authors appear to agree on several important points: the value of formative assessments; the need for training and materials to support such assessments, including a conceptual framework that facilitates the characteristics of comprehensiveness, coherence, and continuity; and, in general, the primary components of such a framework. When scholars working largely (albeit not completely) in isolation from one another reach similar conclusions and build similar models, it is a good sign that worthwhile progress is being made.

CHAPTER 13

The Risks of Coherence[1]

PAMELA A. MOSS

The major premise underlying this volume is that enhanced coherence between classroom assessment and system-level accountability is a good thing—assuming, of course, that the assessments are consistent with sound learning principles. Working from this assumption, four of the five source chapters provide promising assessment and accountability tools that enable and support enhanced coherence; the fifth source chapter, by Black and Wiliam, appears to enact a somewhat different relationship between assessment and accountability that I will address later in my commentary. Although acknowledging the potential benefits of coherence, I draw on critical and sociocultural theory to explore the risks of enhanced coherence, even when the standards, curriculum, instructional practices, and assessments through which it is enacted represent sound pedagogy. Are there ways in which enhanced coherence can undermine important outcomes? In what ways might there be too much of a good thing?

What Kind of Tools Do the Source Chapters Provide Toward What Kind of System?

The focus of my criticism is not on the usefulness of the individual sets of tools but rather on how they might be incorporated into an educational system at the district, state, or national level. What kind of system are they likely to enable, and with what effects?

Three of the five source chapters offer rich examples of assessments that can be simultaneously used in the classroom and aggregated to provide system-level indicators (Foster & Masters, Chapter 3; Frederiksen & White, Chapter 4; Wilson & Draney, Chapter 6). These

Pamela A. Moss is Associate Professor, 4220 School of Education, University of Michigan, Ann Arbor, MI 48109-1259; e-mail: pamoss@umich.edu. Her areas of specialization are at the intersections of educational assessment, validity theory, and interpretive social science.

assessments share many strengths: they offer opportunities for students' engagement in active learning around meaningful activities; they scaffold teachers' (and students') judgments of students' work; they provide the means of documenting progress (or development) over time within classrooms; and they can be aggregated and compared over time and location to provide system-level information about status and progress on the particular learning outcomes. If enacted as intended, there is no question that the information available about student learning outside the classroom would be richer and that the press to perform well on these curriculum-embedded assessments would be far less detrimental than with conventional state-sponsored paper-and-pencil tests. A fourth chapter (Smithson & Porter, Chapter 5) provides an intentionally more generic set of indicators for examining the degree of alignment among standards, curricula, assessments, instructional content, and so on. Although initially intended for policymakers to address questions about policy implementation in the classroom, the system can be and has been used by teachers and local administrators at various levels of the educational system to assist with decisions about curriculum and instruction. Summary graphs and statistics display the degree of alignment between different parts of the system. The fifth chapter, by Black and Wiliam (Chapter 2), focuses more on a professional development model that supports teachers in working collaboratively to develop the practice of formative assessment in their classrooms. Although one could imagine these professional development practices working in conjunction with the tools described in the other four chapters, as Black and Wiliam enact them they support different assessment practices in different classrooms, and coherence with indicators at other levels of the system is indirect and post hoc.

The sort of coherent system Wilson imagines in the opening chapter of this volume involves "the integration of assessment frameworks and methods across all levels of the assessment system, from the classroom to the system level" (p. 3). He called for system-level assessments that are directly usable in the classroom, that could serve as a model for teachers designing their own assessments, and that could "give an appropriate place in the accountability system to the professional knowledge and standing of teachers" by incorporating "teacher judgments of student performance that are the classroom reflection of student learning" (p. 3). Wilson pointed us toward the National Research Council's *Knowing What Students Know* (Pellegrino, Chudowsky, & Glaser, 2001; hereafter KWSK) as a theoretical resource, drawing on psychometrics and cognitive science, for coordinating our various efforts. As the authors of KWSK describe it, "a vision for the future is that assessments at all levels—from classroom to state—will work together in a system that is comprehensive, coherent, and continuous" (p. 9). KWSK, along with four of the five source contributions to this volume, appears to be consistent with this vision. I will call this vision of a "comprehensive, coherent, continuous" system *coherence-through-alignment*. Coherence-through-alignment appears to promote commonality in curriculum frameworks, language, and methods across classrooms and throughout the levels of the educational system (albeit with differing degrees of specificity). The brunt of this commentary, then, explores the risks of coherence-through-alignment. Then, I will sketch out some principles for an alternative vision of coherence—*coherence-through-negotiation-of-meaning*—a phrase appropriated from Wenger (1998). Although most congenial to Black and Wiliam, I imagine how the tools provided in all five of the source chapters might work within a vision of coherence-through-negotiation-of-meaning, a vision with its own risks and benefits that supports more diversity in classroom practice. I do not mean to portray alignment and negotiation of meaning as antonyms. In fact, negotiation of meaning can result in alignment and alignment can encourage negotiation of meaning such that local actors come to "own" the concepts provided in the assessment system. The distinction between alignment and negotiation of meaning is intended to signal a difference in emphasis in the way in which coherence is promoted.

It is important to note that the part of the vision Wilson described— as "harnessing this flood of assessment information . . . of learning *within* the classroom, and as the source of crucial information flowing *out* of classrooms"—is not illustrated in any of the five source chapters (p. 2). Although it appears that teachers were actively and productively involved in the design of the three classroom-assessment systems illustrated, subsequent use of these systems in other classrooms provides a far more limited role for teacher input. Thus, for most classrooms, these assessments will arrive already developed by others and will be implemented by the classroom teacher, whose productive role in the assessment will likely be restricted to activities like judging student work using the guidelines provided, perhaps developing tasks consistent with a predetermined template, choosing the time of implementation, and of course, supporting students in making progress toward the goals. Smithson and Porter are "skeptical" about the possibility of using classroom-developed assessment for accountability purposes: "The challenges to building such a system in a way that guarantees some standardization of results across classrooms and teachers seem insurmountable to us" (p. 128). Earlier work by Wilson (1994, reprised in chapter 1 of this volume) offers teachers the possibility of considerably more flexibility in designing assessments. Even here, however, to be viable, these assessments must enact a common language and curriculum framework across classrooms.

Whether the classroom assessments are externally imposed or locally shaped and harnessed for the larger system, they make classroom practice externally visible in a way—comprehensive, coherent, and continuous—that has not been previously possible. What are the potential consequences of such a system of routine visibility?

A Critical Response to Coherence-Through-Alignment

Critical theory and the research practices it supports illuminate a number of important questions that might be raised about the vision of coherence-through-alignment coupled with potential for "continuous" visibility. At the heart of these questions is an overarching concern with the effects of the assessment and accountability system on the people involved: *"What kind of people do they foster?"* (Scott, 1998, p. 348).

What Is Critical Theory?

Critical theory, as I am using it here, encompasses a diverse constellation of practices and theories that share some common features.[2] An important aim of critical research is to illuminate the dialectical relationship between social structures (like assessment and accountability systems) and local practices (like interactions among principals, teachers, and students or among school board members or legislators)—how each constructs, shapes, or challenges the other. Critical researchers typically ask questions about how social structures and local practices influence conceptions of knowledge or progress, conceptions of self and others, and differences in access to society's good. Analyses involving *different* perspectives, practices, and contexts are central to critical research because they illuminate the categories of thought and action "we" take for granted, situate them in the social historical conditions in which they arose, and allow us to imagine how things might be otherwise. A primary aim of critical research is social change. Although critical research shares this aim with many conceptions of social research, it privileges practices that enable change, not primarily through external controls but rather through action orienting self-reflection. In other words, by helping us become aware of the social forces that shape our categories of thought and action, we can make better informed decisions about how and whether to change our practice (which in turn can affect the social structures within which we live). Critical theory reminds us, as well, that these sorts of questions are as important to ask about social scientists as they are about the people we study (Bourdieu, 1988, 1991; McCarthy, 1994): "social researchers are themselves engaged in socially situated forms of action," and "bringing this to consciousness and examining its implications" is a central role of critical theory (McCarthy, pp. 14-15).

What sorts of questions might be raised from a critical theoretic perspective about a system that privileges coherence-through-alignment, and what evidence might be gathered to address them?

The Genesis and Effects of an Indicator System

I begin with a historical narrative of the use of an indicator system in quite a different context. James C. Scott opens his book *Seeing Like a State* with a narrative of the development of scientific forestry in late eighteenth-century Prussia and Saxony—a narrative that also serves as a metaphor for examining state-sponsored indicator and planning systems, which make local practice visible, and hence manipulable (Scott, 1998, p. 2), from afar. Below, I have cobbled together excerpts from Scott's narrative. I invite readers to imagine the questions that this narrative might prompt us to ask about assessment and accountability programs.

The development of scientific forestry in Prussia and Saxony served the state's need to monitor and manage its resources:

The early modern European state, even before the development of scientific forestry, viewed its forests primarily through the fiscal lens of revenue needs [although] . . . other concerns—such as timber for shipbuilding, state construction and fuel for the economic security of its subjects—were not entirely absent from official management. These concerns also had heavy implications for state revenue and security. (pp. 11-12)

Increasingly precise measurements in scientific forestry enabled the state to engage in systematic planning by achieving a synoptic view of the forest:

The new forestry science was a subdiscipline of what was called cameral science, an effort to reduce the fiscal management of a kingdom to scientific principles that would allow systematic planning. . . .

The final result of such calculations was the development of elaborate tables with data organized by tree size and age under specified conditions of normal growth and maturation. By radically narrowing his vision to commercial wood, the state forester had, with his tables, paradoxically achieved a synoptic view of the entire forest. (pp. 14-15)

Scott notes, however, that much was missing from this abstracted vision of the forest:

Missing, of course, were all those trees, bushes, and plants holding little or no potential for state revenue. Missing as well were all those parts of trees, even revenue-bearing trees, which might have been useful to the population but whose value could not be converted into fiscal receipts. Here, I have in mind foliage and its uses as fodder and thatch; fruits, as food for people and domestic animals; twigs and branches, as bedding, fencing, hop poles, and kindling; bark and roots, for making medicines and for tanning; sap, for making resins; and so forth. (p. 12)

The set of state-sponsored indicators then suggested strategies for forest management:

The fact is that forest science and geometry, backed by state power, had the capacity to transform the real, diverse, and chaotic old-growth forest into a new, more uniform forest that closely resembled the administrative grid of its techniques. To this end, the underbrush was cleared, the number of species was reduced (often to monoculture), and plantings were done simultaneously and in straight rows on large tracts. These management practices . . . produced the monocultural, even-age forests that eventually transformed the . . . abstraction to reality. (p. 15)

This transformation of the diverse, old growth forest to the monocultural, even-age forest made centralized management more viable:

The more uniform the forest, the greater the possibilities for centralized management; the routines that could be applied minimized the need for the discretion necessary in the management of diverse old-growth forests. (p. 16)

And, it resulted in spectacular short-term success:

In the short run, this experiment in the radical simplification of the forest to a single commodity was a resounding success. . . . The productivity of the new forests reversed the decline in the domestic wood supply, provided more uniform stands and more usable wood fiber, raised the economic return of forest land, and appreciably shortened rotation times (the time it took to harvest a stand and plant another). (p. 19)

It was not until after the second round of planting that negative consequences of the system became apparent:

The negative biological and ultimately commercial consequences of the stripped-down forest became painfully obvious only after the second rotation of conifers had been planted. . . . An exceptionally complex process involving soil building, nutrient uptake, and symbiotic relations among fungi, insects, mammals, and flora . . . . was apparently disrupted, with serious consequences . . . [including] thinner and less nutritious soils, . . . more vulnerab[ility] to massive storm felling, . . . and a favorable habitat for all the "pests" which were specialized to that species [of trees]. (p. 20)

Scott attributes the negative consequences in large part to the radical simplicity of the "scientific forest" (p. 20).

Any unmanaged forest may experience stress from storms, disease, drought, fragile soil, or severe cold. A diverse, complex forest, however, with its many species of tress, its full complement of birds, insects, and mammals is far more resilient—far more able to withstand and recover from such injuries—than pure stands. Its very diversity and complexity help to inoculate it against devastation. . . .
  The simplified forest is a more vulnerable system, especially over the long haul, as its effects on soil, water, and "pest" populations become manifest. Such dangers can only partly be checked by the use of artificial fertilizers, insecticides, and fungicides. (pp. 21-22)

This simplified, vulnerable forest led to the development of "restoration forestry" and the need for sustained outside intervention to attempt to remedy the consequences:

"Restoration forestry" attempted with mixed results to create a virtual ecology, while denying its chief sustaining condition: diversity. . . . Given the fragility of the simplified production forest, the massive outside intervention that was required to establish it—we might call it the administrators' forest—is increasingly necessary in order to sustain it as well. (pp. 20, 22)

This narrative of the effects of centralized planning coupled with routine visibility is not an isolated case. Scott's book takes us through case after case—collective farms, planned cities, and so on—that trace the genesis and effects of large, state-sponsored systems that make local practice "legible—and hence manipulable from afar" (p. 2). Although acknowledging the egalitarian and emancipatory intent of such systems and the unjust social orders they attempted to replace,

Scott documents a consistent pattern of failure for social planning that also does not nurture local knowledge and practical skill.

Without denying the incontestable benefits either of the division of labor or of hierarchical coordination of some tasks, I want to make a case for institutions that are instead multifunctional, plastic, diverse, and adaptable—in other words, institutions that are powerfully shaped by metis [that is, "forms of knowledge embedded in local experience" (p. 311)]. . . .

To any planned, built, or legislated form of social life, one may [ask]: to what degree does it promise to enhance the skills, knowledge and responsibility of those who are a part of it? On narrower institutional grounds, the question would be how deeply that form is marked by the values and experience of those who comprise it. (pp. 353, 355)

Scott's narrative raises questions about some potential consequences of a system that privileges coherence-through-alignment and routine visibility: it does not illuminate (at least as currently illustrated) features of the local context that are essential to decision making; it provides opportunity (whether intended or not) for a large-scale *intervention* into local social systems (districts, schools, and classrooms); it supports a single set of centrally determined learning goals across the system (albeit at different levels of specificity for different approaches, with Wilson, 1994, offering the most flexible alternatives for teachers) and thus limits diversity; it enacts (whether intended or not) a particular view of the social world of schools with different responsibilities for different actors and thus reduces opportunity for local actors to influence or shape the system by which they are judged. I will consider each of these issues in turn. In so doing, I will draw heavily on Bryk and Hermanson's (1993) benchmark chapter on educational indicator systems, which uses different theoretical perspectives to raise many of the same issues.

Assessment Systems Are, at Best, Partial Representations

With the exception of Smithson and Porter, there is not much attention paid in the source chapters to how the available information about student learning will be used by decision makers outside the classroom or about what additional information is needed to enable sufficient understanding to make good decisions. In this sense, the set of indicators illustrated in any one of these chapters is incomplete. This is not, in itself, a criticism, as none of the authors intended to illustrate a "complete" indicator system. Questions of the purposes to which the system will be put, however, are crucial to understanding and anticipating its effects; and so I consider them here even though they may reflect concerns about issues not addressed in the source chapters.

Bryk and Hermanson (1993) worry that "although discussions about educational indicators may acknowledge the diverse aims of education, it is nonetheless common to presume that one can focus on the "core of schooling"—academic achievement and the processes instrumentally linked to it—while ignoring everything else" (p. 456). For instance, they note, "there is growing evidence . . . that the social structure of schools influences student engagement and teacher commitment, both of which are linked to students' academic achievement" (p. 456). These concerns raise issues of fairness as well as sufficiency: "Since the information system will shape the nature of . . . contests [over schools' aims and methods], concern must focus on issues of fairness toward all interests in these debates. Without care and sensitivity, seemingly technical decisions can advantage some interests and disadvantage others" (pp. 473-474).

In the classroom, the partial nature of an indicator system is less of a problem, since the teacher has ongoing and intimate knowledge of the social world of the classroom. A student's performance on a particular assessment can be interpreted in light of the teacher's goals, students' interests, established norms and routines, the past experiences of students inside and outside the classroom, the situated meanings of words in the classroom (Gee, 1999), the learning opportunities the assessment follows, all that was said as the assessment was undertaken, the particular uses to which the assessment will be put, and so on.

Harnessing classroom assessment for use outside the classroom entails stripping away the context. Once removed from the classroom to another social context, these indicators cannot be understood in the same way; they require "recontextualization" in the new social context in order for their salience to be adequately understood (Bryk & Hermanson, 1993, p. 458). Bryk and Hermanson outline what a more complete model might look like:

In outline form, a complete model would require a multilevel formulation, which includes at a minimum, classroom-level concepts about student learning, teacher pedagogy, and classroom practices; school level concepts about curriculum organization, academic and disciplinary policy, quality of social relations, adequacy of available resources, and school leadership; and, similarly, key concepts that capture the major support and administrative functions at the district and higher levels of government. . . . The educative influences of larger cultural forces and other social institutions . . . would also have to be included. In addition, the model component for student experiences and outcomes would need an explicit developmental dimension [something, I should note, that three of the source chapters in this volume provide]. The interrelationships among student experiences in the first five years of life, learning in elementary and secondary schools, and adult outcomes including active citizenship, workplace productivity, and personal well-being would also have to be specified. (p. 462)

Bryk and Hermanson caution, however, that "our scientific knowledge about schooling is partial" (p. 462) and that it is "nothing less than a seductive delusion to presume that we could develop a comprehensive indicator model of sufficient intelligence to support instrumental use" (p. 462). By "instrumental" they refer to the use of information "to externally control schools through instruments such as rule writing, administrative sanctions, and incentives" (p. 453). They call, instead, for an "enlightenment" model of indicator use (an idea I will return to in the conclusion).

In this view indicators are of value in that they can broaden our understanding of problems and catalyze new ideas. They can signal new problem areas, offer conceptual frames in which to discuss these issues, provide some useful information for initial brainstorming about possible solutions, and, more generally, inform the broader public. (p. 465)

This use of indicators appears more consistent with what is imagined by the editor and the authors of the source chapters in this volume. Wilson calls for assessment and accountability systems that "give an appropriate place in the accountability system to the professional knowledge and standing of teachers" (p. 3); Smithson and Porter note that "successful data use . . . appear[s] to match many of the characteristics associated with professional learning communities. . . . These characteristics have less to do with the technical skills of interpreting and using data and more to do with the professional culture of the school and the ability of faculty to engage in collegial discussions about practice" (p. 123).

Indeed, practices envisioned in these chapters stand in stark contrast with the instrumental vision of assessment and accountability enacted, for instance, in the federal No Child Left Behind Act of 2001 (Pub. L. 107-110) (see Linn, 2003, and Linn, Baker, & Bettebenner, 2002, for critical reviews). There, schools that do not meet their states' goals for annual yearly progress, in terms of overall and subgroup achievement gains, face increasingly severe requirements and sanctions. Clearly the source chapters in this volume intend a far more enlightened vision of reform. However, even assuming the assessment and accountability tools were *intended* for "enlightenment" rather than "instrumental" purposes, important questions remain about the effects of an assessment system that permits comprehensive and continuous visibility from outside and above. That is the issue I turn to next.

Externally Imposed Assessment and Accountability Systems Entail Interventions into Local Social Systems

Scott's case studies compel us to begin with the testable assumption that any externally imposed assessment and accountability system is an intervention into the social system it seeks to describe. The assessment system highlights certain activities or outcomes as important and worthy of particular attention; it offers a particular vision of progress; and it gives people a language to use in understanding themselves and others. It is not and cannot be a neutral language that simply describes reality: symbolic representations, once incorporated into local discourses, shape the social reality they describe in theory- and value-laden ways.

Let's look for the moment at what are arguably the two most general sets of conceptual tools this volume has to offer: Smithson and Porter's language for describing instructional content and KWSK's assessment triangle. Smithson and Porter characterize their language for collecting descriptions of classroom practice as a "theory neutral tool" (p. 125) with respect to pedagogical and curricular orientation. However, the resulting language, as they describe it, is "based on a two-dimensional model of instructional content consisting of topics and cognitive demand" (p. 105). To what extent can this language be "theory neutral"? Wilson (Chapter 1) asked all contributors to use the assessment triangle from KWSK in order to "consider this complex issue in a coherent way":

According to KWSK, assessment consists of 1) a cognition aspect (the model one has of a student's cognition); 2) an observation aspect (the methods one uses to assess the student's cognition); and 3) an interpretation aspect (the methods one uses to relate the observations to the cognition model). (p. 2)

Although neither Wilson nor the authors of KWSK portray this as a theory-neutral tool, they propose it as a conceptual tool with general relevance for assessment designers. In fact, the authors of KWSK are somewhat more prescriptive: "These three elements," they assert, "must be explicitly connected and designed as a coordinated whole. If not, the meaningfulness of inferences drawn from the assessment will be compromised" (Pellegrino, Chudowsky, & Glaser, 2001, p. 2).

In what ways might these conceptual tools shape the social contexts in which they are used? Perhaps the best way to address this question is to contrast it with a vision of learning that this language ignores. From a sociocultural perspective,[3] learning involves not only acquiring new knowledge and skill, but taking on a new identity and social position within a particular discourse (Gee, 1999; Gee, Hull, & Lankshear, 1996) or community of practice (Wenger, 1998).[4] As Wenger puts it, learning "changes who we are" (p. 5) "by changing our ability to participate, to belong" (p. 227) and "to experience our life and the world as meaningful" (p. 5). Thus, learning is perceived through changing relationships among the learner, the other human participants, and the tools (material and symbolic) available in a given context (Beach, 1999; Chaiklin & Lave, 1993; Cole, 1996; Gee; Gee, Hull, & Lankshear; Mehan, 1993; Wertsch, Del Rio, & Alverez, 1995). From this perspective, evidence of learning cannot just focus on the cognition of the student—what takes place inside the head of the learner, as the assessment triangle would imply; rather it must focus on the *interaction* among the learner, the other actors (e.g., teachers and students), and the symbolic and material resources available. The situation rather than the individual becomes the unit of analysis. As Mehan (1998) notes, "By moving beyond the states and traits of individuals to social situations as the unit of analysis . . . [students' performances can be] recast as collaboratively constructed and continuously embedded in face-to-face interaction in social environments" (pp. 251, 254).

Seen from this perspective, both the assessment triangle and the language for describing instructional practice ignore the social dimensions of learning, the ways in which learning is shaped and demonstrated in interaction with other human beings and with the symbolic and material resources available in the social context. Even Smithson and Porter's notion that cognitive demands and topics can be crossed in a two-dimensional model, such that the meaning of a cognitive demand remains constant across applications to different content, is controversial. (See Beach, 2003, Gee, 2003a, and Greeno & Haertel, 2003, for responses to KWSK from a sociocultural perspective.)

There is, I would argue, no escape from the theory- and value-ladenness of any conceptual tool or indicator system or from the responsibility (acknowledged or not) for having intervened in a social system. When coupled with state authority, and associated rewards and sanctions, as with No Child Left Behind, the power of the assessment system to shape the social realities it describes is greatly enhanced. However, *even in the absence of such tangible incentives*, the power to shape practice remains: "numbers [that] create and can be compared with norms . . . are among the gentlest and yet most pervasive forms of power in modern democracies" (Porter, 1995, p. 45). "They provide legitimacy for administrative actions, in large part, because they provide standards against which people judge themselves" (p. 45). And so it is appropriate to ask about any set of indicators: What does it permit or privilege and what does it exclude or ignore? What does it illuminate, invite, encourage and what does it marginalize or relegate to the background as less important in demonstrating progress or competence? In the next two sections, I focus first on the potential effects of the privileged learning outcomes—knowledge and skills—and second on the identities and social positions they offer actors (teachers, students, principals, district administrators, policymakers, legislators, and so on).

The Indicators Reflect a Single Set of Learning Outcomes

As with any sound curriculum framework, embedded in each of the assessment systems proposed (Foster & Masters; Frederiksen & White; Wilson & Draney) is a coherent set of learning outcomes. The vision of assessment and accountability privileged in this volume—of "the integration of assessment frameworks and methods across all levels of the assessment system, from the classroom to the system level" (Wilson, Chapter 1, p. 3)—implies that the same set of learning outcomes will be expected of all teachers and students within a given system. Presumably this will occur at the state level, but given development costs, the same programs may well be used in many states. While this will likely enhance the quality of education in many schools, it will also likely decrease diversity in learning experiences within the educational system. Of course, all standards-based reform efforts promote common learning goals within the systems in which they are used. However, the comprehensive and continuous visibility the envisioned systems permit will likely give them far more power to reshape the local environment in their own image.

Will we—educators, students, policymakers, and the public at large— be well served by a system that promotes a single set of learning goals? The National Academy of Education Panel on Standards Based Education Reform suggests not (McClaughlin & Shepard, 1995). The panel proposes that sets of standards serve as exemplars: Rejecting the assumption that there is "one best way to define and structure knowledge"

(p. 24) in a field, the panel argues for the value of multiple sets of "coherent, professionally credible" standards in a given domain that could serve as exemplars to state and local education agencies.

Perhaps the greatest long-range risk of centralized planning is that, as the social reality in different contexts comes to resemble the planner's model, we lose opportunities to experience alternative practices and so too our collective memory that things could be otherwise. Our understanding of how people learn is shaped by the way we foster learning. And it is the students in our classrooms who will become the educators, researchers, and policymakers of tomorrow. In fact, a number of sociocultural theorists argue for the importance of studying how learning occurs outside of school and in different cultural contexts in order to gain some purchase on how routinized practices in schools have shaped conceptions of learning.

The Indicators Entail Particular Identities and Social Positions for Different Actors

Moving to the second dimension—the way in which an assessment and accountability system positions those who use it—a related set of concerns arises. As Gee and colleagues describe it, "discourses [like assessment and accountability systems] create, produce, and reproduce opportunities for people to be and recognize certain kinds of people" (Gee, Hull, & Lankshear, 1996, p. 10). Focusing for the moment on teachers, what identities and positions do these assessment systems offer them? Although all of the assessment systems involved teachers in their production, and all seemed intended to honor their professional judgment, they nevertheless limited the role that teachers could (or would likely) play when the system is fully operational in the classrooms of teachers who did not participate in its development. As I noted at the beginning: for most classrooms, these assessments appeared to limit the classroom teacher's productive role to activities like judging student work using the guidelines provided, perhaps developing tasks consistent with a predetermined template, choosing the time of implementation, and supporting students in making progress toward the goals.

Shepard (2003), in a recent response to KWSK, worries that "reliance on technological examples gives an implicit message that good assessment depends on the computer's statistical modeling and data-management capacities. It suggests that teachers need to receive information about typical errors and learning progressions from cognitive experts; and it seems to limit practical implementation to a few . . . modules while we wait for more subject areas to be codified" (p. 172).

Wenger (1998) raises questions about "'ownership of meaning'—that is, the degree to which we can make use of, affect, control, modify, or in general, assert as ours the meanings that we negotiate" (p. 200).

When, in a community of practice, the *distinction between the production and adoption of meaning* reflects enduring patterns of engagement among members—that is, when some always produce and some always adopt—the local economy yields very uneven ownership of meaning. (p. 203; italics mine)

Those whose role it is, consistently, to adopt meaning, Wenger argues, have less opportunity to learn from experience:

A split between production and adoption of meaning thus compromises learning because it presents a choice between experience and competence: you must choose between your own experience as a resource for the production of meaning and your membership in a community where your competence is determined by your adoption of other's proposals for meaning. (p. 203)

Porter (1995, 2003) raises a related issue about the impact of quantitative indicators and predetermined standards on administrators and policymakers: "reliance on numbers and quantitative manipulation minimizes the need for intimate knowledge and personal trust" (p. ix), and it removes from decision makers the need to attend to the unique features of each case and to take personal responsibility for their decisions. As Scott suggests, like the monoculture forest, centralized designs for social systems

tend to diminish the skills, agility, initiative, and morale of their intended beneficiaries. . . . Complex, diverse, animated environments contribute . . . to producing a resilient, flexible, adept population that has more experience in confronting novel challenges and taking initiative. Narrow, planned environments, by contrast, foster a less skilled, less innovative, less resourceful population. *This population, once created, would ironically have been exactly the kind of human material that would in fact have needed close supervision from above.* In other words, the logic of social engineering on this scale was to produce the sort of subjects that its plans had assumed at the outset. (1998, p. 349; italics mine)

Clearly, this is no thoughtful educator's intent, and it is certainly not the intent of the authors of the source chapters, who seek to honor the professional judgment of teachers. It is, however, a potential effect of a single "comprehensive, coherent, and continuous" assessment and accountability system, backed (if adopted at the state level) by state power, that provides a language for local actors to use in understanding themselves and others, and that permits local actions to be visible from afar. Critical theory reminds us always to seek out and learn from the effects of our actions, which may well differ from our intent.

An Alternative Vision of Coherence

The effects of the rich set of tools the source chapters and KWSK offer will ultimately depend on the ways they are incorporated into the social contexts in which they are used. Will they be imposed by the state as requirements that everyone must implement? Or, will they be used as exemplars that teachers, schools, or districts might adopt, adapt, combine with other practices, or reject for alternatives? "How [will] the power to define, adapt, or interpret the design [be] distributed?" (Wenger, 1998, p. 235). The vision of coherence in KWSK—"the integration of assessment frameworks and methods across all levels of the assessment system, from the classroom to the system level" (p. 3)—suggests the press for alignment. In the short term, it is likely that this press for alignment will produce the more widespread effect. It will likely increase the quality of education in many schools and decrease inequities in learning opportunities. These are noble goals we all share. In the long run, however, the potential effects of narrowing both the range of learning experiences and the opportunities for local actors to contribute meaningfully to the way those experiences are conceptualized and judged will, I believe, be more consequential. What will be the disjunctions between system developers' good intentions and what they, in fact, effect? What kinds of people will they foster?

In closing, I'll sketch out some principles for an alternative vision of coherence—one that takes advantage of the rich tools the source chapters offer us but that skirts some of the risks of promoting coherence-through-alignment coupled with comprehensive, coherent, continuous visibility. Following Wenger (1998), I will call this coherence-through-negotiation-of-meaning, or more precisely, coherence through *mutual engagement* in the negotiation of meaning, a vision that comes with its own set of risks. Wenger defines *negotiability* as "the ability, facility, and legitimacy to contribute to, take responsibility for, and shape the meanings that matter within a social configuration" (p. 197). "*Mutual engagement in the negotiation of meaning* involves both the production of proposals for meaning and the adoption of these proposals" (p. 202; italics mine).

A central principle of critical theory is that we learn by encountering perspectives, practices, and social contexts that are different from our own; such encounters make us aware of the categories of thought and action we take for granted, allow us to imagine how things might be otherwise, and encourage us to reconsider our perspectives and practices in light of this knowledge. From this perspective, *diversity is a resource for learning and for social change*. Further, learning and social change occur, not primarily through external controls but, rather, because people have reflected on their experience, come to understand its genesis and effects, and, as a result, have chosen to act differently.

The chapter by Black and Wiliam comes closest to illustrating practices consistent with what I am calling coherence-through-negotiation-of-meaning. Teachers come together around some common issues and resources, supported and challenged by knowledgeable colleagues from *outside* their social context, and they adapt and implement those resources as they choose in their own classrooms. This is similar to a role that Shepard (2003) envisions for the assessment systems illustrated in KWSK and for the teachers who use them:

A different role for teachers might make more sense—one that focuses on teacher learning and increases teachers' repertoire of assessment skills. . . . Why not use existing technology-based models as examples to scaffold teachers' developing understandings of formative assessment? If teachers were helped to analyze and attend to the salient features of technology-based assessments, they could learn to generalize these features to other content areas and instructional units. (p. 173)

For accountability purposes at the school level, teachers might be routinely expected to share with administrators and with one another evidence of their students' learning, their teaching practices, and their reflections on them. Collaborative planning might lead productively to local forms of alignment that permit locally relevant indicators of the form that Wilson imagines in the introduction or to the enthusiastic adoption of any of the programs proposed here. From this perspective, however, the strongest technology-based assessments will be those that not only serve as rich models but also permit local actors to alter the parameters of the program to suit their needs. Indeed, Gee (2003b), who documents the learning potential of computer games, notes that the better programs are those that give players the opportunity to customize their identities.

There are multiple examples of school communities that engage collaboratively in these sorts of practices (see, for example, Darling-Hammond, Ancess, & Falk, 1995; Meier, 1995; Rogoff, Turkanis, & Burtlett, 2001). District administrators might develop policies and practices that support (or at least do not undermine) schools in developing these sorts of learning communities. Darling-Hammond (2001) represents the policy dilemmas as "developing top-down supports for bottom-up reform" (p. xv). Consistent with critical theoretic perspectives, the role of knowledgeable outsiders can be crucial in illuminating limitations of local practices, and district policies can institutionalize such roles. In these ways, accountability at the school level may be more appropriately contextualized with a deep understanding of the social reality students, parents, teachers, and administrators experience. This does not preclude the use of system-wide indicators at the district, state, or national level; it does, however, imagine a smaller, less commanding role, and more "prudent aspirations" (Bryk & Hermanson, 1993) for their use. Darling-Hammond (1994), for instance, envisions

carefully targeted . . . assessments at a few key developmental points that will provide data for informing policy makers about program successes and needs, areas where assistance and investment are needed, and assessment models for local schools. Meanwhile, locally implemented assessment systems—including portfolios, projects, performance tasks, and structured teachers' observations of learning—will provide the multiple forms of evidence about student learning needed to make sound judgments about instruction. (p. 20)

Conceptual tools that assess the nature of alignment between the centralized and local forms of evidence, of the sort Smithson and Porter illustrate, could be productively framed as helping local educators understand the differences in information between the two sources, leaving questions about whether to further alignment to local choice. We should not forget that the National Assessment of Educational Progress (NAEP) was expressly designed and implemented as a low-stakes assessment—to discourage explicit forms of alignment—so it could be used to monitor progress across educational systems with different curriculum frameworks (NRC, 2000). Interestingly, among the concerns represented in the summary of the NRC workshop on reporting district-level NAEP results is that "use of NAEP results at the district or school level has the potential to discourage states' and districts' use of innovation in developing their own assessments" (NRC, 2000, p. 10). Comprehensive and continuous assessment is not necessary for district, state, or national purposes. As Bryk and Hermanson (1993) note, "more information is not always better. . . . The ultimate long-term test of this system is not whether we are better informed but whether we act more prudently. In the shorter term, the best 'test' may be found in the answer to the question 'Is our public discourse enriched (or impoverished) by this new information?'" (p. 476).

One of the most important roles for an indicator system is to help those at one level of the educational system make good decisions that support educational practice at other levels of the system for which they are responsible.[5] Teachers, principals, district superintendents, curriculum coordinators, school board members, state superintendents, state and federal department of education staff, legislators, and so on have different kinds of decisions to make, and the information they will need is likely different as well. Designing an appropriate set of indicators and related practices will depend on a rich, contextualized understanding of what information is needed, how it is used, and what the effects of this use are. Even decision makers at the federal level work within their own immediate social contexts. Those of us who develop assessment and accountability systems need to acquire deeper understandings of the social practices that surround them, not just at the classroom level, but at all levels of the educational system where they are used. (Spillane's program of research on distributed leadership provides a rich, evidence-based example of the sort of research I have in mind; see Burch & Spillane, 2003 and Spillane, Diamond, & Jita, in press).

From this alternative perspective, coherence is achieved, not through actions and structures that promote widespread alignment, consistency, or commonality, but rather *through concerted efforts to understand and learn from our differences* (Moss & Schutz, 2001). "By seriously attempting to understand the insights . . . other perspectives provide, we can begin to educate ourselves and to revise or develop our understanding. . . . Each perspective may develop along its own lines . . . yet in concert with the others, each perspective can refine itself and become more differentiated and more aware of the internal difficulties with which it must deal" (Warnke, 1994, p. 131-132). Of course, this approach has risks, too: the impact of these practices on the larger system will be much more diffuse and likely slower to yield widespread progress on some valued learning outcomes; further, diversity in learning experiences may not as quickly ameliorate inequities in learning opportunities. Administrative structures that support and challenge local learning communities will need to be in place to mitigate these risks. However, as I have argued, the long-term risks of privileging commonality, and thus diminishing local responsibility for design decisions, seem far more consequential and less easily reversible if problems arise.[6]

As Scott (1998) asks, "to what degree does [the system] promise to enhance the skills, knowledge, and responsibility of those who are a part of it? . . . How deeply is [it] marked by the values and experience of those who comprise it?" (p. 355). Under a model of coherence-through-negotiation-of-meaning, the policy goals are to make rich and diverse learning opportunities available; to encourage learning at all levels of the system through ongoing dialogue across different perspectives and contexts about the means and ends of education; and to promote evidence-based critical reflection on the effects of our actions. Diversity together with the meaningful productive engagement of actors at all levels of the educational system represents, in my judgment, our best resources for social change. As Scott reminds us in the conclusion to *Seeing Like a State*, "Diversity and certain forms of complexity, apart from their attractiveness, have other advantages. . . . They may not be as productive, in the short run, . . . but they are demonstrably more stable, more self-sufficient, and less vulnerable" (p. 353).

NOTES

1. As I write this commentary, I am engaged in ongoing discussions with other members of the Idea of Testing Project, an interdisciplinary initiative funded by the Spencer Foundation, focused on expanding the foundations of educational assessment. These discussions with King Beach, Jim Gee, Jim Greeno, Ed Haertel, Carol Lee, Bud Mehan, Bob Mislevy, Fritz Moser, Diana Pullin, and Lauren Young have challenged and advanced my thinking about educational assessment as it is reflected here. A brief description of the project appears in Spencer's 2003 annual report (Spencer Foundation, 2003, p. 18). I am also grateful to Mark Wilson for his insightful comments on an earlier draft of this commentary.

2. Some reserve the term *critical* for perspectives informed by the work of a particular community of theorists known as the Frankfurt school. Here, I follow the lead of other theorists (e.g., Calhoun, 1995; Hoy & McCarthy, 1994) who use the term more broadly to encompass the range of perspectives that share these features, including not only members of the Frankfurt school (like Horkheimer, Adorno, and Habermas), but also drawing on hermeneutic, poststructural, and feminist perspectives (like those of Gadamer, Bourdieu, Foucault, and Harding).

3. While some limit the term *sociocultural* to research that derives from the work of Vygotsky, others use the term more broadly to refer to a constellation of perspectives that attend to the dialectical relationship between social structure and local practice of individuals in context, which is the perspective I use here.

4. This paragraph is adapted from Moss, Pullin, Gee, & Haertel (2002) and Moss (2003). It is the relevance of these ideas to assessment that the Spencer Idea of Testing Project (see reference in Spencer, 2003) is intended to explore.

5. King Beach made a similar point at the October 2003 meeting of the Idea of Testing Project.

6. Even Popper (1944/1985) recommended a "piecemeal" approach to social engineering: "it is difficult enough to be critical of our own mistakes, but it must be nearly impossible for us to persist in critical attitudes toward our actions which involve the lives of many men. To put it differently, it is very hard to learn from very big mistakes" (p. 315).

REFERENCES

Beach, K. (1999). Consequential transitions: A sociocultural expedition. In A. Iran-Nejad & P.D. Pearson (Eds.), *Review of Research in Education, 24*, 101-140. Washington, DC: American Educational Research Association.

Beach, K. (2003). Learning in complex social situations meets information processing and mental representation: Some consequences for educational assessment. *Measurement: Interdisciplinary Research and Perspectives, 1*(2), 149-153.

Bourdieu, P. (1988). *Homo academicus.* Cambridge, UK: Polity Press.

Bourdieu, P. (1991). The peculiar history of scientific reason. *Sociological Forum, 6*(1), 3-26.

Burch, P., & Spillane, J.P. (2003). Elementary school leadership strategies and subject matter: The case of mathematics and literacy instruction. *Elementary School Journal, 103*(5), 519-536.

Bryk, A.S., & Hermanson, K.M. (1993). Educational indicator systems: Observations on their structure, interpretation, and use. In *Review of Research in Education, 19*, 451-484.

Chaiklin, S., & Lave, J. (Eds.). (1993). *Understanding practice: Perspectives on activity and context.* Cambridge: Cambridge University Press.

Calhoun, C. (1995). *Critical social theory.* Oxford: Blackwell.

Cole, M. (1996). *Cultural psychology: A once and future discipline.* Cambridge, MA: Harvard University Press, Belknap Press.

Darling-Hammond, L. (2001). *The right to learn: A blueprint for creating schools that work.* Somerset, NJ: Jossey-Bass.

Darling-Hammond, L. (1994). Performance-based assessment and educational equity. *Harvard Educational Review, 64*(1), 5-30.

Darling-Hammond, L., Ancess, J., & Falk, B. (1995). *Authentic assessment in action: Studies of schools and students that work.* New York: Teachers College Press.

Gee, J.P. (1999). *An introduction to discourse analysis: Theory and method.* London: Routledge.

Gee, J.P. (2003a). Practice, participation, and tools: An alternative starting point. *Measurement: Interdisciplinary Research and Perspectives, 1*(2), e12-e15. Available: http://bear.soe.berkeley.edu/measurement/pubs/toc12.html

Gee, J.P. (2003b). What video games have to teach us about learning and literacy. New York: Palgrave Macmillan.

Gee, J.P., Hull, G., & Lankshear, C. (1996). *The new work order: Behind the language of the new capitalism.* Boulder, CO: Westview Press.

Greeno, J., & Haertel, E.H. (2003). A situative perspective: Broadening the foundations of assessment. *Measurement: Interdisciplinary Research and Perspectives, 1*(2), 154-161.

Hoy, D.C., & McCarthy, T. (1994). *Critical theory.* Oxford: Blackwell.

Linn, R.L. (2003). Accountability: Responsibility and reasonable expectations. *Educational Researcher, 32*(7), 3-13.

Linn, R.L., Baker, E.L., & Betebenner, D.W. (2002). Implications of requirements of the No Child Left Behind Act of 2001. *Educational Researcher, 31*(6), 3-16.

McCarthy, T. (1994). Philosophy and critical theory: A reprise. In D.C. Hoy & T. McCarthy, *Critical theory* (pp. 5-100). Oxford: Blackwell.

McClaughlin, M.W., & Shepard, L.A. (1995). *Improving education through standards based reform: A report of the National Academy of Education panel on standards-based education reform.* Stanford: National Academy of Education.

Mehan, H. (1993). Beneath the skin and between the ears: A case study in the politics of representation. In S. Chaiklin & J. Lave (Eds.), *Understanding practice: Perspectives on activity and context* (pp. 241-268). Cambridge: Cambridge University Press.

Mehan, H. (1998). The study of social interaction in educational settings: Accomplishments and unresolved issues. *Human Development, 41*, 245-269.

Meier, D. (1995). *The power of their ideas: Lessons for America from a small school in Harlem.* Boston: Beacon.

Moss, P.A. (in press). Rethinking validity for classroom assessment. *Educational Measurement: Issues and Practice, 2*(4).

Moss, P.A., & Schutz, A.M. (2001). Educational standards, assessment, and the search for consensus. *American Educational Research Journal, 38*(1), 37-70.

Moss, P.A., Pullin, D.P., Gee, J.P., & Haertel, E.H. (2002). The idea of testing: Expanding the foundations of educational measurement. Unpublished manuscript.

National Research Council (NRC). (2000). *Reporting district-level NAEP: Summary of a workshop.* Washington, DC: National Academy Press.

Pellegrino, J.W., Chudowsky, N., & Glaser, R. (Eds.). (2001). *Knowing what students know.* Washington, DC: National Academy Press.

Popper, K.R. (1944/1985). Piecemeal social engineering. In D. Miller (Ed.), *Popper selections* (p. 304-318). Princeton, NJ: Princeton University Press.

Porter, T.M. (1995). *Trust in numbers: The pursuit of objectivity in science and public life.* Princeton, NJ: Princeton University Press.

Porter, T.M. (2003). Measurement, objectivity, and trust. *Measurement: Interdisciplinary Research and Perspectives, 1*(4), 241-255.

Rogoff, B., Turkanis, C.G., & Burtlett, L. (2001). *Learning together: Children and adults in a school community.* New York: Oxford.

Scott, J.C. (1998). *Seeing like a state: How certain schemes to improve the human condition have failed.* New Haven, CT: Yale University Press.

Shepard, L.A. (2003). Commentary: Intermediate steps to knowing what students know. *Measurement: Interdisciplinary Research and Perspectives, 1*(2), 171-177.

Spencer Foundation (2003). Annual report: April 1, 2002-March 31, 2003. Chicago: Author. Available: http://www.spencer.org/publications/index.htm

Spillane, J., Diamond, J.B., & Jita, L. (in press). Leading instruction: The distribution of leadership for instruction. *Journal of Curriculum Studies.*

Warnke, G. (1994). *Justice and interpretation.* Cambridge, MA: The MIT Press.

Wenger, E. (1998). *Communities of practice: Learning, meaning, and identity.* Cambridge: Cambridge University Press.

Wertsch, J.V., Del Rio, P., & Alverez, A. (1995). Sociocultural studies: History, action, and mediation. In J.V. Wertsch, P. Del Rio, & A. Alverez (Eds.), *Sociocultural studies of mind* (pp. 1-36). Cambridge: Cambridge University Press.

Wilson, M. (1994). Community of judgment: A teacher-centered approach to educational accountability. In Office of Technology Assessment (Ed.), *Issues in educational accountability.* Washington, DC: U.S. Congress Office of Technology Assessment.

CHAPTER 14

Curricular Coherence in Assessment Design

LORRIE A. SHEPARD

As evidence continues to accumulate on the negative impacts of high-stakes accountability testing on instructional practice and student learning, researchers have focused their efforts on the design of new assessment systems that would reverse this trend and instead serve the purpose of improving student learning. In *Knowing What Students Know*, a committee of the National Research Council (Pellegrino, Chudowsky, & Glaser, 2001) laid out a vision of an ideal assessment system that would support effective, ongoing instructional decisions in the classroom and at the same time provide a more complete body of evidence documenting students' accomplishments for policy purposes. A central feature of *KWSK*'s ideal and balanced assessment system is *coherence*. To be coherent (and effective in pursuing the same learning goals), a system of classroom and large-scale assessments must share the same underlying models of learning. These learning models are more exacting than the description of learning outcomes represented in today's content standards because they also describe the pathways by which students develop proficiency.

In this commentary, I argue that coherence in assessment design cannot be achieved without an agreed-upon curriculum and that this shared curriculum is a tall order, requiring much more substantive elaboration and congruence than is necessarily implied by the currently popular term *alignment*. Given that previous attempts to reform large-scale assessments, such as by creating authentic assessments (Wiggins, 1989), have fallen short of grand promises because of practical and political constraints (Fetler, 1994; Kirst & Mazzeo, 1996), it is important to recognize how ambitious the *KWSK* vision is and where it is beyond our present reach. I consider first the impediments

Lorrie A. Shepard is professor of education and chair of the Research and Evaluation Methodology program area of the School of Education at the University of Colorado at Boulder. She is also currently serving as dean of the School of Education.

to coherence in current assessment systems. Then, I examine the projects described in this volume in light of their curriculum-based contributions to assessment redesign.

Impediments to Coherence in Present-Day Assessment Systems

Several factors contrive to make today's large-scale assessments as generic and as detached from curriculum as possible. For example, to appeal to wide markets, commercially developed standardized tests must be sufficiently generic to be useful to states and school districts using a wide range of textbooks and curriculum materials. Most commercial tests cover only basic skills because including special topics or complex problem solving would risk misalignment between test content and the needs of local test selection committees. State assessments have the advantage of being tailored to the content standards of a particular state, but state assessment directors still cannot assume that students have read the same books or studied the same units in science or social studies.

As a matter of fairness, test makers strive to keep irrelevant background knowledge out of test questions. If test items are intended to assess a child's ability to use mathematics in applied settings, problem statements typically avoid the use of highly specialized knowledge from kitchen, carpentry, music, or sports applications and the like. Ironically, we know that context, and the opportunity to connect new learning to prior experience, often helps students make sense of learning and assessment tasks. Similarly, to avoid giving an unfair advantage to one group of students over another, writing prompts are sanitized so that they are equally neutral for everyone. So, students are asked to write a letter to the school board instead of writing about topics they have studied in depth or issues they feel passionate about. More challenging science, mathematics, or history questions may also be made curriculum-free by providing relevant background information in the test materials rather than asking students to draw connections between a new problem and problems solved previously.

Large-scale assessments such as the National Assessment of Educational Progress (NAEP) were purposely designed to be inclusive of all curricula. Whereas standardized achievement tests can be thought of as the intersection—or lowest common denominator—of all curricula, NAEP reflects the union of all possible curricula. The National Academy of Education Panel on the Evaluation of the NAEP Trial State Assessment (1992) emphasized that this *comprehensiveness* feature of NAEP's design, including both new and old content and assessment methodologies, was essential to enable NAEP to track the effects of both traditional and reform-based instructional strategies (National Academy of Education, 1992). Following this same strategy, a number of state assessments originally were designed to be like NAEP, with broad content frameworks used to specify the content at key grade levels, such as grades 4, 8, and 12 on the NAEP.

Despite the intention of representing multiple curricula, items in this type of broad, comprehensive assessment still tend to be generic aptitude-like items, more like questions on the ACT college entrance test than those on curriculum-specific, end-of-course examinations. As political interest has increased in reporting to parents the performance of individual students in every grade, culminating in the No Child Left Behind Act of 2001, states have begun to retrofit their NAEP-like monitoring assessments by filling in the missing grade levels. Once assessments are in place for every grade, it is possible to draw imaginary growth curves by connecting equipercentile points –for example, by connecting the scores obtained by the seventieth percentile student at each grade level. However, in contrast to the desire of *KWSK* that assessments provide information describing the substance of what students must master to move from one level of accomplishment to the next, there is no evidence that either these statistically derived trajectories or aspirational benchmarks represent the pathways of real students' learning gains under conditions of reasonably adequate instruction.

A final example, contrasting the College Board's Advanced Placement and Pacesetter programs, once again illustrates the difference between generic and curriculum-specific assessments but also shows us the kind of curriculum agreement that would be required if the *KWSK* ideal of coherence were to be attempted. Advanced Placement exams are from an earlier era, and while they are based on surveys of corresponding college courses, they are nonetheless more generic than an assessment designed for a specific course. For example, for the AP Biology exam (College Entrance Examination Board, 2003), students are told that they are not expected to have mastered all of the content tested because of the differences in various curricula:

In order to be broad enough in scope to give every student who has covered an adequate amount of material an opportunity to perform well, the multiple-choice section of the examination must be so comprehensive that no student should be expected to attain a perfect or near-perfect score. (p. 32)

In contrast, the Pacesetter program was created in the early 1990s with the intention of increasing access to challenging curricula for a much broader population of high school students. The program was modeled after Advanced Placement, but from the beginning it was understood that providing support for students to achieve these ambitious goals would require that content frameworks and culminating assessments be accompanied by well-integrated curriculum units and embedded assessments, as well as professional development for teachers. In contrast to Advanced Placement, which is based on test frameworks, the Pacesetter program developed a course of study in each area first and then developed embedded and culminating assessments from the course materials. In addition, Pacesetter courses were much more detailed and specific than AP frameworks. For example, the capstone English course was designed from a multicultural perspective emphasizing the cultural and historical contexts of literature. Course assignments also blended literary study with writing instruction with the intention of developing students' voices. As a consequence of this shared specificity, embedded and culminating assessments could be much more focused in the analyses and extensions asked of students. Everyone taking the English course, for example, had read Zora Neale Hurston's *Their Eyes Were Watching God* and had talked about their own identities.

Ideal Classroom Assessment

Black and Wiliam's chapter in this volume (Chapter 2) provides a model of effective classroom assessment as well as a professional development model by which teachers can simultaneously transform their assessment and instructional practices to focus more on learning. While focused on formative assessment, Black and Wiliam's exposition is a thoroughgoing analysis of how learning theory plays out in classroom interactions. Like prior work by Black and Wiliam (1998) and other contributions in the formative assessment literature, this chapter reprises the importance of feedback—tied specifically to features of student work, with clear advice about how to improve—as a powerful tool for improving student learning. However, this chapter goes much further in elaborating how teachers' efforts to adopt formative assessment strategies change the whole tenor of classroom interactions.

A key theme throughout Black and Wiliam's account is the focus on student thinking and "mindfulness," which formative assessment helps to develop (p. 24). For example, in attempting in a fairly straightforward way to get students to talk more, teachers found that they had to ask different questions and that these questions had to be aimed at thinking. As classroom norms changed, both teachers and students benefited from what Glaser has referred to as the "display of thinking." Of course, teachers gain when students make their thinking explicit because then they can build on understandings or address misconceptions. More importantly, as Black and Wiliam found, explaining one's thinking "actually causes learning" (p. 34). Understanding this process was critical for teachers because it helped them move away from the idea that assessment is merely a check on stored information toward a more dynamic view of knowledge building. These practice-based findings are highly consistent with theories of dynamic assessment (Brown, Campione, Webber, & McGilly, 1992) and Vygotsky's (1978) learning theory, on which dynamic assessment is based.

The Black and Wiliam model of professional development is also compelling. The researchers' decision to allow teachers to decide how to modify their instruction to incorporate formative assessment principles is consistent with the literature on professional development whereby teachers themselves are treated as learners, trying to make sense of a new theory. Teachers have a better chance of developing deep understanding if they receive support while trying out these ideas in the context of their own practice.

Black and Wiliam's findings regarding summative assessments and external tests were more discouraging, however. For most teachers in the study, insights from formative assessment did not generalize easily to summative testing requirements. Instead, teachers tended to comply with school-based formal testing requirements by deferring to the simplicity and objectivity of numbers from someone else's test. Teachers also reported all of the familiar complaints about the influence of national high-stakes tests, which despite their awareness forced them to devote more time to lifeless aspects of the curriculum at the expense of more inferential, integrated, and imaginative lessons. Some teachers were able to use summative examinations for formative purposes either by helping students to be more reflective in their preparation or by turning examination results into a learning opportunity. However, these generalizations required as much self-conscious effort and scaffolding as the formative assessment change process itself, both for students and for teachers.

Given that Black and Wiliam did not undertake reform of external examinations, their chapter is silent on the topic of coherence. Nonetheless, they provide one of the best available descriptions of what the ideal, formative assessment, classroom side of a coherent model might look like, and they go further than theoretical articles (Atkin, Black, & Coffey, 2001; Black & Wiliam, 1998; Sadler, 1989) by demonstrating the benefits of moving present practice toward that ideal. Their observations of obvious disconnects between formative assessment and external tests remind us of the incompatibility of current external assessments with *KWSK*'s idealized system.

Curriculum-Based Coherence

Forster and Masters (Chapter 3) describe closely articulated, classroom-level developmental assessments and national survey assessments that they developed in Australia. Quite rightly they ascribe their ability to achieve coherence between the two levels to the use of common progress maps. I argue further that progress maps and accompanying materials serve as a shared curriculum, which ensures that as teachers work to improve student learning, they are simultaneously working to improve performance on the national survey in a way that does not imply the distortion or artificiality of preparing students for external exams found in Black and Wiliam or other studies of high-stakes testing. In addition, because Forster and Masters found a way to embed accountability data collection in the classroom with teachers as judges, they were able to avoid the cost and time constraints associated with more authentic assessments, which have caused the narrowness and inauthenticity of on-demand accountability assessment in the United States.

Progress maps are broad, general descriptions of how proficiency typically develops in a curricular area. They are more specific, however, than the content standards popular in the United States, because, more like rubrics, they also describe the specific features by which the quality of student work may be judged. Progress map descriptors, then, serve both as the anchors for evaluating and summarizing performance for accountability purposes and as the diagnostic indicators that can be used as the specific targets of instructional interventions.

Although adoption of both the classroom-level DART and the national literacy survey, NSELS, allowed teachers to devise their own instruction within the theme of the four- to six-week units, implementation of curriculum-embedded assessments nonetheless required dictating some uniformity in instructional decisions, which has not typically been possible in the United States. (Exceptions include portfolio assessments like those undertaken in Vermont and Kentucky.) In fact, despite their seemingly after-the-fact reflections on the conceptual links between their two separate systems, it should be clear that Forster and Masters built commonality and standardization features into their classroom-level DART from the beginning. In addition to instructionally focused efforts to use multiple assessment methods and to tie student performance explicitly to learning outcomes, DART was designed to ensure that judgments of student work would yield comparable results across schools tied to the national standards framework. Given the commonness of their conceptual underpinnings, it is not surprising that the resulting classroom and accountability assessments were indeed compatible. What is surprising, from a parochial American perspective, is that teachers would readily adopt four- to six-week curricular units of study with accompanying embedded assessments.

Like Black and Wiliam, Forster and Masters also describe the extensive professional development efforts needed to increase teachers' assessment knowledge and corresponding instructional strategies. Importantly, resources available in conjunction with the national survey addressed broad, challenging teaching issues rather than focusing narrowly on improving performance on specific assessment tasks.

Wilson and Draney's chapter (Chapter 6) in this volume provides the most straightforward example of a coordinated, coherent assessment system that is closely tied to curriculum. Like DART, the BEAR Assessment System follows a developmental perspective and is built around a set of progress variables that reflect the way that expertise or increasing proficiency develops for each instructional goal. An assessment system organized around progress maps or progress variables that measure and characterize developing competence in particular subject domains is quite distinct from the cross-sectional and smorgasbord type of large-scale assessments typically used in the United States.

Wilson and Draney emphasize that this coherence between classroom and external uses, represented in their study by link tests, requires a shared understanding of the assessed construct at both the level of the progress dimension and the level of specific assessment tasks and scoring guides. Curriculum provides the common conceptual base. Then, because of the shared curriculum, common content and instructional experiences can be presumed and correspondingly more specific assessments can be developed. Embedded assessments from the Issues, Evidence and You curriculum, therefore, can ask students to reason with and integrate information from previous labs and readings. In the example cited by the authors, the problem "cannot be fully answered without access to the curricular materials that precede it" (p. 138). My point here is that building on a shared curriculum enables development of substantively rich assessment tasks that call on students to reason with and apply content knowledge.

When they shifted to writing items for their link tests, Wilson and Draney developed items that were relatively less curriculum-dependent by providing needed content information in the test question itself. However, in their example, they still preserved a focus on the IEY-defined Evidence and Tradeoffs variable, which in a more typical large-scale assessment would be only one of many item types used to measure a more generic construct such as reasoning from evidence. In our efforts to reconceptualize assessment systems, we have to ask whether curriculum-specific and curriculum-independent assessment tasks do an equally good job of reflecting students' deep understanding and proficiencies. Would questions like those used in IEY embedded assessments be edited out of present-day large-scale assessments because they were too specialized or too specific to the IEY curriculum? And, if they were to be edited out, would the remaining generic test be a good measure of the learning gains for students in the BEAR program?

Frederiksen and White (Chapter 4) provide perhaps the most powerful argument of all as to why data gathered from classrooms would be important for accountability purposes—because they reflect accomplishments on extended problem solving and inquiry tasks and are thereby qualitatively different from the knowledge and skills captured by present-day large-scale assessments. In an earlier study, White and Frederiksen (1998) demonstrated the dramatic benefits of formative assessment, in particular the benefits of self-assessment for helping students internalize the meaning of evaluative criteria. In the present study, they are focused more on improving the accuracy of teacher judgments so that classroom assessments, dependent on these judgments, might be used for accountability purposes as well as for classroom learning.

Regarding the issue of curriculum-based coherence, White and Frederiksen's ThinkerTools Inquiry Curriculum prompts an important observation. To the extent that the constructs being measured are skills and processes rather than science content, the argument that students must have access to the same curriculum to be assessed fairly may not hold to the same degree. The ThinkerTools curricular goals are reflected in broad criteria such as Understanding the Science, Understanding the Processes of Inquiry, Making Connections, Writing and Communicating Well, and Teamwork. It can be argued, with the exception of Understanding the Science, that mastery and fair assessment of these processes is not dependent on a specific curriculum. In fact, general reasoning and communication skills become a different way to create generic, curriculum-independent assessments. The latest national interest in measuring outcomes in higher education, for example, has naturally focused on general education skills—for example, critical thinking, analytic reasoning, and written communication (Benjamin & Chun, 2003)—because of the impossibility of giving common tests to measure the knowledge and expertise gained from myriad specialty courses. The question we should be asking for large-scale assessment and accountability, however, is whether these generic measures are a sufficient representation of the learning goals for science classrooms or colleges and universities.

Frederiksen and White provide some promising data on the consistency of judgments made by teachers using an analytic framework to evaluate student projects. They are interested in obtaining adequate consistency to warrant using teacher judgments for external accountability as well as for student feedback. While the internal consistency approach is interesting, it does not simulate for us how teacher ratings would actually be used at either the classroom or the aggregate level. For student learning, 33 discrete analysis questions may be too many for effective feedback. In studies of effective tutoring, for example, tutors often ignore errors on some dimensions that are out of reach for an individual student while focusing on other areas for improvement that are more central and attainable with support. To evaluate the benefits of analytic scoring for student learning, we would need the same type of comparative study reported by White and Frederiksen (1998) earlier.

At the aggregate level, if classroom projects were to be included in large-scale assessment, it is likely that a score or several scores would be included, with agreed upon weights, in a composite score for each student. To evaluate analytic scoring for large-scale purposes, the question is not whether each rater is internally consistent but whether or not there are systematic differences among them that would bias the resulting composite. More importantly, do the scoring method and the nature of the tasks provide valid evidence of relative proficiency on the learning dimensions, Understanding the Science, Writing and Communicating Well, and so forth?

Conclusion

In this commentary, I have argued that coherence between large-scale and classroom assessments requires a shared curriculum. This observation should not be taken to mean that I am advocating for state-adopted curricula as a means of improving assessment and learning. At the present time, there are too many examples of both narrow and excessive content standards across states to be in favor of giving these frameworks even tighter control over day-to-day instruction. Rather, we should use the models offered in this volume to understand how profoundly different curriculum-based assessments are from current large-scale assessments, and we should resist efforts to use existing assessment frameworks as if they were adequate as curriculum guides.

To move toward the more ambitious ideal of assessment systems built to reflect underlying learning progressions, we should invest in research and development efforts like those described in this volume. Given the field's lack of familiarity with curriculum-embedded assessments, we need more practical experience with such systems as well as more research-based evidence before this idealized vision of mutually supportive assessment systems can be expected to displace existing large-scale assessments. Research programs should be designed to evaluate the technical adequacy of assessments, but more significantly they should focus on key validity questions. Do coherent, curriculum-based assessments provide effective diagnostic feedback to further learning, and do they provide valid aggregate data so as to identify programs where effective learning occurs?

References

Atkin, J.M., Black, P., & Coffey, J. (2001). *Classroom assessment and the National Science Education Standards*. Washington, DC: National Academy Press.

Benjamin, R., & Chun, M. (in press). A new field of dreams: The collegiate learning assessment project. *Peer Review, 5*.

Black, P., & Wiliam, D. (1998). Assessment and classroom learning. *Assessment in Education, 5*(1), 7-74.

Brown, A.L., Campione, J.C., Webber, L.S., & McGilly, K. (1992). Interactive learning environments: A new look at assessment and instruction. In B.R. Gifford & M.C. O'Connor (Eds.), *Changing assessments: Alternative views of aptitude, achievement, and instruction* (pp. 121-211). Boston: Kluwer Academic Publishers.

College Entrance Examination Board. (2002). *Biology: Course description*. New York: College Entrance Examination Board.

Fetler, M.E. (1994). Carrot or stick? How do school performance reports work? *Education Policy Analysis Archives, 2*(13). Available: http://epaa.asu.edu/epaa/v2n13.html

Kirst, M., & Mazzeo, C. (1996). The rise, fall, and rise of state assessment in California, 1993-1996. *Phi Delta Kappan, 78*(4), 319-323.

National Academy of Education. (1992). *Assessing student achievement in the states: The first report of the National Academy of Education Panel on the Evaluation of the NAEP Trial State Assessment: 1990 Trial State Assessment*. Stanford, CA: National Academy of Education.

Pellegrino, J.W., Chudowsky, N., & Glaser, R. (Eds.). (2001). *Knowing what students know: The science and design of educational assessment*. Washington, DC: National Academy Press.

Sadler, R. (1989). Formative assessment and the design of instructional systems. *Instructional Science, 18,* 119-144.

Vygotsky, L.S. (1978). *Mind in society: The development of higher psychological processes.* Cambridge, MA: Harvard University Press.

White, B., & Frederiksen, J. (1998). Inquiry, modeling, and metacognition: Making science accessible to all students. *Cognition and Instruction, 16*(1), 3-118.

Wiggins, G. (1989). A true test: Toward more authentic and equitable assessment. *Phi Delta Kappan, 70,* 703-713.

CHAPTER 15

Structuring Successful Collaborations Between Developers and Assessment Specialists

HERBERT D. THIER

One had to cram all this stuff into one's mind for the examinations, whether one liked it or not. This coercion had such a deterring effect on me that, after I had passed the final examination, I found the consideration of any scientific problems distasteful to me for an entire year.

—Albert Einstein, *Ideas and Opinions*

Designing quality standards-based science materials and models for instruction and getting them used widely in schools is my major professional goal. The current emphasis in education on high-stakes testing and accountability intensifies the need for effective working relationships between instructional materials developers like me and assessment specialists. The five chapters that make up the core of this volume on assessment present a variety of models and approaches for more effectively assessing what students learn as a result of instruction. My challenge is to react to the chapters and the approaches to assessment they emphasize from the point of view of the developer. This task is made easier and more interesting because of the stated and implied agreement in the five chapters on the following principles for quality assessment programs:

1. Current short-answer, machine-scored standardized tests are inadequate as an effective measure of what students are learning.

2. A major purpose of assessment is to help students understand what they know about a subject and, especially, what they don't know and need to learn.

Dr. Herbert D. Thier is Academic Administrator Emeritus at the Lawrence Hall of Science, University of California, Berkeley, and the Founding Director of the Science Education for Public Understanding Program (SEPUP) there.

Parts of this chapter are adapted from *Developing Inquiry-Based Science Materials: A Guide for Educators* by Herbert D. Thier with Bennett Daviss, which was partially supported by a grant from NSF.

3. Another major purpose of assessment is to provide feedback to teachers and developers so that they can collaborate to improve instruction.

4. Assessments need to be embedded in the instructional materials and the teacher must play a central role in the assessment process.

5. Based on assessment theory and practice, it is possible to design assessment approaches that accomplish these goals and also provide necessary evidence of alignment with student, school, district, state, and national expectations for education.

Compare these thoughtful expectations for effective assessment that contribute to learning to the current tidal wave of short-answer, fact-laden, machine-scorable testing taking place in the schools. The challenge is how to bridge the gap in understanding between the popular/political notion of assessment and the learning-centered professional points of view expressed in the source chapters of this volume. Close cooperative efforts between the assessment and development communities can contribute significantly to steering the popular concept of assessment away from comparing scores and toward measuring improvement in student learning.

The focus of this commentary is assessment in science education from a developer's point of view. After discussing the nature of science, the learner, and an approach to instruction called Guided Inquiry (Thier & Daviss, 2001), I will comment on the primary concern of the volume, assessment of learning, and then on the role of assessment in a development project. This sets the stage for an exploration of the leadership role teachers must have in any quality assessment system. Then, based on all of this, I will make suggestions for building true collaborative efforts between assessment specialists and materials developers. Throughout I will suggest ways to better inform education's various publics and hopefully help to bridge the gap between educational assessment as discussed in this volume and educational assessment as emphasized in our daily newspapers.

Science, The Learner, and Guided Inquiry

Quite differently from the case for mathematics and reading/language, standardized testing in science has been almost nonexistent except at the high school level until recently. Even in the high school, standardized testing in science, until recently, was limited to the New York State Regents Exams, the Advanced Placement tests, and a scattering of efforts in California and a few other states. Currently, national and international assessment efforts in science such as the National Assessment of Educational Progress (NAEP), the Trends in International Mathematics and Science Study (TIMMS), and the Programme for International Student Assessment (PISA) are extensively discussed as part of politically inspired educational commitments like First in the World by 2000 and the current No Child Left Behind legislation. Both of these focus on mass testing of representative groups for state and national comparisons with little or no feedback to schools and teachers on the progress of individual students. As part of the current political and academic commitment to accountability, many additional state and national science tests are under development. During the last 20+ years, there has been a significant rethinking of and agreement in principle on the purposes of science education. These purposes have been stated by the American Association for the Advancement of Science (1989) in *Science for All Americans* (based on Project 2061) and by the National Research Council (1996) in *National Science Education Standards* (NSES) in their goals for science education. More important for this discussion, these recommendations are rapidly becoming integrated into state science expectations and guidelines. During the same time period, the number of science courses students are expected to take in high school has increased significantly, with mixed results as stated by Smithson and Porter (Chapter 5). The good news is that enrollments in science and math increased, and Smithson and Porter's 1993 study determined "that these increased enrollments did not appear to compromise the *traditional* curriculum offered in those courses" (p. 114, emphasis added). The bad news is that, according to the same study, mathematics and science courses were still some distance from reflecting the type of curriculum advocated by the national standards in both fields.

In order to better understand the challenges facing developers and assessment professionals in science education, it is important to agree on the nature of science and that our definition of science determines what it is important to assess. An operationally useful definition of science, proposed by Thier and Daviss (2001), is: Science is a way of asking and seeking answers to questions rather than learning answers to someone else's questions. Facts have a necessary role in building a true understanding of science, but they must be given meaning and context that enable students to assimilate them into their personal knowledge structures. PISA uses the following definition as the basis for assessment goals in science:

Scientific literacy is the capacity to use scientific knowledge, to identify questions and to draw evidence-based conclusions in order to understand and help make decisions about the natural world and the changes made to it through human activity.

The NSES uses the following approach to science to define what students should learn from science education: The goals for school science are to educate students to be able to

- Experience the richness and excitement of knowing about and understanding the natural world;
- Use appropriate scientific processes and principles in making personal decisions;
- Engage intelligently in public discourse and debate about matters of scientific and technological concern; and
- Increase their economic productivity through the use of the knowledge, understanding, and skills of the scientifically literate person in their careers. (NRC, 1996; p. 13; see also AAAS, 1990)

The acceptance of this kind of definition for science and what students need to know about science needs to be combined with current understandings about learning theory to structure an effective approach to science instruction. Black and Wiliam (Chapter 2) summarize these understandings as follows: "The main lesson that emerges from constructivist approaches to learning theory is that the key to effective learning is to start from the students' own ideas and then help them to restructure their knowledge in order to build in different and more powerful ideas (Bransford, Brown, & Cocking, 1999; Wood, 1998)" (p. 34). This means that learning is measured not by what students are able to recite or by the books they have read, but by what they are able to do. Thus learning can no longer be defined as taking courses and passing tests, but only as mastery of a subject or skill as demonstrated by the ability to apply concepts and processes flexibly and accurately outside of the classroom. Forster and Masters (Chapter 3) cite three principles, suggested by research on how people learn (Bransford et al., 2000), that when incorporated into teaching result in the improvement of student achievement: (1) Learning is enhanced when teachers identify and work from learners' current knowledge and beliefs; (2) Learning is most effective when it results in well-organized knowledge and deep understanding of concepts and their applicability; and (3) Learning is enhanced by the ability to monitor one's own learning (p. 68).

Science educators and materials developers need to expand the idea of inquiry to a larger one that can be described as *guided inquiry* (Tafoya, Senal, & Knecht, 1980). My definition of guided inquiry is the sequencing and integration of appropriate processes and information, chosen through research, to fashion experiences for students under the leadership of an informed teacher. These experiences should lead students to confront scientific concepts and principles in the context of real-world problems or situations; use data and evidence to reason their way through a particular problem or issue; and reach independent conclusions or decisions justified by the data and evidence.

The concept of guided inquiry in science education gives equal weight to knowledge and skills, retaining a hands-on or activity-based focus that relies on strong content. Sequencing activities in a larger curricular plan or design enables educators to reach their curricular and instructional goals. Placing scientific ideas and processes in the context of actual issues—balancing the risks and benefits of industrial production, for example—can suddenly give formerly abstract concepts meaning within students' own lives, a key element in helping them master knowledge (Thier & Daviss, 2001). Guided inquiry does not ignore or belittle the value of the information that textbooks, databases, and other repositories of facts have to offer. No one, student or adult, can be expected to rebuild the entire structure of science or other disciplines for themselves. But educational research, and a century of experience, has shown us that facts must be given meaning and context that enables students to assimilate the information into their personal knowledge structures.

By rethinking the traditional concepts that have shaped schooling for more than a century, guided inquiry can redefine the roles of students and teachers alike. Students are no longer passive vessels that teachers must labor to fill with knowledge; they are no longer raw material in a process that trains them to look to others not only for information, but also for judgments of its value. Guided inquiry helps teachers to avoid being the all-knowing source of information and lets them become more like facilitators or learning coaches, who help students master the processes of learning for themselves. Students develop the ability to frame problems, ferret out facts, test and assess the accuracy and relevance of those facts, articulate conclusions, and make reasoned, evidence-based decisions. These are crucial survival skills in a world awash in un-refereed information, much of it being peddled by groups promoting partisan agendas. Guided inquiry is one means to the goal of higher quality learning experiences for students.

Learning materials structured around real-life, open-ended challenges engage students emotionally in academic content. That kind of engagement leads them to find meaning in their studies. Materials for guided inquiry lay the foundations of engagement and meaning that lead to the mastery of facts, processes, and higher-order intellectual skills—the kind of learning that our society and economy now demand of every graduate. Guided inquiry is designed to create student interest in and a need to know about the aspect of science under consideration. This is not the kind of learning measured effectively by currently available fact-laden, machine-scorable tests in science.

Assessment of Learning in Science Education

Too often as educators, we assess what is easy to measure and easy to grade—increasingly by using a machine. As a result, conventional curricula focus on facts instead of on concepts and their application. But current standardized, fact-based tests do not and cannot assess the processes and skills that our newest voting citizens and workers will need to know. They also cannot assess how well students are able to use what they have learned to improve their own lives and those of their communities. Of course, standardized tests have legitimate roles. They can signal long-term trends in students' mastery of facts. Given in high school, they also can predict first-year college success because so much of freshman instruction is conducted in large groups and assessed by fact-based tests that can be scored by machines. The fit is perfect, but the shoe itself is wrong.

Our growing understanding of science and the nature of the learner means that assessment should be the fraternal twin of instruction: The two should look as much alike as possible but be designed differently enough so that each fulfills its distinct purpose. Assessments that are more useful (as well as more valid) than conventional standardized tests are successfully being built into inquiry-based learning activities themselves, thus earning the adjective *embedded*. *National Science Education Standards* explains why they should be: "Assessment practices provide operational definitions of what is important; the methods used to collect educational data define in measurable terms what teachers should teach and what students should learn. For example, the use of an extended inquiry for an assessment task signals what students are to learn, how teachers are to teach, and where resources are to be allocated" (NRC, 1996, p. 76). National, politically motivated education improvement programs like No Child Left Behind claim to endorse the national science standards. Currently, however, they focus their efforts on standardized tests of the facts of science included in the standards rather than on the broad encompassing goal of using inquiry to lend meaning, understanding, and reality to those facts for the benefit of the learner.

The embedded assessments such as those suggested by the authors of the five source chapters of this volume, in contrast, weave the tasks on which students are assessed into the learning activities, projects, and investigations that students conduct as routine elements of their learning. The activities designated as assessment tools are carefully crafted to resemble as closely as possible any other day-to-day activity. The traditional multiple-choice, machine-scored, standardized tests currently focused on in state and national testing programs can interrupt learning as teachers and students get ready to take the tests by practicing test-taking skills, drilling repeatedly on the same lists of facts, and so on. Each of the five chapters that make up the core of this volume calls for embedded, authentic assessment as the design for all assessment efforts.

It is important to emphasize that this approach to assessment, as to development, is evolutionary rather than revolutionary. Authentic, embedded assessment is not intended to supplant fact-oriented tests. Knowledge of facts remains one key to knowledge of science or any field. The goal of these new assessment regimes is to augment the measurement of factual knowledge with measurements of students' evolving abilities to understand what those facts mean and to apply them appropriately in making real-life decisions.

Embedding assessments in activities offers three advantages. First, these assessments can measure what the national standards call the "rich and varied" outcomes of science education—not only skills in factual recall but also such accomplishments as "the ability to inquire" and "knowing and understanding scientific facts, concepts, principles, laws, and theories" (NRC, 1996, p. 76). Second, they deduct little time from learning compared to conventional tests, for which learning activities usually cease during the testing period (March or April Madness). Third, they help to eliminate conventional test-taking skills (or lack thereof) as a significant factor that too often conceals a student's actual degree of intellectual achievement.

But embedding assessment is only half the challenge of designing valid, accurate assessment protocols for guided inquiry. The other half is to make the assessments authentic. *National Science Education Standards* describe authentic assessments as "exercises that require students to apply scientific knowledge and reasoning to situations similar to those they will encounter in the world outside the classroom, as well as to situations that approximate how scientists do their work" (NRC, 1996, p. 78).

As an example, consider an assessment event in the guided-inquiry course Science and Sustainability (SEPUP, 2001) for high school students.

A theme of the course is energy use and its impact on issues of sustainability. Through a series of course activities, students examine the principles of energy transfer. In one investigation, students burn equal amounts of ethanol and kerosene (instead of gasoline, for safety reasons) to heat identical volumes of water. The students observe and record the change in temperature in each container of water as well as similarities and differences in how the two fuels burn. Then the students are asked a question: "Chemically, gasoline is very similar to kerosene. How could the results of these investigations affect your decision to buy fuel for your car that combines ethanol and gasoline?"

The question is an assessment item, graded against a five-point rubric that gauges a student's ability to gather and weigh evidence and to use that evidence to make trade-offs. (For example, students learn that ethanol burns more cleanly than gasoline but yields less energy per volume of fuel used.) This ability to weigh evidence and balance advantages and disadvantages of specific choices is not only one of five variables on which students are assessed during the course but also a task that will confront them daily in their lives beyond school. This is one example of the approach to assessment emphasized in the entire course. It is these kinds of assessment that are needed if assessment is to become an integral part of the student's learning experience.

Assessment of a Development Project

The impact of a materials development project is gauged in two parts. First, whether and what students learn (and how well) by using the project's materials must be *assessed*. In guided inquiry, learning is best measured by assessments that are both *embedded* and *authentic*. This is the main emphasis of this chapter. Second, the project itself must be *evaluated*. A project team may be allowed to evaluate itself or, more likely, the project's funder will appoint an external evaluator. Evaluations examine how efficiently the project team manages itself, its work, and the funder's money.

All developers of innovative instructional materials face the same challenge: the more innovative their materials are, the harder it is to find well-established assessment and evaluation methods that will accurately gauge the materials' range of impacts on learning in all its richness. That makes it difficult for a project to provide the kinds of evidence that education's various constituencies need to be convinced of the innovation's value. At the same time, educators in the schools face growing political demands for accountability: their pay and job security is increasingly linked to their students' performances on standardized tests. Therefore, a project's ability to provide detailed evaluation results showing its power to improve learning of both facts and processes becomes crucial if science education based on guided inquiry is to grow and flourish. To meet this challenge, developers can design their materials to fulfill comprehensive new standards while still meeting educators' needs for acceptable scores on standardized tests.

National Science Education Standards set content standards that can provide a useful frame of reference for developers creating science materials for guided inquiry. More and more, these standards are determining the content of courses in biology, chemistry, earth science, and physics. The standards, developed by a committee whose members were drawn from each of the disciplines, are not revolutionary. Indeed, their specific content guidelines form the universe of topics from which questions on standardized tests are drawn. Developers can use this conjunction of new standards and conventional testing forms to create materials able to meet evaluation criteria in both areas. They can accomplish this by doing two things.

First, they must specify which of the content standards their materials embody and at which grade level or levels. This means something other than which content areas their materials "cover." It is too easy to make up lists of standards that materials cover (too often done by wall-papering materials with lists and definitions of technical terms). This approach contributes to the public perception that science education in U.S. public schools is a mile wide and an inch deep. Developers will find it far more useful to compare a project's goals with the specific content standards at the grade level or levels on which the project has focused. Team members can then identify ways in which the materials and the student experiences they are creating will enable students to apply the skills and knowledge specified in each standard in their own lives, as the goals of the science standards demand.

Second, a project team can develop and try out banks of short-answer questions similar to the ones that appear on classroom quizzes and standardized tests. At the same time, the team can develop embedded, authentic assessments that help the teacher measure students' mastery of the higher order skills, mandated by the standards, that the materials have been designed to address.

To accomplish the first part of this step, developers can analyze the sample questions that publishers of the most widely used standardized tests release publicly. Through that analysis, the developers can better ensure that their materials target the ideas and understandings that are both expressed in the content standards and addressed in standardized tests for the grade level or levels on which the project has focused. This needs to be done in addition to making sure that authentic, embedded assessment of students' real learning takes place. Developers need to follow closely the work on redesigning of multiple-choice questions to provide information about student's understanding of the content, as discussed by Wilson and Draney (Chapter 6).

The emphasis a team gives to this kind of review and analysis, and the degree to which the materials developed reflect that analysis, will result from an ongoing conversation among the project team, its assessment specialists, its funder, and also its publisher or producer-distributor. Currently, innovative educational materials in science are distributed primarily by publishers. That is why NSF, the primary funder of innovation in science education materials development, requires every project it funds to develop a working relationship with a publisher for the distribution of the materials. The project decides on its educational goals, designs materials to meet them, and in collaboration with its assessment specialists establishes its own system for assessing student learning. A competent commercial partner knows the market. It can use that insight to help team members shape materials that meet market demands without violating the team's own objectives. For example, a team's proposed assessment might accomplish its goals for measuring its materials' educational effectiveness. But a commercial partner can tell the team that the system is so complex that teachers are unlikely to use it and that the system therefore must be adjusted. A constant conversation among the three constituents will ensure that each understands the demands the others face in carrying out their parts of the project. Working together, the three can create materials that meet the team's goals for content and assessment, help the funder achieve its objectives, and give a producer-distributor materials that address the practical realities of the marketplace. This can all be achieved while using embedded, authentic assessments to track students' real accomplishments.

Teachers are essential to the success of every aspect of project and materials evaluation. Teachers who work with their students in classrooms every day are among the best sources of evidence about how well a project team is doing its job and whether and how effectively its materials are achieving their educational objectives.

Project and materials evaluations that intensively involve teachers are among the most persuasive tools a project team can have to convince educators to adopt and implement its materials. Selling materials to a school does not guarantee that the materials will be used, especially as long as classrooms have doors and teachers can close them, affording them a measure of privacy. The more that leading teachers take part in a project's evaluations and the development of its assessment protocols, the more likely it becomes that other teachers will want to use the project's materials to create curricula in their classrooms.

Teachers as Assessment Leaders

The most effective embedded, authentic assessments are able to help students learn while taking a test and also guide teachers in planning the direction and content of future class sessions. Developing such useful assessment methods is not possible without the leadership, commitment, and participation of teachers. Indeed, this approach gives responsibility for conducting assessment back to the teacher—always the educational leader essential to the success of any program. In discussing this kind of assessment Frederiksen and White (Chapter 4) emphasize that the teachers "also felt that the value of the knowledge they acquired, of how to analyze students' work and of scientific inquiry itself, has important benefits in helping them support their students' learning" (p. 101). Wilson and Draney emphasize that, in building a classroom based assessment system, "teachers must be the classroom managers of the system and therefore must have the tools to run it efficiently and to use the assessment data effectively and appropriately" (p. 139). They further emphasize that teachers must be "involved in the process of collecting and selecting student work; be able to score and use the results immediately, rather than waiting for scores to be returned several months later; be able to interpret the results in instructional terms; and take a creative role in the way that the assessment system is realized in their classrooms" (p. 139).

Forster and Masters state that, based on their research, "classroom teachers can assemble valid student achievement data on a wide range of learning outcomes, if they are provided with adequate tools. Furthermore, with adequate support, classroom teachers can be trained to assess student work with a level of reliability necessary for system-level data collection" (p. 69). This point, reinforced in different ways by the other authors of the source chapters, means that further research and development efforts on authentic, embedded, classroom-based teacher-led assessment can provide the data needed for student, school, state, and national accountability purposes. This would increase the quality and efficiency of the teacher-learner interaction in the classroom because it would no longer be necessary to take time out of relevant instruction to prepare for external tests unrelated to the real goals of the instructional program.

Structuring Successful Collaborations Between Developers and Assessment Specialists

As developers create new kinds of materials to teach students new kinds of skills, they are obligated to help create new ways to effectively assess students' mastery of those new skills. To fulfill that obligation, they must work in close collaboration with assessment specialists to design the most effective ways to assess student achievement resulting from the use of specific innovative materials.

Such collaborations are increasingly common but are not always successful. In reflecting on the cooperative effort by SEPUP developers and BEAR assessment specialists to design an assessment system for the SEPUP Issues, Evidence and You (IEY) course, the following four suggestions evolved that should increase the effectiveness of collaborative efforts between developers and assessment specialists generally:

1. To make embedded, authentic assessment an integral component of a project's materials, the project team must include assessment specialists from the very beginning of the design process.

2. Professionally, developers and assessment specialists wrestle with different issues and pursue different purposes and goals. The goal of the partnership is not to transform developers into assessors or vice versa. Instead, it is to enable members of both specialties to help each other achieve their unique professional objectives by working together to ensure the success of both the development and assessment components of the project.

3. For the partnership to succeed, developers must understand the dictates and implications of the research base that underlies the assessment system they adopt for their project. Similarly, assessment specialists must grasp the practical goals and expected learning outcomes of the materials being developed. Therefore, when the partnership begins, each group must devote time specifically to teaching, and learning from, the other about their specific goals, methods, and concerns.

4. Developers and assessment specialists can smooth and strengthen their working partnership by investing time early in the project

to work together to design one, or even a few, activities. This initial collaboration can not only show each group how the other thinks and works but also fashion a common understanding of the elements that make an activity a good candidate for assessment as well as an effective learning experience.

A lot was learned about assessor-developer relationships through this collaboration, and the value of the collaboration was confirmed two years after SEPUP first tested its new assessment system for IEY. The NSF's 1997 review of widely used middle school science curriculum materials cited IEY's assessment program as an outstanding example of embedded assessment at the middle-school level (NSF, 1997). One teacher, commenting on his use of the system, put it more bluntly: "This isn't the kind of assessment system where a kid can screw around all year and then do fine on a test just because he's smart. This is the kind of process where a kid needs to progressively improve specific skills in order to do well on the assessment" (teacher feedback to SEPUP).

As developers learn to view each aspect of each new activity as a potential assessment item, they can show assessment specialists which components within activities they regard as most important to use as assessment tools. The assessment specialists can analyze those components as well as their context among others in the materials being developed. Developers and assessment specialists then can work together to refine the choices and designs of assessment items. During and after field tests of the materials and their assessment system, the team can collaborate again to review teachers' comments and use the results of classroom experience to further refine and improve assessment items and techniques.

This is not to imply that the needs of assessment must drive the curriculum, but rather that the two, assessment and instruction, must be in step—they drive one another. Using progress variables to structure both instruction and assessment is one way to make sure that the two are in alignment, at least at the planning level. In order to make this alignment concrete, however, the match must also exist at the level of classroom interaction, and that is where the nature of the assessment tasks becomes so crucial.

Conclusion

The goal is to construct an embedded, authentic assessment system for science. Such a system must meet the demands of high-stakes school district, state, and national testing for accountability programs while at the same time providing quality, usable information on the progress of individual students in their developing understanding of science as called for in the goals of the national standards. This is no small task. First, assessment specialists and instructional materials developers must work in close collaboration. Second, research on more effective ways of structuring and using test questions must be continued and made use of by developers and assessment specialists. Third, teachers who have direct and continuing interaction with students and their learning must have a central role in all cooperative assessment and development efforts. The challenge is to change the current focus on fact-based testing. All assessment should contribute to helping students understand how the facts of science are the tools they will use to identify and frame questions, draw evidence-based conclusions, and use their evolving understanding of science to help them make decisions for themselves and, as citizens, for their communities. Last and most important, all professionals involved need to become advocates for the value of embedded, authentic assessment. They need to use their professional status and influence to convince the decision makers, regarding high-stakes standardized testing, that an embedded, authentic approach to assessment can meet their needs while also contributing to quality science education for all students.

REFERENCES

American Association for the Advancement of Science (AAAS). (1989). *Science for all Americans: A project 2061 report on literacy goals in science, mathematics, and technology.* Washington, DC: Author.

Bransford, J.A., Brown, A., & Cocking, R. (1999). *How people learn: Brain, mind, experience and school.* Washington, DC: National Academy Press.

National Research Council (NRC). (1996). *National Science Education Standards.* Washington, DC: National Academy Press.

National Science Foundation (NSF). (1997). *Review of instructional materials for middle school science.* Retrieved July 26, 2000, from http://www.nsf/gov/cgi-binbin/getpub?nsf9754

Organisation for Economic Co-operation and Development (OECD). (n.d.). Programme for International Student Assessment (PISA). Retrieved July 28, 2000 from http://www.pisa.oecd.org

Science Education for Public Understanding Program (SEPUP). (2001). *Science and sustainability: Teacher's guide.* Berkeley: University of California, Lawrence Hall of Science.

Tafoya, E., Senal, D.W., & Knecht, P. (1980). Assessing inquiry potential: A tool for curriculum decision-makers. *School Science and Mathematics, 80,* 43–48.

Thier, H.D., with Daviss, B. (2001). *Developing inquiry-based science materials: A guide for educators.* New York: Teachers College Press.

CHAPTER 16

Student Assessment as an Opportunity to Learn In and From One's Teaching Practice

SUZANNE M. WILSON

> We had the experience but missed the meaning.
> —T.S. Eliot, "The Dry Salvages," *Four Quartets*

The focus of this volume is ostensibly student assessment, including assessments used daily by teachers and those used to judge the effectiveness of teachers and schools. Yet in addition to students and their learning, teachers are everywhere in this volume: Teachers use the assessments, they adapt them to their curricula, they examine and react to student work. Teachers help author assessments, vet them as users and critics, and score student performances. They offer their classrooms as laboratories to test new assessments, change their practices to accommodate them, and learn how to use data and data systems in order to implement them.

Indeed, perhaps one of the most remarkable features of the work these researchers report is how closely they have worked with teachers as collaborators and users. While many projects purposefully included teachers in the work, not all of the collaborations were intentional. As Smithson and Porter (Chapter 5) note, "This steady migration from the realm of policy to the realm of practice was not a deliberate goal on our part, but rather a response to a growing interest among educators and administrators" (p. 124-25). Incidental, accidental, serendipitous, or intentional, it was the teachers' omnipresence in these projects that I was most taken with. In particular, I was struck by the notion that as student assessment became a critical part of teachers' practice, it might also have played an important role in how much teachers were learning from their everyday experiences.

Suzanne M. Wilson is a professor in the Department of Teacher Education at Michigan State University and senior scholar at the Carnegie Foundation for the Advancement of Teaching.

The Challenge of Learning in and from Practice

The education of teachers—which runs the spectrum from prospective teacher preparation to induction experiences to professional development—is an enterprise fraught with complexities. A perennial and central challenge is how to bridge the worlds of theory and practice, and both teacher preparation and professional development have long been criticized for their lack of connection to practice. Yet another challenge lies in experience. Teachers are awash with experience, but whether they learn from that experience—and if so, what they learn from it—is problematic.

Those responsible for helping teachers learn are pushed to get closer and closer to practice, to the dailiness of teaching. But classrooms are noisy places. Teachers must make decisions quickly, with little time to reflect, and their attention is drawn in myriad directions, by each and every student, by the principal or other teachers, by local and state policies and mandates. It is hard to imagine how anyone can learn from his or her own teaching; there is just too much going on. In fact, many scholars, including Dewey (1964), have suggested that immersion in experience might stunt learning for new teachers, so taken are they with the surface, mundane features of teaching.

Thus we have a central paradox in teacher development (from preservice to inservice): Most of teachers' learning comes from and through experiences in schools. But experience can limit learning, in shaping what it is that we—as teachers—can see and comprehend as we go about our practice. Hence, the mere having of experience is not necessarily educative, for to paraphrase T.S. Eliot, we can have an experience and still miss its meaning. The projects discussed in this volume offer a way through this conundrum, for the assessments teachers were using might very well have helped them learn in and from their practice in meaningful and productive ways (Ball & Cohen, 1999).

Before proceeding, I want to note that the kind of teacher learning I focus on here is not that which took place in the professional development that these projects intentionally designed for and offered to teachers. All of these projects worked with teachers, developed resources for the participating teachers, and held meetings to review the assessments or to score items. Those *formal* occasions, intentionally crafted to support teachers' use of the project materials, do constitute an important form of professional development. Smithson and Porter note that their tools for analyzing assessment data provided a "platform for new and innovative approaches to professional development and technical assistance" (p. 122). Forster, Masters, and their colleagues

(Chapter 3) were careful to provide models for teachers throughout their project—models that were developed, one presumes, to guide teachers' use of the assessment materials. These official, intentional opportunities to learn were, no doubt, important aspects of the work.

But here I am interested in other, unofficial opportunities that were created for teacher learning. Specifically, I wonder about how the materials that teachers used changed the very nature of their daily experiences, potentially turning ordinary experiences into educative ones, helping teachers learn in and from their practice in ways that were (perhaps) incidental to the project goals. My conjecture is that their teaching changed in fundamental ways and that the assessments provided teachers with new evidence and texts to inform their practice.

Making Teaching Experience Educative

In *Experience and Education*, an analysis of what emerged under the banner of "progressive" education, Dewey (1938) argues that we need a "coherent theory of experience" if we want to give "new directions to the work of schools" (p. 30). Concerned with distinguishing educative from *mis*educative experience, Dewey proposed that there are two critical features of educative experience: continuity and interaction.

Continuity

There is a conceptual resonance between Dewey's continuity and the assessment work reported in this volume. Wilson and Draney (Chapter 6) remind us that continuity—"a continuous stream of evidence that tracks the progress of both individual students and educational programs over time" (p. 133)—is a critical feature of high-quality assessment programs. While Wilson and Draney focus on the continuity of the *student* assessment systems, let us consider how these projects enhanced continuity in teachers' experiences. Continuity, for Dewey, meant that "every experience both takes up something from those which have gone before and modifies in some way the quality of those which come after" (p. 35). Experience has continuity, Dewey claims, "if [it] arouses curiosity, strengthens initiative, and sets up desires and purposes that are sufficiently intense to carry a person over dead places in the future" (p. 38).

One problem with assessment as it has been traditionally conceptualized is that it is disjointed from teaching. In classrooms, teachers might pause to give a chapter test, then move on to the next unit. In a school, teachers might call a halt to their regular instruction to spend two or three days, maybe even weeks, preparing students to take the state standardized tests and then, when this particular form of March

Madness (as it is known in some states) is over, students and teachers alike resume their focus on the curriculum. Thus, whether assessments have been locally developed or mandated by the state, they have traditionally existed apart from the daily work of teachers and students, separate from learning and teaching. They have traditionally, it seems, been moments of discontinuity.

The work described in this volume paints a very different picture of assessment. Whether teachers are using new kinds of questions in the King's-Medway-Oxfordshire Formative Assessment Project or analyzing fine-grain content maps or progress maps for individual students or groups of students using the BEAR Assessment System, these projects "take up experience" (student learning and performance or the content of curriculum) and re-present it in ways that allow teachers to "modify" what comes after. Forster and Masters argue that the "conceptual bridge between classroom assessment and system accountability is a common assessment system" (p. 69). A byproduct of this new "connectedness" might be that in all of these assessment projects, the use of classroom assessments that are coordinated both with the classroom curriculum and with the larger education system's accountability plan turns teachers' ordinary experiences into opportunities to learn in their classrooms while they are teaching.

How has this happened? By using questions to surface students' prior knowledge early in a science unit, one teacher who worked with Black and Wiliam (Chapter 2) discovered that students had already mastered the content he intended to teach. This allowed him to return to his plans, edit them in light of what students knew, and create a more logical, coherent flow of material for students. In another case in that same project, teachers applied what they had learned about formative assessments to the summative assessments imposed by outside authorities. Pupils and teachers alike became active participants in analyzing the summative tests. In so doing, they transformed the tests from outside agent to educative tool, or as the authors put it, "Students can see that they can be beneficiaries rather than victims of testing because tests can help them improve their learning" (p. 42).

Interaction

But continuity is not the only feature of educative experience, according to Dewey. He also argues for interaction:

Experience does not go on simply inside a person. . . . Every genuine experience has an active side, which changes in some degree the objective conditions under which experiences arc had . . . There are sources outside an individual which give rise to experience. . . . A system of education based upon the necessary connection of education with experience must . . . take these things into account. (pp. 39-40)

Dewey goes on to say that

an experience is always what it is because of a transaction taking place between an individual and what, at the time, constitutes his environment, whether the latter consists of persons with whom he is talking about some topic or event, the subject talked about also being part of the situation; or the toys with which he is playing; the book he is reading; or the materials of an experiment he is performing. The environment, in other words, is whatever conditions interact with personal needs, desires, purposes, and capacities to create the experience which is had. (pp. 43-44)

The projects described in this volume systematically and purposefully changed the transactions between teachers and their environments. They did this in three ways: by introducing tools, by introducing a professional language, and by creating space for reflection and critical appraisal of teaching and learning.

Tools. First, they provided teachers with new tools, which took multiple forms and had varied purposes. Some of the tools were instructional strategies: teachers learned to ask "big questions" and provide comment-only feedback to students. They learned to scaffold students' inquiries and support students as they made their conceptual models explicit. Other tools focused on assessments: teachers on the DART project learned how to evaluate student work and use elaborated scoring rubrics. Teachers who piloted the BEAR Assessment System used scoring guides and progress maps to support their assessments of ongoing student learning.

Still other tools involved learning how to analyze assessment data. On the DART project, materials were developed to inform teachers' work, including the Assessment Resource Kit with its colorful magazines, videotapes, wall charts, and manual. Indeed, the tools for representing what students learn, could learn, and should learn are particularly compelling aspects of these projects. Researchers are taught the maxim "display the data," but few teachers have had the opportunity to learn how to display the data on student learning in powerful ways that go beyond the traditional bar graph or pie chart. On the DART project, teachers used progress maps and learned to compare "graphical, numerical, and descriptive interpretations" (p. 64) against those maps. Smithson and Porter showed how one might use content matrix layouts, as well as content maps and graphs at both coarse- and fine-grained levels. Teachers who worked with Wilson and Draney learned how to read progress maps; those who worked with Frederiksen and White (Chapter 4) learned how to construct maps of each student's inquiry project. These maps gave teachers an opportunity to consider the character and content of every investigation, and they served as a touchstone for then asking and answering assessment questions. In displaying the data, teachers learned to turn numbers and words into alternative representations that captured the progress of individual students, the progress of groups of students, the developmental character of understanding particular topics, and the content of the curriculum. These projects thus provided teachers with a way to make the familiar—the world of classrooms—strange. In so doing, they may very well have made ordinary experience more educative.

Professional language. A second way the projects fundamentally changed the teachers' interactions concerns the development of a professional language for discussing practice. Teachers participating in the DART work used rating scales and marking rubrics to assess student understanding. They developed a graduated view of student learning and could judge whether students were at level 1, 2, 3, 4, or 5. The DART models and the subsequent NSELS work pushed teachers from across Australia to develop a common language for discussing student achievement and a common view of what constituted achievement at different levels.

Smithson and Porter explicitly discuss the development of a "systematic, rich, and multidimensional language for describing instructional content" (p. 105), which they describe as "key to these analyses" (p. 115). They argue that "teachers need such languages to talk among themselves about their intentions and their successes" (p. 115). Teachers who used the ThinkerTools curriculum had to learn to differentiate between a conceptual understanding of science and the cognitive competencies of being inventive, being systematic, using representations and tools, and reasoning carefully. These are distinctions that many teachers would recognize, but seldom do teachers have the opportunity to develop a shared meaning for those terms. Just as the new instructional and analytic tools may have helped teachers see new meaning in their experiences, so too this new professional language and discourse might have also transformed the everyday world of schools into a learning community.

Reflection and appraisal. Third, in enabling teachers to reflect on results, many of these tools provided an opportunity for teachers to appraise the content of their curricula or the alignment between what students have learned and the goals of instruction. These tools created an objective distance between the teacher and students, providing a chance to see and hear students in ways that ordinary experience—as noisy and fast paced as it is—does not allow. For example, when teachers participating in DART began providing more comment-only feedback, they began to notice which assignments revealed students' understanding and which did not. Teachers adjusted some assignments, added some, threw some out. The feedback meant for students created, in turn, feedback to teachers about how productive some assignments were for displaying student knowledge and understanding.

Frederiksen and White describe how teachers using the ThinkerTools Inquiry Curriculum had to learn to use evidence in scoring cognitive competencies. They developed analytic questions as they searched for evidence, and their use of those questions, the authors argue, "provides a way to open up a deep analysis of student work" (p. 94). While most teachers would acknowledge the importance of such analyses, few have either the time or the intellectual tools necessary to do them. By providing the tools, the language, and the space to reflect on what students were learning, these projects may have helped teachers learn in and from their actual practice in ways that go against the grain of traditional school teaching.

Looking Forward: Assessing the Potential Impact of Student Assessments on Teachers

My comments here take the form of conjectures, not claims, for these chapters—while rich in detail about student assessment systems—do not offer evidence about how and what teachers learned while participating on these projects. We know that teachers were presented with models and scoring guides, with assessment resources, and with professional development, but we do not know how those models and materials were presented to teachers. We know nothing of the pedagogies of professional development, intentional or incidental. Did the project leaders theorize about how teachers learn and thus construct professional development for their assessment systems that was shaped by their assumptions about teacher learning? What assumptions were made across these projects about how teachers learn, the materials they would need to do so, and the relationship between the assessments that were offered to them, their use of those assessments, and the meaning they made of them? And what evidence do we have that teachers learned, that they acquired new knowledge of assessment and subject matter, that they changed their beliefs and understanding? These questions go well beyond the focus of this volume, for these projects are in midstream. We will have to wait for subsequent reports to learn about teacher learning in these projects.

Nonetheless, it strikes me that each and every project might very well have altered not only teaching practices (especially those involving student assessments) but also what teachers were able to see in their classrooms, how they were able to process those experiences, and subsequently what they learned from their teaching. In his introduction, Wilson notes that a third challenge faced by the call for coherence in statewide assessment systems is the challenge of creating valid accountability systems that draw upon teachers' professional knowledge. I would argue that the projects described in this volume rose to a fourth challenge as well: the creation of valid accountability systems (both formative and summative) that extended teachers' knowledge—of teaching and learning, of assessment, of curriculum, and of their students. We need not only to develop assessment practices that foster student learning within the curriculum; we need also to develop assessment systems that intentionally foster teacher learning in and from that same curriculum. Teacher educators need to know what they can do to prepare new teachers to both use and learn from such assessments. By changing the very nature of how teachers experience teaching and learning, these projects may have laid important groundwork for this necessary next step.

REFERENCES

Ball, D.L., & Cohen, D.K. (1999). Developing practice, developing practitioners: Toward a practice-based theory of professional education. In G. Sykes and L. Darling-Hammond (Eds.), *Teaching as the learning profession: Handbook of policy and practice* (pp. 3-32). San Francisco: Jossey-Bass.

Dewey, J. (1938). *Experience and education*. New York: Collier Books.

Dewey, J. (1964). The relationship of theory to practice in education. In R.D. Archambault (Ed.), *John Dewey on education* (pp. 313-338). Chicago: University of Chicago Press.

Part Four
ONE STEP FURTHER

CHAPTER 17

A Perspective on Current Trends in Assessment and Accountability: Degrees of Coherence

MARK WILSON

The commentary chapters in Part 3 of this volume have responded to the ideas and perspectives presented in the preceding source chapters of Part 2. In turn, this concluding chapter is intended as a continuing discussion in response to certain of the points raised in the commentaries. In this final chapter I focus on one specific topic that, although not an explicit focus of the preceding chapters, is indeed lurking behind many of them: the impact of contemporary pressures on assessment and accountability in the United States, both nationally and locally. This chapter adds another layer of discussion to the points made by the commentary authors, especially with respect to current issues.

The chapter has two segments. The first is a recapitulation of points made about current issues in the commentary chapters, many of which are reflections of points made in the source chapters. This is in part to set up the ensuing discussion, but also to illustrate very concretely the interactive and generative nature of this volume. The second segment begins with a discussion that points out important distinctions among the different types of coherence mentioned in the previous chapters. This segment concludes with a discussion of how those different types of coherence can be used to analyze certain aspects of the current context of U.S. national assessment and accountability. There are many other important issues that are raised in the commentaries, well beyond

Mark Wilson is a Professor of Education at the University of California, Berkeley. He specializes in measurement and assessment, particularly in education, and also in educational statistics.

what one could adequately respond to in a single concluding chapter. These many other threads of discussion are left dangling, with the intent that they will be taken up by others and prompt further discussion and debate. (One concrete format for such discussions is noted at the end of the chapter.)

Current Issues Raised in the Commentaries

The authors of the commentaries were asked to respond to the source chapters but were not explicitly asked to relate their comments, or those of the source chapter authors, to any specific current issue. As noted by Le Mahieu and Reilly (Chapter 10), the issue of how classroom assessment relates to large-scale assessment is not one that has arisen just recently. They cite literature on this topic going back 20 years or so, and indeed the issue is one that is relevant in any educational system in which there are both classroom and large-scale assessments. Thus, although many of the points made by the commentary authors transcend the current context, quite a few of their points are directly related to it.

Thier (Chapter 15), writing in the context of assessment in science education, provides a contemporary judgment on large-scale assessments: "Current short-answer machine-scored, standardized tests are inadequate as an effective measure of what students are learning" (p. 250). He believes that we need to change "the popular concept of assessment away from comparing scores and toward measuring improvement in student learning" (p. 251). He elaborates on this theme as follows:

Too often as educators, we assess what is easy to measure and easy to grade— increasingly by using a machine. As a result, conventional curricula focus on facts instead of on concepts and their application. But current standardized, fact-based tests do not and cannot assess the processes and skills that our newest voting citizens and workers will need to know. They also cannot assess how well students are able to use what they have learned to improve their own lives and those of their communities. (p. 255)

Thus, in his view, the problems in contemporary science curricula are at least partially due to the large-scale tests that are used to assess them. Suter (Chapter 8) makes similar points, summarizing the findings of Black and Wiliam (Chapter 2) with respect to summative assessment thus: "The pressures to provide a summative assessment inhibited teaching topics that are linked to other topics. Each lesson was restricted in style and imagination. Tying lessons to specific national curriculum statements restricted pupil involvement and enjoyment" (p. 180).

Suzanne Wilson (Chapter 16) sees problems caused by the discontinuity between the classroom environment and contemporary testing practices. She notes:

One problem with assessment as it has been traditionally conceptualized is that it is disjointed from teaching. In classrooms, teachers might pause to give a chapter test, then move on to the next unit. In a school, teachers might call a halt to their regular instruction to spend two or three days, maybe even weeks, preparing students to take the state standardized tests, and then, when this particular form of March Madness (as it is known in some states) is over, students and teachers alike resume their focus on the curriculum. (p. 266-277)

Thier goes on to explicate what he sees as positive roles for large-scale tests:

Of course, standardized tests have legitimate roles. They can signal long-term trends in students' mastery of facts. Given in high school, they also can predict first-year college success because so much of freshman instruction is conducted in large groups and assessed by fact-based tests that can be scored by machines. (p. 255)

But, looking with a broader perspective, he notes,

National, politically motivated education improvement programs like No Child Left Behind claim to endorse the national science standards. Currently, however, they focus their efforts on standardized tests of the facts of science included in the standards rather than the broad encompassing goal of using inquiry to lend meaning, understanding, and reality to those facts for the benefit of the learner. (p. 255)

Shepard (Chapter 14) views the Fredericksen and White chapter (Chapter 4) as illustrating how classroom assessments broaden the range of assessments beyond that of large-scale assessment (in fact, she calls this effect the "most powerful of all"). She says that "they reflect accomplishments on extended problem solving and inquiry tasks and are thereby qualitatively different from the knowledge and skills captured by present-day large-scale assessments" (p. 246). Working along similar lines, Thier agrees with Shepard and elaborates on this point:

Authentic, embedded assessment is not intended to supplant fact-oriented tests. Knowledge of facts remains one key to knowledge of science or any field. The goal of these new assessment regimes is to augment the measurement of factual knowledge with measurements of students' evolving abilities to understand what those facts mean and to apply them appropriately in making real-life decisions. (p. 256)

He goes on to say that

Embedding assessments in activities themselves offers three advantages. First, these assessments can measure what the national standards call the "rich and varied" outcomes of science education—not only skills in factual recall but also such accomplishments as "the ability to inquire" and "knowing and understanding scientific facts, concepts, principles, laws, and theories" (NRC, 1996, p. 76). Second, they deduct little time from learning compared to conventional tests, during which learning activities usually cease. . . . Third, they help to eliminate conventional test-taking skills (or lack thereof) as a significant factor that too often conceals a student's actual degree of intellectual achievement. (p. 256)

However, Shepard also warns that

At the present time, there are too many examples of both narrow and excessive content standards across states to be in favor of giving these frameworks even tighter control over day-to-day instruction. Rather, we should . . . resist efforts to use existing assessment frameworks as if they were adequate as curriculum guides. (p. 248)

In a similar vein, Suter sees the Black and Wiliam chapter (Chapter 2) as making a good case for "many of the pitfalls in creating assessments that serve two masters: administrators, who want rankings for accountability purposes, and teachers, who want formative assessments that they can use to increase student attention to the topic and thereby improve student understanding of their subjects" (p. 180). And Moss (Chapter 13) expounds with considerable insight upon the dangers of too much coherence.

In summary, the commentary authors seem to have reached common ground on a number of points:

1. The current use of standardized tests for large-scale assessment has a negative effect on instruction and curriculum in the classroom.
2. Although there is a legitimate role for standardized tests, there is an essential role for other sorts of tests in expanding the range and depth of assessments and thus reflecting essential outcomes of the curriculum.

3. There is a danger in tying classroom and large-scale assessments too closely together, say, by using the same items for both.

Systemic Coherence and Threat Coherence

Helen Wildy (Chapter 7) makes the salient point that a unifying idea of the source chapters is that "it is possible to bring classroom and large-scale assessments together conceptually in support of student learning" (p. 155-56). In pointing this out, she is highlighting one form of the coherence that was argued for in the NRC report *Knowing What Students Know*: "The conceptual base or models of student learning underlying the various external and classroom assessments within a system should be compatible" (Pellegrino, Chudowsky, & Glaser, 2001, p. 255). I will refer to this as *systemic coherence*—where there is a high degree of consistency between the underlying frameworks for the large-scale and classroom assessments—and make clearer the meaning of that term by contrasting it with an alternative form of coherence, *threat coherence*. A summary of the different types of coherence is provided in Table 1.

TABLE 1
Degrees of Coherence

Level of Coherence	Description
Threat	The large-scale assessment is used as a driving and constraining force, straightjacketing the classroom instruction and curriculum to adherence to a specific state curriculum.
Systemic	"The conceptual base or models of student learning underlying the various external and classroom assessments within a system should be compatible" (Pellegrino, Chudowsky, & Glaser, 2001, p. 255).
Conceptual	Assessments at the classroom and large-scale levels share a common underlying framework.
Information	Assessments at the classroom and large-scale levels share a common underlying framework, and information from both classroom and large-scale assessments is used by the accountability system.
Item	Assessments at the state and classroom levels are the same.

Systemic coherence is not the only form of coherence that one might find in an accountability system. Indeed, a more basic and probably more common form of coherence is what I will refer to as *threat coherence*—that is, where the large-scale assessment is used as a driving and constraining force, straightjacketing the classroom instruction and curriculum to adherence to a specific state curriculum, resulting in classroom assessments that are either parallel to the large-scale assessments or irrelevant for accountability. Essentially, classroom assessments become just a small component of coherence in this case—the straightjacket is directly imposed on classroom curriculum and instruction via the large-scale assessments, and classroom assessments are expected to follow suit. The import of this view was once made clear to me by a member of the State Board of Education for California, who said that the tests used for accountability do not have to be particularly good tests; they just had to serve their purpose—which was to ensure that teachers teach the standards as tested by the state! It is interesting to note that, in cases where large-scale assessments are used in this way, coherence need not be systemic in the way described above; it need only convey the right sort of threat to the classroom. Note that this threat will not be effective unless the large-scale test is also used in a way that makes the classroom in at least some way (either directly, through the teacher, or indirectly, through the school) subject to the sanctions of an assessment system. For example, a standardized test that does not actually measure *any* standard can be used for accountability if it is "based on" the standards (i.e., test items can be individually mapped to specific standards) because the threat of inclusion of each and every standard will control the curriculum in the classroom. This is consistent with what Suter observes when he notes that Black and Wiliam (Chapter 2) found that teacher concerns about the validity of the national test "seemed to undermine the purpose of assessment" (p. 179).

In the current U.S. context, where the No Child Left Behind Act of 2001 has accelerated the imposition of state assessments in mathematics and reading into every classroom in every state (with science to follow in 2007), threat coherence is very much a reality. Although there are notable exceptions (see the examples in NRC, 2003), a common way that states have been complying with the legislation is to adapt or develop large-scale standardized tests (Erpenbach, Forte-Fast, & Potts, 2003). Typically, these sample quite lightly from those state standards that are easily assessable with multiple-choice items. But regardless of the quality of these multiple-choice items, there are, as Thier and Black and Wiliam note, important aspects of school curricula that are not adequately assessable by multiple-choice tests. In addition, the sheer number of standards addressed in any given test (upward of 100 in some states) ensures that the results cannot be used to gauge student accomplishment in a way that is useful in the class-room or the school for educational planning. All that is knowable on the basis of these tests is that students are doing better, worse, or about as well as their peers on very broad areas such as "math" or "reading."

Note that the argument here is not against the use of tests for monitoring, as described in several of the source and commentary chapters. It is instead directed at the problems of bringing a useful degree of interpretability to assessments. The importance of this point goes well beyond assessments, however, because the assessment prob-lem really arises from a curriculum problem. This matter has been brought to national attention by William Schmidt and his colleagues, who, in their analyses of many curricula from around the world, have developed an apt description for U.S. curricula: "a mile wide and an inch deep" (Schmidt, McKnight, & Raizen, 1997). They found that, compared with the curricula in other countries (specifically, mathe-matics and science curricula), U.S. curricula do not develop a deep understanding of subject matter. Instead they tend to spread attention across a very broad set of domains, doubtless to satisfy as many people as possible. Typical standardized tests reflect this curricular reality (as they must, in order to survive in the marketplace).

One recent attempt to address this issue has been the report of the Commission on Instructionally Supportive Assessment (CISA, 2001), which outlined nine major requirements for accountability systems. Although all of these requirements are important, three of them are particularly relevant for this discussion. The first is, "A state's content standards must be prioritized to support effective instruction and assessment" (p. 4). Thus the assessments must address only a small number of standards so that neither teachers nor students are over-whelmed by what is to be taught and assessed. This requirement clearly relates as much to curricula as to assessments. The second requirement is, "A state's high-priority content standards must be clearly and thor-oughly described so that the knowledge and skills students need to demonstrate competence are evident" (p. 5). In other words, the assessed standards have to be concretely described so that teachers (and even students) can understand the nature of what is to be taught in classrooms, and the standards need to be expressed in clear and plain language so that busy teachers can, indeed, actually take the time to use them. The third requirement is, "The results of a state's assessment of high-priority content standards should be reported standard-by-stan-dard for each student, school, and district" (p. 5). Thus every standard assessed must be measured well enough to permit teachers and their students and those students' parents to find out which particular standards have or have not been mastered by the students (see also Popham, 2003, for more details).

A second, parallel approach to this issue is illustrated in two of the source chapters, those by Forster and Masters (Chapter 3) and Wilson and Draney (Chapter 6). Rather than repeat the descriptions here, the reader is directed to look back over these two chapters to review the quite detailed accounts of this approach and the examples of its realization. In very brief summary, however, the chapters, according to Wildy, focus on the idea of the "developmental 'progress map' of achievement, which links simultaneously to system accountability and classroom assessment" (p. 156). This provides an interpretational thread for all aspects of the assessment system and focuses attention on aspects of the curriculum that are crucial for later development. Subsequent to the development of system-level agreements about progress maps, assessments and reporting systems would need to be developed to make them useful for classroom and large-scale use.

Neither of these approaches could be accomplished by a mere add-on to the current assessment systems as implemented under the No Child Left Behind legislation. Both require serious attention and work on state curricula and their assessments. The potential benefit is that both would address the list of problems described by the commentators, as summarized in the previous section of this chapter and amply illustrated in the source and commentary chapters.

Conceptual, Information, and Item Coherence

Within the concept of systemic coherence as described above, one can think of several different degrees of strength of the coherence. At the weak extreme, which I will refer to as *conceptual coherence*, the assessments at the classroom and large-scale levels share a common underlying framework. Examples would be the progress variables described in the Forster and Masters chapter (Chapter 3) and the Wilson and Draney chapter (Chapter 6) and the reduced set of prioritized standards as envisaged under the CISA requirements described above. At the other extreme is what I will refer to as *item coherence*, where the actual tests and student responses used at one level would also be used at the other. For example, one instance of item coherence would be using the results of locally developed items as the data for large-scale assessment. The system currently being developed in Nebraska (the School-based Teacher-led Assessment Recording System—STARS) conforms to this level

(NRC, 2003). Note that these different levels of systemic coherence are hierarchical. An implementation that satisfied the higher levels would necessarily satisfy the lower levels; thus, an example of item coherence would also necessarily be an example of conceptual coherence.

A level of coherence midway between these two extremes—one that I will call *information coherence*—would share a common framework and share information between the classroom and the large-scale levels but would not necessarily use the same tests or results at the two levels. The community of judgment that I described in Chapter 1 is an example of an assessment system with information coherence. Rather than attempt to summarize that material here, I urge the reader to look back over the relevant section of the chapter: The interlocking nature of the flow of information is described there, and Figure 2 in that chapter illustrates the multiple ways that different types of assessments could contribute to such a system. The key aspect of the community of judgment is that it is designed to take advantage of the particular strengths of different sources of information. For example, where instructional validity is viewed as being important, assessments that are close to the classroom are used. But, in order to ensure comparability across classroom contexts, information on consistency and verifiability must also be available, and that might come from large-scale tests or from judgments by outside experts. Of course, it would also be possible to design a community of judgment along the lines of the Nebraska STARS, where the teacher judgments would simply be aggregated to serve as accountability measures. But a more likely approach would be one that would share certain aspects of item and conceptual coherence.

For example, several varieties of information-coherent assessment systems have been used at various times in different Australian states (Wilson, 1992). One is typified by the process of statistical moderation of teachers' in-class judgments. Under this model, teachers in each school judge their students on locally developed assessments using centrally developed guidelines. The students are also given a centrally developed test on the same material (i.e., the test is developed using the same framework as the local assessments, but perhaps using a more restricted item format). The test results are used to statistically moderate the school distributions (i.e., the mean and variance for the teacher's assessments for each school are linearly transformed to be consistent with the mean and variance for their school on the test). But the within-school values are kept the same as the teacher assessments. Thus, the relative scores of students within schools are determined by the teachers' assessments, but the between-school variability is determined by the centrally developed test (McGaw, 1977; McGaw, Warry, & McBryde, 1975). A different variant of such a system is currently employed in the state of Queensland, where the effect of the statistical moderation has been lightened so that any differences between the teachers' assessments and the test are used *only* to flag inconsistencies that are then followed up with an audit (NRC, 2003). Another variant on such an information-sharing system could use a work-sampling arrangement, with "experts" judging the teachers' assessments of samples of student work; these could then be used as a basis for statistical moderation, or monitoring, as above.

Concern over the problems of item coherence surfaced at several points in the commentaries. Doubts voiced by Shepard and Suter (echoing those of Black and Wiliam) have already been mentioned. LeMahieu and Reilly noted,

Each case that seeks to expand the utility of classroom assessment in service to accountability does so with the well-intended goal of rendering accountability contingent upon assessments that are coherent with classroom goals and practices. However, a certain cautionary tone in the authors' writing betrays a reluctance to commit to the position that one assessment can serve both purposes wholly. (p. 201)

Smithson (Chapter 12) explicitly argues against item coherence, citing problems with both feasibility and desirability. Specifically, he doubts whether teacher assessments on performance assessments can be trusted in cases where individual assessment purposes such as grade promotion and graduation are concerned, or where accountability purposes such as rewards and sanctions for school districts, schools, and teachers themselves are concerned. Shepard sees a further problem with item coherence. She argues that coherence at the conceptual level or above requires a shared curriculum, and she views this curriculum as being much more constraining than current conceptions of test alignment would indicate. In particular, she considers a framework such as a progress map to be more specific than current versions of state curricula as expressed through standards, potentially leading to an undesirable amount of curricular uniformity.

Of course, these are debatable matters. For some it might seem a bit odd, for example, to doubt (as Smithson does) the validity of teachers' judgments of performance assessments in a high-stakes context when we certainly allow them to decide students' grades, which are routinely used for making high-stakes decisions about those same individual students. And whether or not adoption of a framework based on progress maps is unduly restrictive would depend very much on their generality. If one considers the possibilities raised by systems that have information coherence rather than item coherence, then any debate on such matters in the abstract becomes dubious. The potential complexities and the way they interact with a given context would make it impossible to seriously argue a case beyond a specific assessment system and context. The doubts discussed above are important ones, however, and would need to be addressed in any planned implementation of a system based on either information or item coherence.

The application of these concepts of coherence to the current context under the No Child Left Behind legislation leads one to ask what varieties of coherence can be found in different states. The legislation itself does not opt for any particular one of the levels of coherence described above—the "alignment" of tests to state standards can be satisfied by any level of coherence, from threat coherence to item coherence. Although most states are acting at a level of threat coherence, others are attempting to achieve coherence at higher levels (see NRC, 2003). In fact, Nebraska has been authorized to institute a system that is planned to be item coherent. Thus, the scope of possibilities is very broad. Unfortunately, given the scale of the systems that states are required to institute, and given the constant problems of funding, the most likely outcome is that states will satisfy the No Child Left Behind requirements in the cheapest and simplest way possible, which will likely mean that threat coherence will remain the norm unless serious efforts are made to develop alternative models and strategies and to fund initial implementations of such alternatives. Reading broadly through the chapters of this volume, and specifically, reading the extracts cited in this chapter, make clear that 1) the accountability and assessment systems currently predominating across the states under No Child Left Behind are based on an approach that will not foster the sorts of instruction and learning that are desperately needed for the education of citizens in the 21st century and 2) alternative approaches are available that can make positive use of the strength of the relationship among assessment, instruction, and learning and can thus be a catalyst for educational improvements that go beyond the accountancy aspects of accountability.

Conclusion and Invitation

The discussion in this chapter demonstrates clearly that the interactions between the source chapters and the commentary chapters have generated important and interesting points of view and, especially, disagreements. This chapter has been focused on just one specific issue, the contemporary national assessment context in the United States, but the discussion is wide ranging and has prompted ideas and arguments that have a wider application. Certainly the source and commentary chapters raise many other issues that could have been discussed in this chapter and are worthy of debate. Therefore, this small paragraph should not be seen as a conclusion, but rather an invitation for continuing debate and discussion. In that spirit, an online forum (http://bear.soe.berkeley.edu/NSSE/) has been constructed for readers to exchange their thoughts and views. Please log on and participate.

Author's Note

I would like to thank Robert Calfee, Karen Draney, June Hartley, and Debra Miretzky for their comments on an earlier draft of this chapter.

References

Commission on Instructionally Supportive Assessment (CISA). (2001). *Building tests to support instruction and accountability: A guide for policymakers.* Retrieved December 12, 2003, from http://www.nea.org/accountability/buildingtests.html

Erpenbach, W.J., Forte-Fast, E., & Potts, A. (2003). *Statewide educational accountability under NCLB: Central issues arising from an examination of state Accountability Workbooks and U.S. Department of Education reviews under the No Child Left Behind Act of 2001.* Washington, DC: Council of Chief State School Officers.

McGaw, B. (1977). The use of rescaled teacher assessments in the admission of students to tertiary study. *Australian Journal of Education, 21*(3), 209-225.

McGaw, B., Warry, R., & McBryde, B. (1975). *The Queensland grade 12 study report No. 2, validation of aptitude measures for the rescaling of school assessments.* Brisbane: Research Branch, Department of Education.

No Child Left Behind Act of 2001, Pub. L. No. 107-110, §115, Stat. 1425 (2002).

National Research Council (NRC). (1996). *National Science Education Standards.* Washington, DC: National Academies Press.

National Research Council (NRC). (2003). *Assessment in support of instruction and learning: Bridging the gap between large-scale and classroom assessment.* Workshop report. Washington, DC: National Academies Press.

Pellegrino, J., Chudowsky, N., & Glaser, R. (Eds.). (2001). *Knowing what students know: The science and design of educational assessment.* National Research Council Division on Behavioral and Social Sciences and Education Committee on the Foundations of Assessment. Washington, DC: National Academies Press.

Popham, W.J. (2003). *Crafting curricula aims for instructionally supportive assessment.* Retrieved December 15, 2003, from http://education.umn.edu/nceo/Presentations/CraftingCurricula.pdf

Schmidt, W.H., McKnight, C.C., & Raizen, S.A. (1997). *A splintered vision: An investigation of U.S. science and mathematics education.* New York: Kluwer Academic Publishers.

Wilson, M. (1992). *The integration of school-based assessments into a state-wide assessment system: Historical perspectives and contemporary issues.* BEAR Center, University of California, Berkeley: BEAR Research Report (Re-issued May 2000).

Index

RECENT PUBLICATIONS OF THE SOCIETY

1. The Yearbooks

103:1 (2004) *Developing the Teacher Workforce.* Mark A. Smylie and Debra Miretzky, editors. Cloth.

103:2 (2004) *Towards Coherence Between Classroom Assessment and Accountability.* Mark Wilson, editor. Cloth.

102:1 (2003) *American Educational Governance on Trial: Change and Challenges.* William Lowe Boyd and Debra Miretzky, editors. Cloth.

102:2 (2003) *Meeting at the Hyphen: Schools-Universities-Communities-Professions in Collaboration for Student Achievement and Well Being.* Mary M. Brabeck, Mary E. Walsh, and Rachel E. Latta, editors. Cloth.

101:1 (2002) *The Educational Leadership Challenge: Redefining Leadership for the 21st Century.* Joseph Murphy, editor. Cloth.

101:2 (2002) *Educating At-Risk Students.* Sam Stringfield and Deborah Land, editors. Cloth.

100:1 (2001) *Education Across a Century: The Centennial Volume.* Lyn Corno, editor. Cloth.

100:2 (2001) *From Capitol to the Cloakroom: Standards-based Reform in the States.* Susan H. Fuhrman, editor. Cloth.

99:1 (2000) *Constructivism in Education.* D. C. Phillips, editor. Cloth.

99:2 (2000) *American Education: Yesterday, Today, and Tomorrow.* Thomas L. Good, editor. Cloth.

98:1 (1999) *The Education of Teachers,* Gary A. Griffin, editor. Paper.

98:2 (1999) *Issues in Curriculum,* Margaret J. Early and Kenneth J. Rehage, editors. Cloth.

97:1 (1998) *The Adolescent Years: Social Influences and Educational Challenges.* Kathryn Borman and Barbara Schneider, editors. Cloth.

96:1 (1997) *Service Learning.* Joan Schine, editor. Cloth.

96:2 (1997) *The Construction of Children's Character.* Alex Molnar, editor. Cloth.

95:1 (1996) *Performance-Based Student Assessment: Challenges and Possibilities.* Joan B. Baron and Dennie P. Wolf, editors. Cloth.

94:1 (1995) *Creating New Educational Communities.* Jeannie Oakes and Karen Hunter Quartz, editors. Cloth.

94:2 (1995) *Changing Populations/Changing Schools.* Erwin Flaxman and A. Harry Passow, editors. Cloth.

93:1 (1994) *Teacher Research and Educational Reform.* Sandra Hollingsworth and Hugh Sockett, editors. Cloth.

92:1 (1993) *Gender and Education.* Sari Knopp Biklen and Diane Pollard, editors. Cloth.

91:1 (1992) *The Changing Contexts of Teaching.* Ann Lieberman, editor. Cloth.

91:2 (1992) *The Arts, Education, and Aesthetic Knowing.* Bennett Reimer and Ralph A. Smith, editors. Cloth.

Order the above titles from the University of Chicago Press, 11030 S. Langley Ave., Chicago, IL 60628. For a list of earlier Yearbooks still available, consult the University of Chicago Press website: www.press.uchicago.edu

2. The Series on Contemporary Educational Issues

This series has been discontinued.

The following volumes in the series may be ordered from the McCutchan Publishing Corporation, 3220 Blume Drive, Suite 197, Richmond, CA 94806. Local phone: (510)758-5510, Toll free: 1-800-227-1540, Fax: (510)758-6078, e-mail: mccutchanpublish@aol

Academic Work and Educational Excellence: Raising Student Productivity (1986). Edited by Tommy M. Tomlinson and Herbert J. Walberg.

Adapting Instruction to Student Differences (1985). Edited by Margaret C. Wang and Herbert J. Walberg.

Choice in Education (1990). Edited by William Lowe Boyd and Herbert J. Walberg.

Colleges of Education: Perspectives on Their Future (1985). Edited by Charles W. Case and William A. Matthes.

Contributing to Educational Change: Perspectives on Research and Practice (1988). Edited by Philip W. Jackson.

Effective Teaching: Current Research (1991). Edited by Hersholt C. Waxman and Herbert J. Walberg.

Moral Development and Character Education (1989). Edited by Larry P. Nucci.

Motivating Students to Learn: Overcoming Barriers to High Achievement (1993). Edited by Tommy M. Tomlinson.

Radical Proposals for Educational Change (1994). Edited by Chester E. Finn, Jr. and Herbert J. Walberg.

Reaching Marginal Students: A Prime Concern for School Renewal (1987). Edited by Robert L. Sinclair and Ward Ghory.

Restructuring the Schools: Problems and Prospects (1992). Edited by John J. Lane and Edgar G. Epps.

Rethinking Policy for At-risk Students (1994). Edited by Kenneth K. Wong and Margaret C. Wang.

School Boards: Changing Local Control (1992). Edited by Patricia F. First and Herbert J. Walberg.

The two final volumes in this series were:

Improving Science Education (1995). Edited by Barry J. Fraser and Herbert J. Walberg.

Ferment in Education: A Look Abroad (1995). Edited by John J. Lane.

These two volumes may be ordered from the Book Order Department, University of Chicago Press, 11030 S. Langley Ave., Chicago, IL 60628. Phone: 1-800-621-2736; Fax: 1-800-621-8476.